Praise for *THE GIRL I LEFT BEHIND*

"An important book. I know of no book like it."

—JILL KER CONWAY, AUTHOR OF
THE ROAD FROM COORAIN AND *TRUE NORTH*

"Bolstered by contemporary statistics and an excellent memory, Nies details the life changes she experienced alongside countless other women during a decade of secrecy, boys club politics, and outright lies. . . . In her punchy memoir, Nies demonstrates that equal rights for women in the workplace did not just happen. . . . The book's narrative style—blunt, unflinching, honest—serves the story well. . . . Both educational and entertaining with a wry, ironic wit evident throughout."

—*KIRKUS REVIEWS*

"Talk about the personal being political: Nies has written a fascinating account of her personal experience interwoven with her observations of a pivotal decade of political and social history. . . . Nies's story is about political and personal awakening."

—ELLEN STEINBAUM, *BOSTON GLOBE*

"Dense and energetic. . . . Public and private history, *The Girl I Left Behind* is addressed not to Nies's contemporaries, who recall all too clearly the days of dismissive inequality, but to their ambitious daughters, who have no idea how recent ancient history can be."

—AMANDA HELLER, *BOSTON GLOBE*

D0188012

"Future chroniclers of the period may place the drug and hippie scene as, historically, mere decorative fringe to the women's movement that came out of the 1960s. . . . Nies's combination period history and memoir is a highly valuable first-person record of a woman who finds herself, and the movement she grew with."

—*Publishers Weekly*

"Refreshingly candid. . . . Nies's personal take on the ripple effects of the women's movement—both on those involved directly and those who followed—is honest and engaging."

—Deborah Donovan, *Booklist*

"Judith Nies has written a rare and delightful memoir—gripping, personal, and historic. The story of the girl she left behind dramatically illustrates the rapid personal and complex social change of the sixties. Her lively account even illuminates usually dull Washington politics. It is a book for every age: those who lived parallel lives as well as young men and women who want to understand their roots and today's culture."

—Clare Crawford-Mason,
author of *The Nun and the Bureaucrat*

"The life experiences she relates so freshly (including political parallels to this era's war) make this book captivating for students of the political and cultural history of the sixties. Highly recommended."

—Lisa Nussbaum, *Library Journal*

"Colorful exchanges, including one with Congressman Tip O'Neill at a Capitol Hill Weight Watchers meeting, invigorate her new memoir."

—Jan Gardner, "Shelf Life," *Boston Globe*

"Nies moves nimbly between descriptions of her unique personal situation and recollections of the more general climate for women. . . . A potent reminder of how much things have changed—and stayed the same."

—Margaret Quamme, *Columbus Dispatch*

THE GIRL I LEFT BEHIND

ALSO BY JUDITH NIES

Nine Women: Portraits from the American Radical Tradition
(first published as *Seven Women*)

Native American History: A Chronology

War Crimes and the American Conscience
(with Erwin Knoll)

American Militarism 1970
(with Erwin Knoll)

THE GIRL I LEFT BEHIND

A Personal History of the 1960s

JUDITH NIES

HARPER ● PERENNIAL

NEW YORK ● LONDON ● TORONTO ● SYDNEY ● NEW DELHI ● AUCKLAND

HARPER ● PERENNIAL

A hardcover edition of this book was published in 2008 by Harper, an imprint of HarperCollins Publishers.

P.S.™ is a trademark of HarperCollins Publishers.

THE GIRL I LEFT BEHIND. Copyright © 2008 by Judith Nies. All rights reserved. Printed in the United States of America. No part of this book may be used or reproduced in any manner whatsoever without written permission except in the case of brief quotations embodied in critical articles and reviews. For information, address HarperCollins Publishers, 10 East 53rd Street, New York, NY 10022.

HarperCollins books may be purchased for educational, business, or sales promotional use. For information, please write: Special Markets Department, HarperCollins Publishers, 10 East 53rd Street, New York, NY 10022.

FIRST HARPER PERENNIAL EDITION PUBLISHED 2009.

Designed by Renato Stanisic

The Library of Congress has catalogued the hardcover edition as follows:

Nies, Judith.
    The girl I left behind : a narrative history of the Sixties / Judith Nies.—
        1st ed.
    xiii, 354 p., [8] p. of plates : ill. ; 22 cm.
    Includes bibliographical references (p. [339]–344) and index.
    ISBN: 978-0-06-117601-2
        1. Nies, Judith, 1941– . 2. Feminists—Washington (D.C.)—Biography.
        3. Nineteen sixties. 4. Washington (D.C.)—Biography.
        5. Massachusetts—Biography. 6. New York (State)—Biography.
        I. Title.
CT275.N6675 A3 2008
975.304092B 22   2007047964

ISBN 978-0-06-117602-9 (pbk.)

09 10 11 12 13 WBC/RRD 10 9 8 7 6 5 4 3 2 1

FOR THE NEXT GENERATION

Contents

If we do not know our own history, we are doomed to live it as though it were our private fate. —HANNAH ARENDT, POLITICAL PHILOSOPHER

Prologue: Remapping the Sixties

The photo shows a girl of perfect surfaces—every hair groomed, a dazzling smile, an artful composition of pearls, cashmere, and Italian tailoring. She waves out at the unseen viewer, her hand casually framed by the New York skyline spread out behind her like a Hollywood stage set. She is on the deck of an ocean liner, and the shadow of the ship's photographer slips in as part of the composition. Unknowingly, she is poised at a precise and crucial historical moment, so in hindsight, the composition conveys a certain emotional geometry. It is 1965, and I am on a ship coming into New York harbor.

When my then twelve-year-old daughter asks me about the photo, I tell her I am a living artifact of cultural history: an American history book with two feet. That answer makes her laugh but doesn't satisfy her. "But I thought the sixties were a hippie time," she protests. So I tell her the 1960s became "The Sixties" much later. While we were in it, we were inventing our lives—trying to find jobs, become adults, grow up. Not everyone was a hippie, I say. The truth is that my own life in the sixties, like that of the rest of the country, was confused and turbulent. I tell her how I started out in New York but ended up in Washington; how even though I used to have my hair cut at the same Georgetown salon as Jackie Kennedy, I marched in peace demonstrations against the Vietnam War. I tell her how she was born on an estate that used to belong to Marjorie Merriweather Post, once the richest woman in America. I explain that the girl in the picture—and we were all girls, no matter our age—was later employed as a speechwriter in Congress and worked every day with people who are now quoted on the front page of the *New York Times*—although probably not as often as they would like. They became ambassadors, secretary of state, cabinet officers, investment bankers, people in the news. She laughs when I tell her a project of the NOW Legal Defense Fund designated me a pioneer feminist, one of the vanguard of the 1960s women's movement.

But no, she objects, that is not what she wants to know. That is history. She wants an explanation of the disconnect. She wants a story. She wants to know how I changed, why I left the life reflected in the photograph. We page through glamorous scenes in the photo album—a large wooded estate, the gracious driveway with tall pine trees, the fashionable women, and the well-groomed men with long sideburns. Now we live outside of Boston in a working-class neighborhood of two-family houses with tiny lawns, many surrounded by chain-link fences. She wants to know why I went to Washington in the first place. What did I do there? Why did I leave? "Aren't you always telling me we are a product of our choices?" she asks.

Well, yes. But the explanation of choice presents a far more complex narrative challenge. I tell her that choices can be elusive. They don't always lead in the direction we think. The sixties are said to have been about sex, drugs, and rock and roll. But they were also about the Vietnam War, the civil rights movement, and women's liberation. I explain that things she takes for granted, like girls' sports and women doctors and women judges, were rare until twenty-five years ago. The more interesting question is: How did those changes happen? Did they "just happen," as some people think, or did they happen because women actively fought against the dynamics of exclusion? Looking back, I think the 1960s were really about consciousness, a unique moment when *I* became *we*. I was at a juncture of that consciousness, a point of intersection where personal story becomes history.

PART I

Expectations

CHAPTER ONE

"They Want You to Answer Some Questions"

Fall 1970

My marriage was almost ordinary. Sex, money, in-laws—we had the usual problems, my husband and I. But in one respect my marriage was, I think, unusual.

"Holcomb and Southern called me into their office this afternoon," Mac told me one evening while we were discussing the events of the day in the way that married couples do. "And they opened an FBI file this thick." Here he raised the flat of his hand some five inches above the kitchen table.

"Who are Southern and Holcomb?" I asked.

Mac explained that they were security agents at the Treasury Department.

"Whatever did you do," I asked, "that would cause the FBI to compile such a thick dossier on you?" My husband was an economist. He worked in the Treasury Department in a special trade group in the secretary's office. His father was a New York banker, and he came from a tidy, conventional family where dinners were always preceded by two ritual cocktails—the second of which was called a dividend—and conversation rarely ranged beyond travel, real estate, and Wall Street. Mac was fairly conventional himself, neither altruistic nor excessively patriotic. Politically, he usually played the pragmatist to my assigned role as ideologue. We had met in Italy in 1965 when we were both in graduate school.

"Oh, no," my husband said. "You don't understand. The file was on *you*." That "you" hung ticking in the air between us. Me? I felt a shiver of distress, as though I were in a rowboat on a calm river and my nervous system had suddenly registered the quickening of deep, treacherous currents.

Our kitchen was colorful and cozy, filled with bright colors and big splashy flowers. I had painted one wall a vibrant cherry red and hung a large stretcher covered with a vivid Marimekko fabric from Finland. Another wall was covered with political artwork that I had collected: a poster from Eugene McCarthy's legendary presidential campaign of 1968, signed by the artist, Peter Max; a poster for the first Earth Day, April 22, 1970, which used the word *environmental* for the first time; a satirical cartoon of Vice President Spiro Agnew's celebrated tongue twisters. ("Nattering nabobs of negativism" was my favorite.) Agnew was Richard Nixon's vice president, and technically, President Nixon was my husband's employer, although he had started working in the government when Democrat Lyndon Johnson was still president. The men of the Nixon administration were not known for possessing a sense of humor.

From our kitchen window, I looked out over acres of woods. To be truthful, our living situation was unusual. We occupied the carriage house of the old Post estate on Macomb Street in northwest Washington, D.C. Tregaron, as the place was called, was a once magnificent property that had belonged to Marjorie Merriweather Post, who in the 1940s and early '50s had been America's richest woman and Washington's defining hostess. The property embraced twenty-two acres abutting Rock Creek

Park and was a Washington landmark. When a colleague of
mine from Capitol Hill left for New York to work in the legal
department at CBS, he had passed the Tregaron apartment on to
us. After a decade of neglect, the buildings had tilting porches
and missing shutters, the land was overgrown with kudzu, and
the underbrush was occasionally punctuated with marble statuary that had toppled to the ground. To this day, the estate remains a remnant of the original District of Columbia—the
ungraded Maryland farmland that a Revolutionary War general
and a Georgetown lawyer sold to the infant government for a
new federal capital that geographically might bridge the divide
between North and South. (The previous two capitals of Philadelphia and New York had too many freed blacks and relatively
lenient slavery statutes that troubled the rich, slave-owning
founders from the South.)

Two centuries of real estate development around its borders
had left Tregaron's hills, creeks, and gullies largely untouched.
The habitat of memory remained intact. It was a place that ac-
commodated ghosts and spirits.

"So what did you say to Holcomb and Southern?" I asked. "I
mean, why am I part of your security clearance?"

"They said it was just routine. They always include family
members in a security check."

Still in our twenties, my husband and I were new to Washington and the demands of married life. Long before we married,
we had lived together in Rome for a year, during which the two
noteworthy events were his fellowship at the Bank of Italy and
my abortion in the shadow of the Vatican. We both had short
résumés. On the surface, my husband and I appeared to be a
good match. In the checkbook of race, education, and religion
that sociologists love to calculate, we seemed to balance. We
were both white, had attended good suburban public high

schools, and had graduated from good colleges and the same graduate school. We both had been raised in and departed from the Catholic Church: we were lapsed Catholics—or Catholics in recovery, as we might say today. In fact, huge gaps and ellipses in our backgrounds made us susceptible to very different influences.

Mac had gone to Yale without a scholarship and could afford to spend summers in interesting internships. His parents had friends who were connected to law firms, consulting firms, banks, and foundations. Dinner-table conversation at his house often turned to promotions, career paths, networking. He knew the places where people "summered." Where I came from, *summer* was not a verb. Summer was a time when I worked as a camp counselor or a waitress and saved money for college. My father was a foreman in a factory. I had worked since I was fourteen and had gone to college as a scholarship student. Although I had one aunt who had married rich, she had died when I was thirteen, and my father's family had fought like rabid dogs over her will. In short, our differences had to do with that complex combination of income, education, wealth, and occupation that determine the nuances and subtleties of the rigid, but invisible, class structure in America.

"And besides, I thought you already had a security clearance," I said.

"There are different levels within security clearances," he explained evenly. "I need a clearance upgrade."

"But why do you need an upgrade? You've only been there for six months." I had the feeling that all the facts were not on the table. Mac was charming, but he was not direct. I had learned that when he seemed to be at his most open and unguarded, he was often at his most manipulative.

"I'm in a special trade group. We're going into new areas of international trade, and it requires a higher level of security clearance than I had before."

I suddenly remembered his boss, whom I had met a few months earlier in our kitchen, when he came to a Sunday-afternoon party that we gave. Very fit, very focused, very intense, he left me with my hand awkwardly extended in midair after Mac introduced us.

"I don't believe in shaking hands with women," he told me with total self-assurance.

I was astonished. "Do you prefer kissing?" I had asked.

I was gratified when he appeared to be taken aback, at least momentarily. He seemed to have no small talk and no sense of humor.

"What sort of man doesn't shake hands with women in this day and age?" I asked Mac after the party. "At least I didn't ask if he were a Hasidic Jew or a Muslim. He doesn't seem like an economist," I continued. "There's something off about your boss. Spooky, actually. Is he former military?" I asked. Mac didn't answer.

Now as we sat discussing my FBI folder, I was remembering Mac's silence about his spooky boss.

Mac's job before he moved to the Treasury Department had been as an economist with the Export-Import Bank of the United States, a government bank that insures American corporations undertaking theoretically risky international deals—those that involve unstable currencies, restive workforces, and government coups. Later I learned that the "new area of international trade" in question concerned the construction of nuclear power plants in foreign countries. At the time, everything nuclear was secret. Most still is.

"So how did you leave it with Southern and Holcomb?" I asked, hoping somewhat naively that Mac had made some gesture of protest when confronted with a five-inch-thick FBI file on his wife. "What was the outcome?"

"They want you to answer some questions," he said casually, as if it was no big deal. He took a folder out of his briefcase and handed it to me.

I knew something about security clearances because I worked as a speechwriter and congressional aide to the ten congressmen who were the leading opponents of the Vietnam War.* Based on national security, the White House and executive agencies denied Congress all kinds of information, much of it already printed in the nation's newspapers. In fact, the definition of *security* was a moving train. Threats to America's security changed from one day to the next—the Russians, the Chinese, the Vietnamese, the Cubans. Defining national security was one of the prerogatives of a governing class.

That there was a ruling establishment in Washington I understood both from my work and from the place where I lived. Marjorie Merriweather Post had created at Tregaron a place that belonged to permanent Washington—a place where people do not leave after elections or a change in administrations.

WHEN I WAS YOUNG, I'd learned about foreign relations as a subject of the marriages of kings and queens. Then, when I was older, I'd discovered that what counts are treaties, the balance of power, and economic strategies. But as I sat in our cozy kitchen on that evening, listening to my husband tell me about my FBI

---

* The ten congressmen who organized in an ad hoc group were Don Edwards, George Brown Jr., and Phil Burton from California, Ben Rosenthal and Bill Ryan from New York, Bob Kastenmeier from Wisconsin, Don Fraser from Minnesota, John Conyers Jr. from Michigan (still in Congress and chair of the House Judiciary Committee), Bob Eckhardt from Texas, and Ab Mikva from Chicago.

file and reading through three pages of carefully typed security-clearance questions on high-quality bond paper, I realized that marriages were indeed important to the conduct of America's international affairs. Our government had specific cultural expectations for the wives of men who were entrusted to carry out America's role in the world. Having a certain kind of wife was part of Mac's job description. His interagency trade group worked with George Shultz, then at the Office of Management and Budget and soon to be named secretary of the treasury. Shultz would be as indispensable to President Nixon as he would become to the Bechtel family—the family-owned Bechtel Corporation built nuclear power plants around the world—and later to President Ronald Reagan as secretary of state.

I opened the folder and in shock read the questions, most of which related to the period from 1966 to 1968 when I had worked for a tiny peace organization, the Women's International League for Peace and Freedom (WILPF) which had been founded in 1915 to protest World War I and to work against the arms race. It was my first job after graduate school. The questions revealed that I had been under surveillance during my entire two-year tenure there.

I couldn't know then that the Federal Bureau of Investigation had launched a vigilante counterintelligence operation called COINTELPRO (Counter Intelligence Program) aimed at quashing dissent and preventing the growth of "dangerous" ideas in dissident organizations. According to FBI director J. Edgar Hoover, the new women's groups that were springing up across the country—health care collectives, welfare rights organizations, antinuclear groups, environmental associations, women's liberation groups—were communist inspired. I sometimes had joked that my telephone had been tapped and meetings infiltrated, but I hadn't really visualized the reality of it. In fact, Hoover had sent thousands of informants into the new women's organizations, a movement he found particularly alarming. I tried to imagine the scene where Holcomb and Southern, two intelligence officers with the typical lantern-jawed look, interrogated my husband for hours about my work for WILPF, an organization few people I knew took seriously because it never had more than six thousand members nationwide and was always teetering on the edge of a financial abyss.

When I took the job as the legislative director of WILPF's Washington office in 1966, soon after finishing graduate school in international affairs at Johns Hopkins School of International Studies, it was the only professional job I could find. At the time nonsecretarial jobs for women were almost nonexistent and SAIS (rhymes with "ice"), as the School of Advanced International Studies was called, did not help place its female graduates. It had no women professors to help women negotiate the professional world of international affairs. When representatives from the oil companies and international banks (which says something about who was running U.S. foreign policy) came to interview students about future employment, the dean's secretary, Priscilla Mason, hurriedly removed my name from the interview sign-up list, explaining, "Women students aren't allowed to do these interviews." Not one of my male classmates was told to start his career as a secretary or a volunteer, but that's what I was advised. Women were supposed to marry well, dress well, and entertain well. Washington women of a certain class were supposed to volunteer to work for charitable social organizations, hold good dinner parties, and weave the cultural web that linked men with common values and aspirations. Like military wives, our husband's rank was our rank. Although in 1970 we were no longer wearing Jackie Kennedy's pillbox hats, we were learning to cook veal Prince Orloff from Julia Child's *Mastering the Art of French Cooking*. Madeleine Albright, a SAIS classmate for one year, was volunteering for fund-raisers at the Cathedral School, where her children were enrolled, and was years away from her first paying job on a Senate staff. All in all, we were supposed to be mini–Mrs. Posts.

So it was refreshing to work for a woman's organization. To be honest, I also felt peace was a good idea.

"Did you mention invasion of privacy, First Amendment freedoms, principles of liberty, or the right to dissent?" I asked Mac.

It is a rule of both journalism and life that to ask the right questions you have to know 95 percent of the answers. Clearly, Holcomb and Southern knew all the answers, which is what I told Mac. "Those questions aren't about information. They're about intimidation, complicity, the imposition of control." At least I think I said this. I might have only thought it. At one level, I was intimidated. The process is *meant* to be intimidating.

"Did you say anything about how the Women's International League is the oldest women's peace organization in the country and that two of its founders won the Nobel Peace Prize?" I asked. "The *only* American women to ever have won the Nobel Peace Prize. And why is the FBI investigating an organization that has never been on the attorney general's list?" The attorney general's list was compiled during the McCarthy era and included over one hundred organizations believed to be "Communist, Subversive or Fascist." What we didn't know then, of course, was that FBI director J. Edgar Hoover viewed peace as subversive and feminism as the equivalent of communism.

I had seen Hoover once. He was in the parking lot at the racetrack at Pimlico where Mac and I had gone on a Saturday afternoon when we first arrived in Washington. Hoover was talking with three or four men. He was short and pudgy, dressed all in gray, with a fedora on his head. To me, he looked like one of the newspaper photos of a KGB agent. Hoover was notorious for spending many afternoons at racetracks around Washington. He always bet at the two-dollar windows but sent his aides running to the hundred-dollar windows to place bets for him. I once told Mac a funny story that a Washington reporter had told me about how Hoover had put comedian Groucho Marx under surveillance because he thought he was related to Karl Marx.

I was no longer laughing.

At some level, I knew that no matter how this particular security upgrade turned out, one of us was going to be looking for another job—or another spouse. These were not problems I could send to the Can This Marriage Be Saved? column of the *Ladies' Home Journal*.

I knew without asking that Mac had not said anything to Southern and Holcomb about freedom of speech. In government circles, it is considered tacky to talk about the Constitution and the Bill of Rights. In Washington, a man is his security clearance. It is a matter of rank and standing. A failed clearance marks the end of a government career, and my husband was deeply ambitious. I felt strongly—and with absolute certainty—that the whole problem was a misunderstanding. It was simply not possible that in my short, poorly paid, low-status, professional career of four years, two of which had been spent working for duly elected congressmen, I had done anything significant enough to warrant a security file five inches thick.

I was wrong. In many ways, mine was the quintessential dilemma of the 1960s, the moment in which the personal became indistinguishable from the political. I would have to make a choice, and that decision would dictate the future course of my life. Treasury Department intelligence officers were, after all, in my kitchen, interrupting my dinner. How was I to respond? In some dim way, I must have sensed that this was a transforming moment, a moment in which I would have to take an action whose consequences were unforeseeable—the proverbial leap into the abyss.

Over the next few months, I gnawed obsessively at the bone of what I came to call "The Questions." The Questions made me review all the choices I had made in my not-yet-thirty-year life span. Should I answer them all? Should I answer some? Should I answer them only from public sources? Should I get a lawyer? But if I hadn't done anything wrong, why did I need a lawyer? What authority did Southern and Holcomb have to intrude in my life? Why had my husband put me in this impossible position? What would happen to my husband's career if I didn't answer them? What would happen to mine if I did? Then I remembered Mac's tightly wound boss who didn't believe in shaking hands with women. My husband's employers might have told you that I was a threat to national security. But I will tell you that, at that moment in history, the very notion of security itself was a concept that was up for grabs.

"Where," I asked the civil liberties lawyer who had been recommended to me, "is the written federal policy on the security requirements for wives?"

"Let's talk about you," he answered. "Tell me what you do for work now."

CHAPTER TWO

The Most Interesting Job in Washington

Fall 1970

S o, doll," Phil greeted me as I came into his office one morning in the fall of 1970, a few weeks before Mac told me about my FBI file, "what's on the agenda for today's meeting?" The Honorable Phillip Burton, congressman from San Francisco, was leaning back in his chair, stocking feet up on his desk, phone receiver cradled between ear and shoulder, waiting for his caller to come back on the line. I was there as the staff person for the ad hoc congressional group of liberal congressmen for which he served as one of the chairmen. As soon as I started to answer him, he held up his hand like a policeman stopping traffic and started barking into the phone.

"What do you mean it's a communications problem? We're fucking communicating right now." Burton loved conflict and the rough-and-tumble of argument. Although he talked like a longshoreman, I learned from one of his staff that his father had been a doctor.

As Phil's voice boomed, the vibrations bounced off the walls. He ran his free hand through his hair until it stood wildly on end. I waited. Even when you were on the same side of an issue

with Phil, he was combative. It was his nature. I knew he would
not end the conversation until he had gotten what he wanted.
Everything I learned about power and influence, I learned on
the job. I learned much of it from Burton, one of the key leaders
of the anti-Vietnam War forces in Congress and considered by
many to be a political genius. His close friend and fellow Californian Don Edwards once described him as "gruff, irreverent,
sentimental, idealistic, cunning, brilliant, abrasive, charming." I
would add bold. And sexist. But at the time, sexism was a concept still to be named. Women were supposed to be decorative.
If I hadn't looked like a cheerleader, I never would have gotten
the job. If I hadn't been married, I might not have taken it. A
single, unmarried woman was seen as prey. (A woman I knew
who worked on a Senate committee told me that one of the
senators routinely left his hotel room number in her hotel mailbox when the committee held out-of-town hearings and threatened to have her fired when she didn't show up.)

A man with a huge presence, a voice without volume control,
and an unapologetic love of political combat, Burton arrived in
Congress with a reputation as a unique political talent and the
youngest person ever elected to the California Assembly. Intense, often scowling, and always intimidating, a movie version
of his life would have to star Jack Nicholson. Despite the tough-
ness, he was a soft touch for difficult causes and had a fabulous
sense of humor. He had no patience, however, for liberals who
settled for glorious defeats or "educating the public." He loved
to win. He knew how to win. And he expected to win. Burton
was unusual for a liberal because he both loved power and was
willing to master the minutiae of the legislative process. He
knew how to extract the first from the second. He also loved the
House. In this he was quite different from Lyndon Johnson,
with whom he was often compared. (Johnson left the House as

soon as he could run for the Senate, describing the gap between the House and Senate as "the difference between chickenshit and chicken salad.")

Burton's breathtaking ambition, given the power of the opposition, was to become Speaker of the House, a goal which he would come within a whisper of achieving. But first, he needed to extract control of the House from the hands of seniority-heavy southern Democrats by changing internal operating rules. Contrary to Carl von Clausewitz's famous dictum about war being the continuation of politics by other means, politics in the South meant the continuation of the Civil War by other means. In 1970, the racist, conservative, "solid South" was still solidly Democratic. (Today it is solidly Republican, largely because of the passage and enforcement of civil rights legislation by Democrats. When President Lyndon Johnson signed the Civil Rights Amendments of 1965, he reminded his colleagues that they were probably handing the South over to the Republicans.) Southerners dominated the internal workings of the House, including the rules and committee assignments. Burton's tactics included strengthening old institutions and inventing new ones, such as the small group of ten liberal congressmen I worked for. Burton's strength was that he knew how to forge coalitions of idealists, pragmatists, conservatives, liberals, amateurs, and professionals. He knew how to count, and he respected the politics of majorities. He always tried, however, to make sure he had organized the majority ahead of time. In 1976, Burton came within one vote of being elected House majority leader, a key step on the escalator to becoming Speaker. *Washington Post* political columnist David Broder pronounced it the second most important election in the country after the presidency. Its significance lay in the changes that Burton and a coalition of nonsouthern Democrats had made in the rules sufficient to break the southern stranglehold over seniority and committee assignments. Unfortunately, Tip O'Neill, in his first act as Speaker, upheld the old rules by securing the majority leader's post for Texan Jim Wright by *one vote*. Wright's weakness as a leader eventually led to his forced resignation and the so-called Republican revolution. (The seeds for change, however, had been sown. Nancy Pelosi was elected to Phil Burton's seat in 1987 and did not shy away from leadership roles. She ran for House whip, then Democratic majority leader, and twenty years later, in 2007, became Speaker of the House, the first woman and the first Californian ever to hold the Speaker's chair.)★

Until the late 1960s, the recipe for success in the House was "to get along, go along." Phil Burton did neither. He was loud in his opposition to the prowar House leadership; he was constantly maneuvering to change House rules; and he amplified his own position by always claiming he spoke for numerous uncounted congressmen. He had arrived in Congress in 1964 at the age of thirty-eight with a reputation as a legislative *enfant terrible*. Two liberal Democratic congressmen, Bob Kastenmeier of Wisconsin and Ben Rosenthal of New York, instructed Don Edwards, as a fellow Californian, to see what he could find out about Burton, who had been elected to Congress in a special election.

Instead, Burton captivated Edwards and instructed him to invite Rosenthal and Kastenmeier to dinner. Shortly afterward, when they were among the only congressmen voting to cut off appropriations for the House Un-American Activities Committee

---

★ Nancy Pelosi was active in San Francisco politics and in Phil Burton's campaigns. In 1983 Burton died of heart failure and his wife, Sala, succeeded him in a special election. When Sala became ill in 1986 she chose Nancy Pelosi to succeed her. Pelosi ran for election in a field of thirteen candidates, had Burton's contacts to call on, and won her congressional seat in 1987.

(HUAC), they became regular dinner companions. A year later, following the first vote to withhold increased appropriations for the war in Vietnam, they added more members, all Democrats, and decided to meet more formally to strategize. Unlike other congressional groups that organized along party issues, they were known simply as The Group.

The common denominator among ten congressmen I worked for (the group started as eight, eventually expanded to ten) was their profound opposition to the Vietnam War and a willingness to go on the record opposing it—unlike many congressmen who opposed it privately but not in public. Since the war had been authorized—not by Congress but by President Johnson's executive order known as the Tonkin Gulf Resolution—Congress had taken few recorded votes. The standing committees in Congress refused to hold hearings. Burton was among those willing to chair ad hoc hearings that kept congressional opposition to the Vietnam War on the six o'clock news and on the front pages of newspapers. (This would be the equivalent to a group of Republican congressmen forming a special committee to hold hearings against the Iraq war while the war was going on.) My job was to act as a speechwriter, coordinator, and all-purpose staffer to build the group's reputation and make the congressmen's individual positions seem larger and more influential. I rotated offices and was paid a month or two at a time from each individual congressman's payroll. I started out working in Bob Kastenmeier's office, then moved to Ben Rosenthal's. After four or five months I moved on to Don Fraser's office and then to Ab Mikva's. Along the way I learned about Wisconsin progressives, New York factionalism, Minnesota's lake country, and Chicago's South Side.

As the 1960s turned into the 1970s, the war in Vietnam got

louder and nastier. America sent more than a million soldiers to Vietnam. Fifty-seven thousand died; another estimated fifty thousand committed suicide afterward from drugs, alcohol, automobile accidents. The U.S. military dropped as many bombs on Vietnam as in all of World War II; killed one million Vietnamese soldiers and another three million civilians; used napalm on civilian villages and chemical defoliants on plants; and introduced the word *ecocide*. But still no one in government could explain with any lucidity why we were in Vietnam. In 1969, Richard Nixon was inaugurated as president, elected on a promise to bring the troops home, and within a year he had expanded the war into Laos and Cambodia.

"Okay," Phil said, banging down the phone, "let's go. We need to pick up Eckhardt on the way."

"Shoes?" I suggested, pointing to his stocking feet.

"Right." It was not yet ten in the morning and already he was rumpled, with tie askew, a wrinkled jacket collar, haystack hair.

Off we went down the wide marble corridors of the Cannon House Office Building on our way to a meeting of the ten congressmen, an ad hoc group whose membership did not appear on any official list of congressional bodies. As a group, the congressmen were able to support one another in taking unpopular stands, amplify their individual voices, and develop long-term legislative strategies. They came from urban districts all over the country—San Francisco, San Diego, Queens, Madison, Minneapolis, Detroit, Houston, Chicago—many with universities in their districts. Edie Wilkie, who worked for another congressional organization and would later marry Don Edwards, told me I had "the most interesting job in Washington."

Phil, always in a rush, was striding purposefully ahead and, in his booming baritone, was greeting every congressman we saw.

I scrambled to keep up, my arms filled with file folders and fat three-ring notebooks. Today it's common to see male politicians accompanied by female aides in short skirts and long hair, but in 1970 it was unique. Burton, however, always attuned to power nuances, had grasped that a woman legislative assistant brought him a certain amount of curiosity and attention, even though I never had work space in Burton's office. He prided himself on being ahead of the curve. But aside from my attention-getting value, Burton and I got along because he thought I had good political instincts and was knowledgeable about foreign policy and the Vietnam War. He once observed that I had a man's résumé.

"How's that?" I asked.

"Because you've traveled a lot. Studied foreign affairs. Know languages. You're an anomaly," he announced. This was over dinner at the Rotunda, a restaurant on Capitol Hill where he ordered drinks two at a time, double martinis for him and scotch for me. It was true that I had traveled and worked hard at my job, but since I didn't know what *anomaly* meant and didn't want to ask, I couldn't clarify his observation. While it was also true I had a graduate degree in international studies and had traveled outside the United States and knew a lot about the underside of how American foreign policy was conducted, it was equally important that I had good connections with the women's organizations that arrived in Washington by the bus- and trainload to lobby Congress against the Vietnam War. Although these women were outside the formal political framework, they were a formidable presence in the antiwar movement. I was also young, an advantage at a time when America's universities were boiling with rebellion and the slogan of youth was "Don't trust anyone over thirty." I was still under thirty. My other advantages were that I knew Paul Gorman, the young man who had held the job before me—he had been a Yale classmate of my husband's—and that I could be hired at two-thirds of his salary (a discrepancy I found out only after a year on the job).

Except for the ten congresswomen in the House and one woman in the Senate, Margaret Chase Smith—who theoretically could go everywhere (except the House gym and swimming pool)—the marble corridors of the House and Senate office buildings were filled with men. Women on Capitol Hill were desk-bound—as secretaries and case workers were supposed to be. Work was done by women; deals were made by men. No one could imagine it any differently. Few arenas in American life, except religious institutions, were more sex segregated than American politics.*

I was one of only a handful of professional women on Capitol Hill (I counted four on the House side). I wrote speeches, organized hearings, sent out press releases, edited publications, fielded press requests, helped draft legislation. I coordinated with legislative aides in other offices. Day in and day out, I attended meetings

---

* The 91st Congress (1969–1971) had one woman senator and ten congresswomen. In all U.S. history up to that point, only seventy-two women had served in Congress, and almost all had arrived as widows of their deceased congressional husbands. Both women senators of the 1960s, Maurine Neuberger (1960–67) and Margaret Chase Smith (1948–72) had arrived with the "widow's cloak," although Smith started in the House. Consequently, women's interests were barely represented. Another decade would pass before the first woman was elected to the Senate in her own right, when Nancy Kassebaum was sworn in as a senator in 1979. In the House no woman had chaired a significant committee, regardless of seniority. Martha Griffiths, a brilliant legislator, was given the chair of the House Beauty Committee, which supervised the beauty salon and barbershops. In 1973, when Lindy Boggs took over her deceased husband's seat in a special election, attitudes had begun to change. She was given a post on the Appropriations Committee and spearheaded legislation giving women access to credit and mortgages and providing government pay equity for women. By the time the 110th Congress was sworn in on January 20, 2007, there were sixteen women in the Senate and seventy-one in the House, a remarkable improvement but still far behind other Western parliamentary democracies. Nancy Pelosi, first elected to Congress in 1987, filling Sala Burton's seat, became the first woman in history to hold a major leadership role in the House and is currently the first woman Speaker of the House.

where every other face at the table was a man. Women were supposed to be seen and not heard. If I expressed an opinion too
forcefully, someone would remark, "Boy, I'm glad I'm not married to you." Sometimes they expected me to get the coffee. They
always expected me to take notes.

Those years I worked in Congress, from 1968 to 1973, were
among the most politically violent years in Washington's history, save perhaps for the Civil War. The Vietnam War created
an atmosphere of such raw and volatile feelings that, between
the soup and the main course, a dinner party could disintegrate
from a cordial gathering of friends into a lacerating fight over
wasted lives, ambitious careerists, and an unwinnable war. This
atmosphere was why the scarce number of antiwar congressmen
found shelter together. Their collaboration gave them a national
network that transcended parochial interests and battles.

"What's on the agenda for this morning?" Phil inquired as
we headed toward Bob Eckhardt's office. He didn't wait for an
answer. "I hear we're being sued. Kastenmeier told me that guy
you invited is suing us."

"Threatening to sue," I countered quickly. I had learned to
move quickly away from a defensive position. In any argument
with Burton, I was a sure loser.

"I don't even remember this Ellsberg person," he said. "What's
his beef?"

"He didn't like the way I edited his remarks," I began. "But,"
I continued quickly, "the real problem is that he disappeared.
He never answered his mail or his phone calls. He got a transcript like everyone else but never made any changes or sent it
back. He just disappeared. Now the book is out, and he wants to
change his remarks."

On February 20 and 21, 1970, the group of congressmen had
sponsored a widely publicized hearing on war crimes and the

application of the Nuremberg principles to the Vietnam War. The actual topics had included the My Lai massacre, treatment of prisoners of war, bombing of civilian areas, use of herbicides and chemical gasses, Operation Phoenix, and programs such as "pacification," "search and destroy," and the forcible resettlement of civilian populations. Underlying the actual topics was the premise that the Vietnam War had passed beyond anyone's control. It was a historic hearing, and the congressmen notified participants in advance that they planned to issue a formal congressional report and to publish the proceedings in book form by a trade book publisher in New York.

As the group's chief and only staff person, I worked with other congressmen's staffs to send out the invitations, coordinate responses, make all the physical arrangements, and write both the congressional report and the book. At the actual war crimes hearings, I assisted Nobel laureate Philip Noel-Baker with his hearing aid and arranged for Nuremberg prosecutor Telford Taylor to sit to the right of the microphone. I chatted with Hannah Arendt (*Eichmann in Jerusalem*) and Hans Morgenthau (*Power Among Nations*) and was astonished to see them laughing like college students. I greeted movie stars and businessmen and rock promoters and demonstration organizers. Before the hearing, I provided the congressmen with intelligence estimates that said the Vietnam War was unwinnable, that its strategy was based on false assumptions, that there was no military solution to the political problems of Vietnam, and that high-tech weaponry cannot pacify a country. Dan Ellsberg, an analyst at the Rand Corporation, had been a last-minute addition to the hearing's invitation list.

"Who's Ellsberg's lawyer?" asked Phil.

"Marty Garbus," I answered. "He's a well-known First Amendment and civil liberties—"

"And what does Ellsberg want? What's the remedy?" From Phil's point of view, the merit of Ellsberg's complaint was secondary to finding the right person to fix the problem.

The hearings had gone on for two days. Discussions were intricate; more than forty participants filled the hearing room and addressed a series of complex questions about international law and the responsibilities of soldiers, commanders, public officials, and citizens when their government committed acts determined to be war crimes.

Ellsberg's beef was that he wanted to edit his remarks, an impossibility since the book with his remarks was already in print.★

"He seems to want us to include more of his prepared statement—"

Phil didn't wait for me to finish the sentence. Or more likely he already knew the answer. He bounded into Bob Eckhardt's office without knocking.

"Nadine wants to have a real Texas barbecue," Eckhardt was saying as I entered. Bob Eckhardt was the first Texas politician I had ever met. He was the newest member of the group. With his flowing mane of hair, three-piece white linen suits, and large blue-and-white polka-dot bow ties, he seemed to be a stereotype of a southern politician. But he had serious eyes. And his looks were deceptive.

"Barbecue in Georgetown. You have to be kidding me," Phil said.

★ In 1999, when I interviewed Ellsberg, he said he wanted his statement that he could be considered a war criminal included as part of his remarks. He acknowledged that he had never answered his phone calls or his mail, saying he was in transit between the Rand Corporation and the Center for International Studies at MIT. The eventual remedy took the form of an errata sheet that the editor, Aaron Asher, included in each copy of the book, *War Crimes and the American Conscience.*

"Nadine does the best ribs. She's been planning the menu."

Political food is a subject in itself. Nurturing. Comforting. Down-home. Even though politicians who are successful in Washington find "home" an elusive concept.

"And what about wives? Nadine needs to know if wives are invited."

"Ribs are messy," Burton contemplated.

Bob Eckhardt was known for two things: supporting most of the progressive legislation that the petroleum industry in his Houston district opposed and riding his bicycle at a stately pace to meetings on Capitol Hill. A legal scholar who had written two books on constitutional law, Eckhardt was often mentioned as a potential nominee for the U.S. Supreme Court. He was smart and talented, and Phil Burton respected talent above all. Under Burton's sponsorship, Eckhardt eventually became the first southerner to chair the progressive Democratic Study Group.

"No wives," said Burton. "It doubles the number of people. Makes the conversation too diffuse. I want focused conversation. And no husbands," he said to me directly. At another dinner where spouses were invited, I had watched him size up my husband with the deceptive ease of a skillful politician. Mac, who could be very engaging, mistakenly thought he'd charmed him. But Phil had correctly judged Mac as a pragmatist. He could work with pragmatists, but he didn't respect them unless they had real passion. Lack of passion he did not respect.

These group dinners were always at one of the congressmen's homes and were social, intimate, boozy, and fun. They were about mouth-to-ear matters, as Chinese philosopher Sun Tzu described the personal nature of political culture. Casual conversation might touch on J. Edgar Hoover's gambling addiction or rumors about whether Francis Cardinal Spellman was homosexual and a cross-dresser (he was both, as was Hoover). The real inside conversation, however, was about health, the wild card in every person's career. When one congressman died, the others' first questions were: Where's his office? What's his committee assignment? Everyone moved up a notch. "Dr. Death eventually visits everyone," Ben Rosenthal observed dryly when he saw I was shocked at their irreverence.

These were not sentimental men. It was Ben Rosenthal's dictum that gossip created reality in Washington. He usually proposed inviting reporters to the group's dinners. "If the press doesn't report it," he insisted, "it might as well not have happened." Previous guests had included Tom Wicker, then head of the *New York Times* Washington bureau, and David Halberstam, author of *The Best and the Brightest*, the Pulitzer Prize–winning book that described how the macho men of the Kennedy administration backed into the Vietnam War with little knowledge of Vietnamese culture or Chinese politics and history. Phil Burton didn't trust reporters, so, unlike Rosenthal, he was rarely quoted in the press.

Rosenthal's main interest was promoting a new cabinet agency for consumer affairs, which was why the invited guest for the barbecue evening at Bob and Nadine Eckhardt's house was to be Ralph Nader, then at the height of his fame over his successful campaign for automobile safety. Against the opposition of the Detroit auto industry, the most powerful lobbying group in Washington, Nader had successfully advocated for seat belts, air bags, and other passenger safety features. Big Auto fiercely resisted—on the usual corporate arguments of the crushing costs and that no evidence existed proving such measures would save lives—but in the end Nader's legislation for increased automobile design safety passed and over the years has saved millions of lives.

"We have to get to Kastenmeier's office," Burton said. "We can talk about the dinner on our way over. Kastenmeier said he wanted us to start on time for once." Bob Kastenmeier was the senior member of the group. He had the biggest office and was the most thoughtful. When he held the group meetings, everyone tried to show up on time.

Later, I remembered Phil Burton's remark about wives and focused conversation, because, at the actual dinner, he propped up his stocking feet on a brocade sofa in Eckhardt's lovely Georgetown home and fell sound asleep while Nader was talking. "It's okay," Ben Rosenthal said, waving his cigar without missing a beat when Nader paused and looked in Phil's direction. "We never let him snore in public. Go on."

Rosenthal, a congressman from Queens, New York, was the fastest wit in the group and the funniest observer of Washington culture. "Have you ever noticed how WASP first names are like last names?" he asked me, pointing to a State Department roster that might have included the names Averill Harriman and Strobe Talbot and Winston Lord. "Not until this moment," I told him. Ben was also the most media savvy, the most relaxed in front of a television camera, and the only one with a full-time press secretary. He was constantly quoted in the press. He was also well connected to a group of wealthy, liberal New York businessmen who had raised money for the group's sponsorship of the war crimes hearings since there was no congressional budget from which to draw.

Just as we were leaving, Eckhardt's administrative assistant entered the office to show him an article that had run in that day's *Houston Chronicle*.

Phil Burton fastened the assistant with an intense stare. "Are you happy in your work?" he barked.

The speechless assistant stood by Eckhardt's desk looking bewildered. Happiness is not part of the job description of a Capitol Hill staffer.

After a long pause, Phil annouced emphatically, "It's important to be happy in your work." He rose out of his chair. "Let's go."

Burton was a man who was happy in his work.

Phil never asked me if I was happy in my work. He asked me different questions: How did you get here? Where did you come from? Where do you want to go from here? These were questions I frequently asked myself.

CHAPTER THREE

The Godfather

Summer 1962

In July 1962, I was looking at the world through the windows of a restaurant called the Landfall, in Woods Hole, Massachusetts, a weathered waterfront building (still there) located next to the pier where the ferry leaves for the islands of Martha's Vineyard and Nantucket. The Landfall sits on pilings out over the water with an ocean-facing wall of glass, and when the tide is high and the wind blows from the east, the ferries dock at an angle that makes them appear as though they're about to crash through the restaurant's windows. On those nights, the open-mouthed ferry hovers ominously outside the windows like an enraged, prehistoric beast—engines racing, lights blinking, ropes dangling over the sides. Diners have been known to leap up from their tables and run for safety. Then, abruptly, the propellers reverse, the ferry disappears into its slip, the diners return to their seats, and the hum and chatter of the restaurant resume.

It was on a night of the hovering ferry that the man who would later call himself my godfather appeared. At the time, it seemed like a minor diversion in a youthful summer. But later,

I saw it as destiny's smile—a dramatic turning point that sent my life in a new direction. Hollywood has instructed women well, after all, in that particular narrative. A strange man walks into a woman's life and transforms it. As the old adage has it, there are only two stories in life: a stranger comes to town or the heroine takes a trip.

"Call me Ray," he said, when I came to take the order. He and his wife, Connie, sat at a table by the window. He wore dark, heavy-framed glasses and had a New York accent and New York self-assurance. "We're on our honeymoon. Aren't we, Connie? The second marriage. For both of us. A triumph of hope over experience."

I laughed, as I was supposed to. It was a line from Oscar Wilde that he must have used before but that I had never heard. I thought he was extremely clever. Connie confided she was in the fashion business. I thought they both looked and talked like people out of the *New Yorker* magazine, my only contact with the culture of Manhattan. By that point in the summer of 1962—it was the middle of July—I had learned that New Yorkers were by far the best tippers. I had developed an easy banter with out-of-state visitors.

"Are you on your way to the Vineyard for your honeymoon?" I asked. The island air is balmy and soft in summer, a logical spot for a honeymoon.

"Nope," said Ray. "We're staying right here in Woods Hole." He named the only good motel in Woods Hole. "So. Tell us. What's to see? Be our guide."

I blinked. Woods Hole is a village south of Falmouth on the outer elbow of Cape Cod, known mainly for its ferry service to the islands and the Woods Hole Oceanographic Institution. Summer residents came mainly from the Smithsonian Institution or the National Academy of Sciences. At some earlier pre-air-conditioned period, the Smithsonian gave the scientists the opportunity to buy a small plot of land and build a cottage in order to continue their research outside the malarial conditions of a Washington summer. I was surprised Ray and Connie had chosen to honeymoon in a place they knew nothing about.

"Well, there's Nobska Light, if you want to take photographs," I said while serving a basket of hot Portuguese bread, a local specialty. "And there are the antique shops on the road to Falmouth," I continued when I brought the chowder, careful not to spill it into the saucer. "Then, of course, if you like marine biology, which not everyone does, there's the museum and lab connected with the Marine Biological Laboratory. I like the pool with the seals." I spent a lot of time watching the seals. I also spent time playing pool at Captain Jack's, which I did not mention because I suspected billiards was not their style.

By the end of June, I had developed a successful routine for the tourists. I had learned a basic rule of American life: you must have a story. A talent for self-promotion is a key part of our national character. Our clean-cut crew of waitresses and bartenders were all hustling. We realized that these summer visitors wanted a story from the "locals," and not just any story. They wanted stories of uplift, of dedicated young people working their way out of the provincial working classes into the American dream.

So we weren't just hapless college students working in a restaurant. We were on our way to medical school, or we were saving for a trip to Europe, or we were going into the Peace Corps in Africa. This was the early 1960s, in what everyone believed was the American century. These visitors, many of whom came from other states on vacations they waited eleven months for, wanted to give advice. They wanted to tell us the consequences of roads not taken and possibilities not seized. They wanted to enter that elusive magic of a Cape Cod summer, those brief eight weeks of a New England year when the velvet air evokes a magical lightness of being and we all understand Henry James's epiphany that the most beautiful words in the English language are *summer afternoon.*

So when Ray and Connie asked what my plans were, I told them I was on my way to San Francisco and an exploration of the American West. I wanted to see the country. The road and the automobile were the American experience. Like virtually everyone else in my generation, I had read Jack Kerouac's *On the Road.* As a girl, my mother had lived in the same French Canadian Catholic section of Lowell, Massachusetts, as the Kerouac family. (And my grandmother retired to the same French Canadian section of St. Petersberg, Florida, where Kerouac's mother retired and where Kerouac eventually died at the age of forty-seven.)

They nodded sympathetically.

I was a twenty-year-old summer waitress who had just graduated from Tufts University with a degree in history. I had doctored my birth certificate so I could serve liquor (the legal drinking age in Massachusetts was twenty-one), and I was thoroughly uncertain of what useful work I could do in the future. I was in a frame of mind that I thought was temporary but would become permanent—the false cheerfulness of someone who was operating with forged papers and waiting to be found out.

Ray and Connie ate at the Landfall every night for an entire week. And every night they requested me as their waitress. If I didn't have a table free at my station, they waited in the bar until I did. They always ordered several drinks each, selected the most expensive items on the menu, and left a generous tip. By the third night, I felt like we were old friends.

Ray told me he worked for a foundation in New York. The Kaplan Foundation. Cultural affairs. "Saving Carnegie Hall and that kind of thing," he said. His part-time vocation was Democratic party politics. He wanted to know if I was interested in politics. I said I was.

"Who did you support for president?"

Had I been more sophisticated I might have wondered why a wealthy New Yorker was spending his honeymoon in a motel in Woods Hole instead of in one of the handsome hotels on Nantucket or Martha's Vineyard and talking to a waitress about politics. But I wasn't, and I didn't.

"Tell me again the name of that college you went to, where Adlai Stevenson was your graduation speaker?" Ray asked one Saturday night as I served them grilled swordfish. Ray's request for a double-thick slice had made the chef furious because he had to spend time cutting it during the busiest hour of the busiest night of the week.

"Tufts University," I answered. I had told him about Adlai Stevenson when he asked if I was interested in politics. Truthfully, I didn't know much about politics. Nor did my friends. During the Nixon-Kennedy straw election at our college in the fall of 1960, Goose Goss and her friend Paula had stuffed a man's suit with pillows, mounted a full-size photograph of Nixon's head from a *Time* magazine cover at the neck, and arranged two hands in white gloves holding a stuffed pink sock as a penis. The campaign banner above it read YOU CAN'T LICK OUR DICK.

We laughed so uproariously that someone in the dorm threatened to report us to the college authorities. Nixon won the presidential election at my college.

"The women's part is called Jackson College for Women," I continued. I didn't say it was pretty much a townie school then. The students mostly came from towns around Boston and small Massachusetts cities. Many were like me, the first in our families to go to college. I was from Swampscott, a small fishing town eighteen miles north of Boston, named for the long vanished Squamscot Indians. It was not quite part of the tony North Shore nor the fashionable bedroom community it is now. From the window of my high school homeroom, I saw fishing boats go out every morning. A few Jackson students came from New York and Pennsylvania, and the most exotic Tufts student in our class came from Hawaii. The one or two African American women (who were called Negroes) were given single rooms whether they wanted them or not.

"What did you major in?"

"History."

"What did you do there that was special?"

Had I answered honestly, I would have told him my most memorable event was the day I stood up in my geology class and flawlessly recited all thirty-two rock layers of the Grand Canyon, astounding the teacher and myself. I might also have told him about the time I attended a live concert by Ray Charles, who brought the sounds and rhythms of an unknown world to Medford. I might also have mentioned how I turned down membership in a sorority because they didn't accept Jews (or blacks). But I instinctively knew that for this audience my "story," like any good American story, required uplift and progress, so I said something about being on the debating team, which was true, and how my team never lost a debate. Also true.

"What courses did you like the best?"

"Writing," I answered without hesitation.

"But you weren't an English major?"

"No, but I was the Jackson editor on the *Tufts Weekly,* the school newspaper." I told them about a half dozen editorials I had written on the harmful health effects of smoking that had won a prize for the newspaper. (I didn't tell him that I wrote the articles while puffing away on the free cigarettes that the cigarette companies gave out at the college dining rooms after dinner. "If we hook you in college," the distributor told me, "you'll smoke our brand for life.")

"What else did you write about?" Ray asked, very interested.

"Well, I also wrote a series of editorials proposing that the college administration get rid of the housemother system and all the rules for women. The men's dorms had hardly any rules." The rules were called "parietals," and my editorials proposing their elimination had been astonishingly controversial. In the 1960s, men and women went to college under two entirely different social systems. Men had no curfews and few rules; women had to be in by ten o'clock every weeknight and by midnight on the weekends. Women couldn't wear slacks unless there was a blizzard or the mercury dropped below zero. No men in the women's dorms. Parents had to write a letter of permission if a woman student was to be away overnight. Any infractions of those rules, enforced by a system of grim housemothers, and you were hauled up before a dorm council. I knew about this because I occasionally skipped out the back door with my college boyfriend to be able to go to events during weeknights. I used to wedge a shoe in the back door to keep it from locking, then slip back in after curfew. We went to the fights at the Boston Garden, night baseball games at Fenway Park, and bars in the old Scollay Square. These outings made me realize what a much bigger and more complex world the male students experienced. Tragically, I was eventually caught and sent immediately to the dean's office. She put me on probation for the last three months of my senior year.

"Interesting," Ray said, nodding approvingly. "But why did you major in history instead of English, since you like writing so much?"

No one had ever asked me these questions before. I had no idea what my real talents or inclinations were. I had also gone to art school and learned how to do oil paintings, but I had never thought of being an artist. Why had I majored in history? The truth was that I didn't have a literary imagination. I liked real events. Although I often put quotations from Milton on the title pages of my history papers, I didn't think I had any talent for literary symbolism or decoding the imagery in *Paradise Lost*.

Ray focused me with a laserlike attention when I told him about my Russian history class and my honors thesis about the Soviet secret police. He seemed fascinated with my choice of subject and asked many questions. He wanted to know more about how the czar's secret police had metamorphosed into the communist KGB. He also wanted to know how I had researched my account of the Russian show trials of the 1930s. He seemed enthralled when I told him how I became interested in a photograph of the czar's children, four beautiful daughters and the hemophiliac prince who seemed to know that a somber destiny awaited them. The czar was inept and did not have much talent for governance.

"How did you do your research?" he asked again. I told him I had gone to Widener Library at Harvard and read unpublished dissertations on microfiche. He nodded intently. No one, including the professor who read it, had ever seemed as fascinated with my honors thesis. Even though students had heard rumors that all Russian studies professors were contacts for U.S. intelligence agencies, particularly the CIA, it didn't seem possible that my youthful professor, Mr. Metropoulos, just out of graduate school and still working on his PhD, could have had any secret government connections.

So there we were in the middle of the Landfall restaurant

with names like Dzerzhinski and Menzhinski trilling from our lips while I swooped back and forth to the kitchen, emerging with plates filled with lobsters, steamed clams, and other marine favorites of New England shores. Ray Rubinow and I might have been two figures in a sepia photograph of the period known as the cold war.

In the early 1960s—the height of cold-war tensions between the United States and the Soviet Union—the Russians occupied the same space in the public mind as Islamist terrorists do today. The covert war between the two countries was no less real because it was out of sight. My dialogue with Ray Rubinow reflected a certain type of conversation in which all discussions of the larger world were focused on weaponry, missiles, communism, the Soviet Union, and "how to beat the Russians."

"So what are your career plans?" Ray asked again a few nights later. Career? I had never thought about my future in terms of a career. Women didn't have careers. Where I came from, women got jobs, were chosen, got married. "What do you plan to do in the fall?" he asked. "Still planning to go to San Francisco?"

I had a boyfriend who wanted to go to California. The appeal of that particular boyfriend was that he wanted to be a writer. It didn't occur to me to be a writer myself. Women didn't have literary aspirations. I didn't know of any women writers. "I plan to travel," I said. I was serving dessert—baked Alaska, a Landfall specialty and a quintessential dessert of the 1950s—an ice cream pie heaped high with baked meringue, browned briefly under the broiler, and topped with a sauce of fresh strawberries. I told them I wanted to see the Grand Canyon and the Hoover Dam, places I'd been saving pictures of since I was ten. I didn't know that urbane New Yorkers had never seen the Hoover Dam or the American West, nor did they plan to. Their orientation was toward Europe.

"But what about graduate school?" Ray persisted, returning to his theme. "Didn't you tell me you'd been accepted at a graduate school in Washington?"

Well, yes, I had. My mother, who did not like my talk of San Francisco and who hated the domesticity she felt she had been forced into, had sent me a graduate school application with everything filled out except my signature. Had she been asked, she would have been one of the *90 percent* of mothers polled by George Gallup in 1962 who said they did *not* want their daughters to repeat their lives. On the other hand, my mother didn't know what a different life might look like. I had signed the application and sent it in without giving it much thought. I don't remember having had to include a transcript of my grades. I did ask the one woman professor I had for a reference. (In four years of college I had only one tenured woman professor.)

When the school's interviewer came to Boston, I planned to tell him that my application was a mistake and I couldn't afford graduate school. But the interviewer, Dean Philip Thayer, had consumed far too many martinis at his lunch at the Harvard Faculty Club to listen to me, and I was too respectful of authority to interrupt his soliloquy on daffodils and the delights of spring in Washington. During my "interview," he gave me no opportunity to say a word, thanked me for coming, and concluded by wandering out of the room. A week later, I received my official letter of acceptance from the Johns Hopkins School of Advanced International Studies. I had never written back to acknowledge the school's acceptance letter.

"Frankly," I confessed—Ray and Connie seemed like old family friends by then—"I don't have any money to go." Graduate school was never a real possibility in my mind. The only woman I knew in my college class who was going to graduate school was Verona Gomez, the daughter of New York Yankees pitcher Lefty Gomez. She planned to become a doctor and was going to medical school.

"What's the name of that graduate school?" Ray asked.

"SAIS," I answered. "Rhymes with 'ice.' It's part of Johns Hopkins but in Washington not Baltimore. It stands for—"

"School of Advanced International Studies." He finished my sentence with a big flourish and outstretched arms. "Amazing! The new dean is one of my very best friends. Fran Wilcox and I went to graduate school together in Geneva years ago. I even have a young protégé from Princeton whom I've sent to him. I'm like a godfather, you know," he confided. "I don't have children of my own. We like to help out young people when we can. Don't we, Connie?" He went on to tell me about the school, about his protégé, and about how exciting and innovative the SAIS program was. "International studies," he said. "It's the future. You'll love it."

I nodded. Although I had told him I wanted to travel, *travel* was no more real to me than graduate school. Travel, as Phil Burton would later point out, was a privilege largely enjoyed by men. Air travel was extremely expensive and undertaken mainly by businessmen. And the communication barriers for everyone—no credit cards, no easy access to telephones, no Internet—required hard work to overcome. Consequently, foreign countries were much farther away than they are today. I barely had traveled outside New England. I had taken a few trips to New York City with my childhood friend Patty Bresnahan. We traveled by bus, bought standing-room tickets to Broadway musicals, and slept in the apartment of Marcia Hubbard, who had been my "big sister" during my freshman year at the University of Massachusetts. (I transferred to Tufts because I hated being in the middle of all that farmland, disliked the fraternity/sorority culture, and wanted to be close to a city.) And I had gone to Pittsburgh with the college debate team. I had never been on an airplane. Airplane travel was for the wealthy business classes.

"You know what I'm going to do?" Ray seemed excited. "As soon as I get back to New York, I'm going to write to Fran Wilcox saying I've met you and tell him that I know you'll be a terrific addition to the school. Right, Connie? Don't you think that's a good idea?"

"Fabulous," said Connie.

TWO WEEKS LATER, IN August 1962, care of the Landfall, I received a carbon copy of Ray's letter to Dean Wilcox. The envelope had a return address in small black raised letters: The Kaplan Foundation, 55 Fifth Avenue, New York. Boy! I showed it to the bartender, Dr. Pharasles. This was the big time. It seemed like the *New Yorker* come to life. The letter introduced me to the dean, said I would be a superlative addition to the incoming class, and expressed the hope the dean would keep an eye out for me. It was my first letter of introduction. Who could question such a good connection?

The bartender was a senior at Rutgers in his mid-twenties but was called "doctor" because he willingly dispensed all kinds of advice on any subject. He was a former marine and, I thought, extremely worldly. "No question in my mind," he said. "You should go. Maybe this Rubinow guy will be a sugar daddy. Or maybe he's tipping off the dean that he found him a nice piece of ass." Dr. P. did tend to see everything as a sexual transaction. "Don't make the mistake of thinking that because it's academe it's any different from this bar," he warned. "Listen, everyone has a hustle. Buy some new clothes," he advised. "If Jean Seberg can go from Kansas to Hollywood, courtesy of Otto Preminger, you can go from Swampscott to Washington, courtesy of this Rubinow guy. Besides, what are your other options?"

Here he made a most persuasive point. My other options were General Electric in Lynn or the United Shoe Machinery Company in Beverly, where my father and my uncle worked. At over a million square feet, the Shoe, as it was called, was the largest factory in the country. One of my cousins, who worked there during the summers, warned me never, ever to go through its doors. I felt my future was a window that wouldn't open.

Also in August my boyfriend and I broke up. I had fourteen hundred dollars in the bank—all from summer tips. It represented one year's graduate school tuition but no living expenses. It was too late to apply for a student loan.

So a week later, I wrote to Dean Wilcox, mentioned meeting Ray Rubinow, and said I was looking forward to enrolling in the fall. With shaking hands, I wrote a check for the first semester's tuition—seven hundred dollars from my tip money. It was the largest check I had ever written. I added something about my hope that financial aid might be possible in the future. At the very least, I figured that I would have a chance to spend a semester in Washington, D.C. At the very worst, I would have to drop out. In my mind, it was a travel opportunity rather than a career decision.

Ten days later, I was on a plane looking down at the U.S. Capitol and the Potomac River. I was twenty years old, terrified, and excited. I had little money and, unlike most of my future classmates, no network of family friends to call on. I had the name of a women's hotel on Sixteenth Street and the telephone number of a distant family acquaintance who owned a men's clothing shop on Connecticut Avenue. My tip money was not sufficient to rent an apartment or buy food or stay for the second semester. I would figure something out, I thought.

If I could have looked into the future through that oval air-plane window, I would have seen myself six years later working in that same complex of Capitol buildings and reading copies of articles from the *New York Times* and *Ramparts* magazine, where the name of the Kaplan Foundation caught my eye as though it had been printed in neon ink. The Kaplan Fund had been identified as one of several CIA front organizations that channeled money into student, cultural, and political organizations. The largest recipient had been the international section of the National Student Association, but many other American organizations had been involved. A picture of J. M. Kaplan accompanied an earlier *Times* article. Mr. Kaplan had made his fortune in sugar and started his foundation with the proceeds from the sale of the Welch's Grape Juice Company. What could be more American than Welch's grape juice? The news stories followed the announcement by a powerful Texas congressman, Wright Patman, to hold hearings over the alleged domestic operations of the CIA. By then I was a little more sophisticated about CIA recruiting techniques. Several of my graduate-school classmates had gone to work for the CIA. (The CIA was interested in women because the Russians had women in prominent leadership and professional positions—they had lost 20 million people during World War II, more than any other nation. The lack of American public women made the United States look socially backward.) Patman had abruptly announced the cancellation of his hearings once CIA officials briefed him. But in 1967 the CIA had no such leverage to bring to bear on *Ramparts* magazine. New sources kept emerging to explain how the CIA had illegally channeled funding into all kinds of domestic organizations, including the AFL-CIO's Institute for Free Labor, the Center for International Studies at MIT, publishing houses, research institutes, as well as many other business, church, university, cultural, student, and women's groups.

Ray Rubinow was true to his word and stayed in touch with me, always offering cheery advice and potential connections, as needed. He identified himself as my godfather to anyone who asked.

Was it possible, I wondered in 1967, that my godfather's unusual choice of Woods Hole as a honeymoon spot might not have been random? Did he know more about me than I knew about him?

The question I had failed to ask during that fateful summer of 1962 was how could Ray Rubinow know that I would be such a terrific addition to a school of international studies from the way I served clam chowder and Portuguese bread?

Washington, 1962

The iconic images that dominated the media in 1962 were of the touch-football playing JFK and the extraordinary fashion chic of the photogenic Jackie—especially her camera-designed wardrobe, paid for by the Hollywood-savvy Joe Kennedy. In this media context, the formation of a commission to study the economic, social, and political position of women in America was decidedly not sexy. The President's Commission on the Status of Women did not receive much press notice. The White House announced its formation a week before Christmas, in 1961, the first year of Kennedy's presidency. Early in 1962 Kennedy appointed Esther Peterson, a labor lobbyist from Minnesota, as director, and Eleanor Roosevelt as chairman.

In the fevered presidential campaign summer of 1960, John F. Kennedy, the Democratic nominee, had made a trip out of New York City to the upstate town of Hyde Park. His destination was not the grand mansion owned by the Roosevelt family but an unpretentious cottage at the end of a long dirt road where Eleanor Roosevelt lived. Called Val-Kill, the cottage originally had been remodeled by Eleanor in the 1920s to get away from the pressures and social duties of the big Hyde Park mansion where her mother-in-law reigned as hostess. The media characterized Kennedy's visit as a courtesy call to the widow of a former Democratic president.

"Courtesy" actually had little to do with it. Eleanor Roosevelt was still as knowledgeable and as connected as any political boss in the country. Kennedy, who knew he was facing a knife-edge election against Richard Nixon (he would win by only 118,000 votes), wanted Mrs. Roosevelt's support and her political networks at his disposal.

Eleanor Roosevelt was not enthralled by the Kennedy candidacy. She had supported one of his opponents, Adlai Stevenson, and had been heard to remark that she wished young Kennedy had "less profile and more courage," a canny reference to insider gossip about his book *Profiles in Courage,* which was widely believed to have been ghostwritten and paid for by his father, as well as his failure as a senator to support civil rights legislation. Kennedy needed to court her.

The forty-three-year-old Kennedy and seventy-six-year-old former first lady had tea in her living room, surrounded by photographs of her prominent friends, many of whom had participated in some of the most historic events of the century. No Kennedy aides were present. Mrs. Roosevelt's secretary was out. No notes were taken. No one knows exactly how the conversation went, but Mrs. Roosevelt had operated at the highest levels of power, and she understood how politics worked: just before Kennedy departed, a photographer came to take their picture.

The candidate, who had never shown a glimmer of interest in women (save as bed partners) or in women's rights, soon announced his plan to set up the first Presidential Commission on the Status of Women. He promised that the precedent-setting commission would be housed in the Labor Department, and would have a staff, a budget, and the full support of the president. By the end of his first year in office he had issued Executive Order 10980, establishing the commission. The preamble and list of duties of the commission could have been written by Eleanor Roosevelt herself. ("Whereas in every period of national emergency, women have served with distinction in widely varied capacities but thereafter have been subject to treatment as a marginal group whose skills have been inadequately utilized." And: "Expanded services may be required for women as wives, mothers, and workers, including education, counseling, training, home services, and arrangements for care of children during the working day.") By March 1962, the twenty-member commission began work.

The commission benefited greatly from Mrs. Roosevelt's Rolodex, which provided many of the names to set up the remarkable network of women who served both on the federal level and on subsequent state commissions. Contrary to conventional wisdom, these were not all white, upper-class, professional women. Most had been active in radical political and social movements—particularly labor, child welfare, and civil rights. These women were veterans of the left and the labor unions, lobbyists for trade associations, case workers on Capitol Hill, and leaders from women's church organizations and minority organizations like the National Association of Negro Women. They included activists who had worked for child welfare legislation, education reform, and peace initiatives in international affairs. Many had worked in Washington and understood how social movements can eventually rewrite laws. Like Esther Peterson herself, the majority came from the Protestant Midwest, where strong labor unions, progressive farmers, and liberal teachers' organizations produced a population of women who were knowledgeable about discriminatory laws, political negotiations, working conditions, and inequitable taxes. They would provide the invisible floor on which the still infant feminist movement would stand.

To change the laws that institutionalized women's subordinate status, they needed to gather the kinds of statistics that had never been gathered on a national basis by an official governmental agency. As economists frequently point out, you can't change what you can't measure. New policies require metrics.

In 1962, women in America were still excluded from serving on juries, an exclusion the Supreme Court unanimously upheld so as not to interfere with women's functions as wives, homemakers, and mothers. Women were excluded from appointments to high-level federal jobs even when uniquely qualified. Women were denied credit and mortgages by banks unless they had a male cosigner. Women teachers were not allowed to teach in public schools if they became pregnant, and some school systems refused teaching jobs to married women. Airline stewardesses were forced to resign when they got married or reached the age of thirty-one, whichever came first. Women rarely received tenured professorships, jobs in educational administration, or admission to law, business, engineering, architectural, or medical schools, most of which had 5 percent quotas for women applicants, on the grounds they were using up a seat that should be taken by a man. Women earned fifty-eight cents on the dollar that men earned for the same work. In a room of a hundred practicing doctors, fewer than five would have been women. The number of women judges was less than 1 percent. Unless she were Katharine Hepburn, it was unthinkable that a woman would wear slacks except in the privacy of her own home. The commission documented that women's status in education, in the professions, and in the American economy was in rapid decline.

In the process of compiling this information, the Commission on the Status of Women formed a crucial link between the suffrage generation of the 1920s and a new emerging generation of feminists. Although the *Sputnik* crisis of 1958 had pushed politicians, scholars, and business leaders to proclaim loudly that the United States must enlist its best minds in the struggle to win the space race and beat the Russians, Mrs. Roosevelt pointed out that even at the most efficient functioning of our educational and social order, America had access to less than 42 percent of its best minds.* Women (51 percent of the population) and African Americans (14 percent, male and female) were systematically excluded from studying the sciences or entering technology-related professions. In response to these articulate criticisms of reality, the FBI director J. Edgar Hoover placed Mrs. Roosevelt under surveillance. (When she died in 1962, Eleanor Roosevelt's FBI file numbered more than eight thousand pages.)

Members of the earlier feminist generation were far from dormant. Three in particular were creating a revolution in consciousness about cities, nature, and the home. Jane Jacobs, in *The Death and Life of Great American Cities* (1961), struck a blow for history and stood up against an entire generation of architects

---

* In 1957, the Russians launched *Sputnik,* the first satellite to orbit the Earth. This achievement by Russian scientists gave credibility to the idea that the Russians were becoming dominant in rocket technology and winning the space race, a race that meant Russians could also launch intercontinental missiles. The *Sputnik* crisis sparked a national debate over America's failures in teaching math and science in the public school system.

and urban planners to halt the scourge of urban renewal that
was demolishing neighborhoods and the centers of old cities in
favor of suburbia and malls. Rachel Carson, one of the first professional women to work as a publications specialist in the Fish
and Wildlife Service in the Department of the Interior, published *Silent Spring* (1962), a book that took on America's chemical industry, the efficacy of "better living through chemistry,"
and environmental awareness. In the process she created a radical rethinking about our faith in industrial agriculture and our
lack of environmental intelligence. And Betty Friedan, a former
graduate student in psychology and labor journalist, wrote *The
Feminine Mystique* (1963), in which she challenged both Freudian
psychology and postwar America's policies emphasizing wom-
en's domestic role as the American Dream. Friedan put into
words the forces of consumer capitalism that kept an entire generation of women at the margins of America's economic and
public life. Her radical proposition was that being a wife and
mother should not be the totality of a woman's existence. Millions of women who read her book said exactly the same thing:
"It changed my life."

By the end of 1962, Congress had before it 432 pieces of legislation relating to women's rights. It was behind-the-scenes
work by women who promoted and lobbied for these bills on
equity for women. Edith Green, a former teacher and congresswoman from Oregon, introduced the Equal Pay Act, which
proclaimed the right to equal pay for equal work. Congress
passed it in 1963. (As a practical matter it didn't have great effect; women still did "women's work" for "women's wages," but
it was a law on the books that could be enforced at a later date.)
President Kennedy revised the 1870 law that prohibited women
from holding high-level federal government positions. A year

later the Supreme Court revised its ruling that women could be excluded from serving on juries.

Although I was unconscious of these new ingredients that were being stirred into the national political stew, I was aware something was wrong. After I graduated from college in June 1962, I expected my hard work and education to bring me opportunity and success. Instead, I couldn't find a job. The only employer who came to my college to recruit was the telephone company. "A customer-service job will be a good job for a year or two before you get married," the recruiter assured me.

A successful college woman of the era was supposed to have an engagement ring on her finger by the end of her senior year. What we see is what we can become.

But suppose there was no one to marry?

CHAPTER FOUR

The Honorable Schoolgirl

October 1962

I had been a graduate student of international studies for exactly six weeks when the great power nuclear confrontation known as the Cuban missile crisis erupted on October 16, 1962. Most historians agree that the Cuban missile crisis was the twentieth-century moment when the world came closest to nuclear war. By the time the crisis officially ended on October 28, I knew I had a mind-set very different from my classmates.

I had arrived at school—SAIS then was housed in a dingy town house on Florida Avenue, a marginal neighborhood that had long ago seen its best days—that first day of the blockade to find students and faculty huddled around the television set in the student lounge.

Everyone seemed to be in a trance.

"What are we watching?" I had to ask twice.

"Russian freighters heading to Cuba," said my friend Harry. I had met Harry the second day of school when he offered to drive me out to Chevy Chase, Maryland, to interview for a position as an au pair for a French American family. The Russian freighters were plowing through the Atlantic Ocean. Then the scene on the screen shifted, and we saw warships flying American flags.

"Quarantine," someone said. The warships belonged to the U.S. Navy, and they were fanned out in the seas around Havana harbor. "It's not a blockade. There's a diplomatic difference between a quarantine and a blockade."

"Do the Russians know that?"

Another voice explained that the Russian freighters were carrying nuclear missiles intended for installation in Cuba. The American ships were there to make sure the missiles didn't get delivered. For all practical purposes, it was a blockade.

"What happens if the Russian freighters don't turn around?" I asked. Long silence. That, of course, was the question that was being asked around the world. It was one of those questions that would send world politics in a new direction. Cuba, that little sugarcane island ninety miles off the coast of Florida, had suddenly emerged as the center of the world.

Americans were not the only ones watching television that day. Nuclear war had abruptly emerged as an alarmingly real possibility, and people in many countries recalled that the United States was the only power that had used a nuclear bomb. People saw their lives being held hostage by two great powers. Walter Cronkite, a voice of authority on the *CBS Evening News,* at a time when 90 percent of the American population got most of their international news from network television, asked in resonant tones whether "America was on the brink of World War III, only this time it will be nuclear." The next day, conservative newspaper columnists Joe and Stewart Alsop predicted "a worldwide nervous breakdown" over the global atomic future.

For the next three days we stayed glued to the televised news. Although I didn't yet realize it, my generation was the first to see world events unfold in real time on television. The Soviet freighters stopped on the high seas, but they didn't turn around. Their cargo of missiles was destined for bases that had been secretly constructed in Cuba by the Soviet Union following America's wondrously incompetent and ill-conceived invasion of Cuba the previous April. An army of Cubans in exile—trained in Florida, Louisiana, and Guatemala by the CIA—invaded Cuba on a marshy landing spot on the Cuban coast known as the Bay of Pigs. Tipped off by spies who had infiltrated the exile groups, Fidel Castro's well-armed military was waiting for the invasion. Over eleven hundred of the Bay of Pigs soldiers ended up in Cuban prisons. American planners for the Bay of Pigs, relying on unreliable intelligence, assumed that the invasion would inspire a popular uprising, the assassination of Fidel Castro, and the thanks of a grateful liberated Cuban nation. (Forty years later the same kind of bad intelligence and faulty assumptions would doom America's invasion of Iraq.) Instead, Cuba asked the Soviet Union for protection against future American invasions, and the missile bases were the consequence.

While President Kennedy ordered the U.S. Navy to blockade Havana harbor, he continued to negotiate with Soviet premier Nikita Khrushchev. The outcome was uncertain. It seemed that, although we had a youthful, athletic president with great hair and a refreshingly self-deprecating sense of humor, he was willing to risk a global nuclear war. I thought it was insane. But the habit of being a "good student" kept me quiet.

Within the school, the Cuban missile crisis was discussed as the steady use of force and a line drawn in the sand. The players were characterized as "weak" and "strong," with the denouement something like the shootout at the O.K. Corral. I heard much discussion about who had the president's ear and how the muscular intellectual blows had been struck. In the media, it was "an eyeball-to-eyeball confrontation and the other guy blinked." Word leaked out that Adlai Stevenson, then ambassador to the United Nations, who had advocated negotiation, was being characterized as Chamberlain at Munich, Mr. Peace-at-Any-Price. It was all very macho in a WASP kind of way.

The long-term result was that the fundamental absurdity of postwar nuclear arrangements bubbled up into many people's consciousness. The United States and the Soviet Union were the two superpowers that controlled the world nuclear system. With the possibilities of 30 million deaths in the Soviet Union, 20 million in the United States, and radiation sickness and fallout streaming around the equator, the realities of nuclear annihilation played an active role in global consciousness. (In some nuclear war scenarios, mortality estimates went as high as 160 million.)

Images of vaporized buildings and the human shadows from postnuclear Japan made a mockery of America's civil defense programs and public school "duck-and-cover" drills. To be told to "duck" (under the desk) and "cover" (your head) in the face of a nuclear attack seemed a cruel hoax. Japan was the only country that had experienced nuclear devastation, and images from the nuclear aftermath at Hiroshima and Nagasaki had begun to percolate into America from European magazines. Grassroots antinuclear movements were building in Great Britain, France, Italy, Germany, Scandinavia, and Japan. Within the United States, a group of students from the University of Michigan spoke for many young people when they wrote a manifesto that began, "We are people of this generation . . . looking uncomfortably to the world we inherit." Their statement, written in Port Huron, Michigan, in 1961, launched Students for a Democratic Society (SDS), formed the beginning of the New Left, and cultivated a voice for a student protest movement that spread to campuses across the country.

Whatever else may be said about the dynamics driving the social upheavals of the 1960s—the demographics of the baby-boom generation (born 1945 to 1964), economic prosperity combined with great poverty, inflation, de facto segregation of African Americans in the North, Jim Crow laws in the South—the Cuban missile crisis jolted people out of the endless present of American life. People around the planet feared—with good reason—the real possibility of nuclear war.

I was not the only person trying to get my mind around nuclear war calculus. In a nuclear war, there were no civilians. We were all in the military. During the five days of the standoff between the Russian and the American superpowers, the *Bulletin of Atomic Scientists,* which had published a Doomsday Clock since 1947, moved the hands of the clock to one minute to midnight, as a symbolic illustration of how close the world was coming to nuclear war. (Afterward, the minute hand slowly went back to twelve minutes to midnight, where it remained until the early 1980s, when President Reagan's rhetoric about the evil empire and Congress's huge increases in military spending convinced the Russians that the United States was planning a preemptive nuclear strike. In 2007, the minute hand of the clock again moved forward to five minutes to midnight, when nuclear scientists stated that "the world stands at the brink of a second nuclear age.")

After the Cuban missile crisis had been resolved, I saw an article in the *Washington Post* that said President Kennedy's willingness to keep negotiating with the Russians had been greatly influenced by a book he had been reading. The book was Barbara Tuchman's history of the opening days of World War I, *The Guns of August,* a story that examined how the secret treaty system among the European powers transformed what should have been the third Balkan war of 1914 into the Great War and the War to

End All Wars, later known as World War I. The *Washington Post* reported that it was Ms. Tuchman's descriptions of the ineluctable momentum of the war's progression—despite the best efforts of many of Europe's leaders to stop it—that influenced President Kennedy to keep negotiating rather than issuing ultimatums. I immediately went out and bought *The Guns of August*. When I read the opening lines from the book, they changed my life. Here, I thought, is someone who is asking the right questions of history and diplomacy. And what's more, the historian was a woman.

> *So gorgeous was the spectacle on the May morning of 1910 when nine kings rode in the funeral of Edward VII of England that the crowd, waiting in hushed and black-clad awe, could not keep back gasps of admiration. Together they represented seventy nations in the greatest assemblage of royalty and rank ever gathered in one place and, of its kind, the last.*
>
> *The muffled tongue of Big Ben tolled nine by the clock as the cortege left the palace, but on history's clock it was sunset, and the sun of the old world was setting in a dying blaze of splendor never to be seen again.*

My discovery of Barbara Tuchman and her influence on Kennedy's decision making was not a shared point of view among my classmates. Foreign affairs is a career choice for the upper class. Graduate school was the first time I was asked, "Where do you summer?" and "Where did you prep?" Male, WASP, prep-schooled, networked—these students were mostly children of wealth and privilege who were being prepared to take their places in financial institutions, international banks, law firms, foundations, and think tanks that make up the universe of America's foreign policy establishment. A woman historian who

was unaffiliated with an Ivy League institution was not someone they saw as influential.

"What is Porcellian?" I asked my friend Harry.

"A final club at Harvard," Harry answered. Then he had to
explain to me what a final club was. At Tufts, there had been no
final clubs.

Class is the feature of American life that dares not speak its
name. Theoretically, the very openness, fluidity, and social het-
erogeneity of American society are qualities supposed to prevent
anything as rigid as a "ruling class" or a "ruling elite." In fact,
there is a foreign policy elite, and the policies they decide on are
more or less impervious to democratic controls. The faculty at
SAIS supported the key players in the Kennedy administration and were quite enthusiastic about military intervention in
Southeast Asia, which turned into the Vietnam War. Forty years
later, another SAIS faculty supported the invasion of Iraq. Paul
Wolfowitz (SAIS dean from 1993 to 2002), a protégé of both
George Shultz and Paul Nitze, provided the theory for preemptive war and America's unilateral invasion of Iraq, now
viewed as the most disastrous foreign policy decision in American history.

It was slowly dawning on me that I was a triple outsider:
blue-collar family, second-tier college, and a woman. The most
troublesome aspect by far was my gender. My first conscious
realization of my secondary status as a woman came when I was
invited to a SAIS dinner at the Cosmos Club. These invitations
were extended to students on the basis of social skills or connections. In my case, it was because of my godfather's connection
with the dean and the generous grants given to the school by the
Kaplan Foundation. The school sponsored evening lectures by
prominent members of the foreign policy establishment that
included pre-event dinners at Washington's most exclusive

men's club. I received an invitation to attend the dinner for former Secretary of State Dean Acheson, then an attorney and man of influence at the white-shoe Washington law firm of Covington and Burling. I was quite excited as I walked up to the Gilded Age mansion near Dupont Circle. Modeled on the Petit Trianon built for Marie Antoinette at Versailles, the Cosmos Club was the preeminent club for Washington's establishment. I arrived on time wearing a good dress, pearls, and heels and reached for the handle of the ornate glass and wrought-iron main door.

"Hold on. Hold on. You can't go in there." The doorman rushed over and held up his arm, barring the entrance.

"But I have an invitation," I said, looking in my purse for the letter.

"You have to go around to the Ladies' Entrance," he told me, pointing to the back of the building.

Ladies' Entrance? This confused me. I'd never heard of a Ladies' Entrance.

"This entrance is for members only," he said emphatically. Although I was still unaware that members did not include women, Jews, or blacks, I immediately grasped that I was dealing with far more than how to get from point A to dinner.

I was seated between a classmate on one side—a wealthy Brazilian with patent leather hair whose main topic of conversation was the frequent suggestion that we have sex because "we are both tall"—and an empty chair on the other. After the soup course, a silver-haired man smoothly slipped into the vacant chair. He apologized for being late, informed me that he was a former U.S. ambassador to Germany, and said his tardiness was not of his doing. Leaning in close, he confided, "I was held up at the White House." Then, with crinkling eyes and a knowing smile, he added, "So I told my wife to call ahead and say I'd be late. After all, isn't that the purpose of a wife?"

"Mmm. But of course," I murmured. "How fascinating."

If the Cuban missile crisis revealed that I had a different mind-set than most of my classmates, the social experience of the Cosmos Club triggered a new wariness about how women were perceived. As one of only two women students at the dinner, I became an observer rather than a participant, a cast of mind that would became habitual. When I looked around the Cosmos Club dinner table, I turned into an anthropologist doing fieldwork among natives of a highly stylized and ritual culture. I was not wrong. It is a ritual culture.

In 1962, Jackie Kennedy was the iconic wife who seemingly was content to bask in the reflected glory of her husband. Julia Child had just published *Mastering the Art of French Cooking* the previous year and as a result had begun to wean Americans away from meat and potatoes and overcooked vegetables. We were all learning to cook veal Prince Orloff and were wearing dresses with big buttons and three-quarter-length sleeves. We did not know that Mrs. Kennedy was extremely intelligent; or that her wardrobe had been fashioned by Hollywood designers for the photographer's lens; or that her husband was a man with a life-threatening illness, troubling extracurricular sexual appetites, and a father rumored to have connections with organized crime. The Kennedys seemed glamorous and cultivated, and Things French were all the rage.

Few women spoke in public or had oratorical skills. Even the first lady spoke in a whispery, girlish voice, as women were supposed to. I began to notice that our professors rarely called on women in class. If a woman student—never more than three or four out of a class of twenty or twenty-five—gave a confident answer that might have differed from what the professor was expecting, she was quickly dismissed with sarcasm or condescension. "You must have gotten that idea from the Style section of the *Post.* Try reading the political news." There were no women professors to serve as role models or mentors, and few of the male professors were noted for their generosity toward women students. Several were notorious for their active antagonism and harassment of women students.

One, for example, was Paul Linebarger, who taught Chinese studies. He was as thin as a string and had idiosyncrasies such as popping out his glass eye if he felt students weren't paying sufficient attention to his lectures. He was known to make disparaging remarks about any women in his classes, most of whom dropped out. His misogyny was so pronounced it merited mention in one of the school's publications: "The eccentric and colorful Paul Linebarger . . . infamous for not wanting women in his classes because they were distracting." Two decades later, this type of "eccentric and colorful" treatment of women would be defined as sexual harassment and the creation of a hostile environment. Gossip had it that Linebarger, who had been born in China when his father was an adviser to Sun Yat-sen, wrote spy novels under the pseudonym Cordwainer Smith and had worked as a courier for the CIA.

Then there was E. A. J. Johnson, who strode into class wearing tall leather riding boots, form-fitting jodhpurs, and a rakish beret. At first, I thought he was rushing to class from the stables and hadn't had the time to change his clothes after riding. But it turned out he simply liked costumes and frequently came to class wearing his riding outfit. He also carried an elaborately carved walking stick and sometimes swept into parties wearing a hooded cape with a red satin lining. (Someone once introduced him as Zorro.) E.A.J., as he was called, had been a political affairs officer for the Supreme Allied Expeditionary Forces during World War II and later was the third-ranking official in the U.S. military government in Korea. He taught a wide-ranging course about the United States in the postwar world that students nicknamed "Wide Wide World."

Other members of the old guard included William C. Johnston Jr., who taught South Asian affairs and had once been chief public affairs officer for the U.S. embassy in India, and former dean Philip Thayer, the professor who had interviewed me at the Harvard Faculty Club, who taught international law. These gentlemen—warriors of the cold war—frequently had lunch at the Cosmos Club, a lunch that included numerous martinis. Students learned to have academic conferences in the morning.

With a few notable exceptions, our professors were not scholars. They were men who had once served in high government positions and were part of Washington's foreign affairs establishment. They were men, still enchanted with the possibilities of living abroad with cooks and servants and big houses and private clubs. On assignments in foreign lands, they were men for whom life still held the promise of being where history was about to happen. At home in Washington, they lived in modest three-bedroom houses and had to get up in the morning to walk the family dog.

My professors seemed to dwell in a region where the mists of colonialism swirled around them. And although they disparaged colonialism, they did seem to approve of the ambitions of empire. They saw American foreign policy as supporting democracy and free trade around the globe. If we were forced into military confrontations because of our 650 military bases around the world, it was a necessary result of hard-nosed power politics against a ruthless, unscrupulous enemy. Later, I realized how ill-equipped our professors were to predict the outcome of the course they were mapping in Southeast Asia and our ill-fated war in Vietnam. In other universities, respected scholars—R. W. Van Alystyne (*The Rising American*

Empire) and William Appleman Williams (*The Tragedy of American Diplomacy*)—analyzed America's role in the world quite differently.

Curiously, the course that I was least enthusiastic about—propaganda—led me to discover a seed that would bloom in the future. It was taught by George Allen, the former head of the United States Information Agency (USIA) in Dwight D. Eisenhower's administration, who was a golfing buddy of Eisenhower's and an easygoing teacher as he explained America's efforts in "democratic education" around the world. (We never called it propaganda.) For the course's required research paper, I decided to study the Nuclear Test Ban Treaty, then making its way through Congress (it was eventually ratified by the Senate and signed in Moscow in August 1963). I told Allen I would explore how the Soviet and American views on the treaty were portrayed in the press. Since I didn't read Russian, I wrote to the head of "press affairs" at the Soviet embassy, who seemed delighted to be interviewed by an American student. (This interview might have marked the start of my FBI file, since the FBI photographed everyone going in and out of the embassy, except for the embassy's annual May Day party of unlimited vodka and caviar, which was the highlight of the diplomatic season.) Only later did I learn I should have written a letter to Dean Francis Wilcox, informing him of my interview at the Russian embassy. When I told Allen I had forgotten to write the letter, he told me not to worry. He thought an embassy interview was very enterprising of me. Next, I interviewed some of the people who were lobbying on behalf of the treaty in Congress. To my astonishment, many of these lobbyists turned out to be women, even though American women at this time were supposedly nonparticipants in the public world. Where did these women come from? Who were they? What motivated them to take on an issue as complicated and sophisticated as a nuclear treaty?

It began with milk. In 1961, families in many neighborhoods began finding "Dear Neighbor" notes slipped in between their milk bottles. Like millions of Americans, my family had glass bottles of fresh milk delivered two or three times a week—the kind of milk we now buy in expensive natural-food stores. Signed by a group identifying itself only as the Women Strike for Peace (WSP) Radiation Committee, the letters warned, "This milk could contain strontium 90, which is very dangerous to children. Strontium 90 causes leukemia in children."

Strontium 90 was a chemical by-product of the radioactive fallout that came from aboveground nuclear testing. It entered the atmosphere during nuclear test explosions, traveled by wind, mixed with rain and snow, fell to the ground, percolated into the water table, was absorbed into vegetation (including grass), and was ingested by cows. Strontium 90 entered the human food chain through milk, and children were particularly vulnerable because they drank large quantities of milk. As small amounts of strontium 90 built up in children's bones, it caused leukemia and other childhood cancers.

When doctors first began diagnosing unusual clusters of childhood leukemia in unrelated sections of the country, they theorized that contaminated groundwater was the source. But this explanation contained several unanswerable questions: How could the same contaminant be found in different states that were served by distinctly separate watersheds? Although the government admitted nothing about the medical effects of atmospheric nuclear tests, scientists familiar with nuclear medicine believed that there was legitimate cause for alarm.

The government denied everything. In fact, the Atomic Energy Commission (now part of the Department of Energy) denied that nuclear tests were even taking place—even though the United States had conducted more than two hundred tests since 1945, averaging over fourteen a year. In the mid-1950s, after the Pacific Islands were determined to be no longer viable, the location of the tests moved from Pacific atolls to the empty spaces of Nevada deserts. (The other proposed location was Cape Hatteras in North Carolina.) Although the nuclear tests, called "events" as in "event Annie," were conducted at the remote Nevada testing grounds, winds carried radioactivity thousands of miles from the sites. Air currents did not respect state lines or national borders. Reports of contamination were coming from as far away as Canada.

As Terry Tempest Williams later wrote in her book *Refuge,* she came from a family of one-breasted women because everyone in her Utah family lived downwind of the nuclear tests, "atomic events" that they didn't know were taking place. Every one of the women in her family eventually was diagnosed with breast cancer. The state of Utah had cooperated with the U.S. government in keeping quiet about the effects of nuclear fallout on those living downwind of the tests. Many of those "downwinders," like Williams's one-breasted female family members, came down with cancer or leukemia.

The public opposition to nuclear testing by the women of Women Strike for Peace was all the more remarkable because any dissent from official policy was considered both unpatriotic and communist-inspired and could provoke an investigation by the House Un-American Activities Committee. Women Strike for Peace first reached the public eye on November 1, 1961, when they called for women across the country to stop the basic duties of homemaking as a way to protest nuclear testing and preparations for nuclear war. The unexpected result was public demonstrations by an estimated fifty thousand women in sixty cities and communities across America. The public demonstrations seemed to explode in an active invasion of public spaces—courthouses, city halls, town commons, the United Nations, the White House—by previously invisible women. Naturally, within five weeks the leaders had been called to testify before the House Un-American Activities Committee.

Elise Boulding, then a young professor's wife with five children, later recalled the November 1961 antinuclear demonstration in Ann Arbor, Michigan, as one of the most exciting and pivotal moments in her life. (Her husband, economist Professor Kenneth Boulding, had influenced some of the students who wrote the Port Huron Statement.) Born in Norway to a mother who had been active in the European peace movement, Boulding was an active Quaker. But she had not seen American women taking a public role in debating matters of war and peace. Like her, most of the demonstrators were white, middle-class mothers and housewives who decidedly did not fit the portrait of "communist subversives." The events of that day motivated her to go back to college, complete her graduate degree in sociology, and devote her considerable intellectual energies to peace education and women's studies. Her master's thesis, published the following year, was called "Who Are the Women of Women Strike for Peace?" (Boulding would eventually get her doctorate, become a pioneer in the field of peace research, become chair of the Sociology Department at Dartmouth, and be named a nominee for the 1990 Nobel Peace Prize.)

The idea for the strike began with women members of the Washington, D.C. branch of the Society for a SANE Nuclear Policy (SANE). Frustrated with the refusal of the all-male board members to call a nationwide demonstration for peace, women met in Dagmar Wilson's living room and decided to organize their own one-day women's strike for peace. Using their personal address books and contacts reaching across the country, the Washington women sent out a call for women to stop whatever they were doing on November 1 and "strike for peace." Over fifty thousand women participated, and their pictures, with baby strollers and banners, were in newspapers across the country. They brought a new style of humor and laughter into political debate, one that they soon had opportunity to illustrate before the House Un-American Activities Committee.

These women of Women Strike for Peace were not feminists. Dagmar Wilson identified herself as "just an ordinary housewife" rather than the successful children's book illustrator that she also was. They saw no need to examine women's rights or women's participation in government. They admitted they did not know the history of the women's rights movement. They saw their work as public housekeeping and based their public standing on moral motherhood in a nuclear age. As mothers and as protectors of children, they believed it was their moral obligation to speak out against the effects of nuclear testing. To that end, they educated themselves on nuclear science, radiation fallout, weapons systems, and testing protocols. They enlisted the help of technical advisers, wrote letters to editors, circulated petitions, and wrote op-ed pieces. They cultivated relationships with state and federal legislators. Since there was no platform for legitimate public dissent about nuclear foreign policy, public officials called them communist dupes and subpoenaed their leaders before a congressional committee.

By the time I was writing my paper, Dagmar Wilson and other WSP leaders had already appeared before the House Un-American Activities Committee. Wilson's articulate and intelligent testimony—prepared in part by Telford Taylor, the former war-crimes prosecutor at Nuremberg—made her congressional inquisitors look foolish. Suggesting that "better dead than Red" did not constitute a viable foreign policy, she made a brilliant end run around the Red-baiting congressmen by saying she had no idea if any WSP members were communists because WSP was a movement, not an organization, and didn't keep membership lists. At the same time women supporters changed the dynamic in the hearing room. They arrived with baby strollers and children, many wearing flowered hats and white gloves. Some of them carried bouquets of flowers and offered them to the congressmen. Every time one of their members was called to appear they stood. They spontaneously burst into applause when the chairman quoted Lenin and Khrushchev and said, "The fact that communists have infiltrated peace organizations does not mean that all members . . . are communists or communist sympathizers."

President Kennedy received a delegation of WSP members at the White House as part of a women's peace delegation and said afterward that he "found them sincere."

The treaty to ban aboveground nuclear testing passed the U. S. Senate in 1963 largely because of public pressure. Conservative senators criticized Kennedy for giving in to "the mothers' vote." Senator Maurine Neuberger of Oregon was the only woman on the floor of the Senate and refuted the conservatives: "We have been told that Senate ratification of the test ban treaty will be more a tribute to . . . the 'mothers' vote' than a rational reflection of our national self-interest. There is, indeed, a mothers' vote but it is not a sentimental vote. . . . It is a vote cast for the genetic future of mankind."

Spring 1963

I did well academically at SAIS. In any course where I was able to write a paper, I got an A. I did, however, have to drop international economics to keep up my grade point average. I learned that anything to do with the Soviet Union was well received, so I recycled my paper on the Soviet secret police and got high marks for political astuteness as well as good research. These subjects were not my natural inclination. I was engaged by other questions. In our course on American diplomatic history, for example, I was interested in the treaties with the Indians. One of America's very first treaties had been negotiated with the Delaware Indians to reward them for helping George Washington and his troops survive the winter at Valley Forge. They had been promised a sawmill and representation in a future Congress. What happened to the Delaware Indians? I wanted to know. (My father said there was Indian blood in our family and that there had been a lot of intermarriage among Indians and the Europeans in Swampscott and Marblehead.) This was not a scholarly interest I could pursue because I had a more important nagging question: Where was this all leading? After I wrote a check for my second semester's tuition at SAIS, which wiped out my savings, the next pressing question was: How and where would I get a job?

In the spring of 1963, I signed up for interviews with the international banks and oil companies that sent their recruiters to the school. That was when the dean's secretary crossed off my name. "Women students are not allowed to do these interviews," she said frostily.

"But what do women do for jobs?" I asked her. No one could answer that question directly. I inferred that we were still supposed to be secretaries, but in international or national security agencies. I was getting the idea that female graduates were supposed to be office wives: we would be smart and capable and well educated but wouldn't want promotions or raises in salary.

Whenever I had the opportunity, I asked one of the second-year women students about her future plans. Valerie and I often rode the same bus back and forth to Chevy Chase, Maryland, where we both lived—she with her parents, I with a French family as an au pair. During our long rides up and down Connecticut Avenue, she told me about the literature she was reading (*Doctor Zhivago*), her fiancé in medical school, and her job interview as an intelligence analyst for the CIA. "If I pass my lie detector test, I plan to take it," she told me. "I think I'll be able to influence policy," she said. I looked doubtful. But Valerie was engaged and would be getting married soon. Another friend, Ann, was interviewed by the CIA but failed her lie detector test because she lied about having had an abortion. "It was a hard choice," she said, "between personal privacy and the electronic mind reader. If I answered honestly, I could have been rejected on moral grounds."

Another time, I struck up a conversation with a classmate who looked like a second-year student. It turned out that Madeleine Albright was also a first-year student, a doctoral candidate in Russian studies, but had been out of college for five years while she married and had twins. When I told her I was from Boston, she asked if I ever shopped in Filene's Basement. I did. We had a few things in common. We both had been raised Catholic, although she said she had converted to the Episcopal Church when she married. We had gone to small New England colleges, where we both had scholarships, although she had gone to Wellesley, part of the women's Ivy League. We both had family members who had been in politics, although hardly at the same level.

Her father had been in the Czech diplomatic corps and had served as Czech ambassador to Yugoslavia before World War II and to the United Nations afterward. He was founder and head of the International Affairs Department at the University of Denver. (Another accomplished student her father would train was Condoleezza Rice.) My grandfather had been a representative in the Massachusetts legislature and the plumbing inspector for the town of Swampscott. My father had once worked for United Fruit and had been to Cuba, but now he was a foreman at the United Shoe Machinery Corporation in Beverly. She had gone to private boarding school, not public high school. She was bright and charming, with a surprising sense of humor. I thought she might hold some clues to the looming question of where I might look in the Help Wanted section at graduation time.

But, alas, a career or even a job was not one of her concerns, although she would go on to become America's first woman secretary of state. When I asked her what she would do with her doctoral degree, she was vague. "Maybe a think tank. Maybe teach." She was going slowly, she said. Her husband had a demanding career as a journalist. She described her husband as a newspaperman, but Joe Albright was heir to the *Newsday* newspaper fortune and came from one of the wealthiest families in the country. I was not the first to get the impression she was burnishing her accomplishments to add luster to her husband's career. I didn't sense much incipient feminism. (One of her later biographers, Ann Blackman, would describe her as an "opportunistic feminist.")

When I inquired why the school didn't insist that women students be able to interview with the companies that came to recruit or what the rationale was for the Ladies' Entrance at the Cosmos Club, she waved her hand. "Don't take it personally," she said. It was a minor price of admission, she seemed to imply. Savvy about how the Washington game was played, she knew what it took to become a member of the club, a membership whose value was unquestioned.

Was this a club I wanted to join? And if so, at what price? This conversation raised larger questions that I was able to formulate only vaguely. Were there any women anywhere in America engaged in foreign policy? If so, what were they doing? Another classmate had speculated that the women students were being channeled to the CIA, which needed smart people who wouldn't press for promotions or higher salaries. This was not Madeleine Albright's view of things.

We talked about her children. She said she was worried because one of her twins was speaking only Spanish because the nanny was Spanish. I hope I didn't look as shocked as I felt. In Swampscott, no one I knew had a nanny, and it startled me to think that a mother might not be able to converse with her own children in her native language. On the other hand, it revealed the true nature of our social status. She *had* an au pair. I *was* an au pair.

I remembered that conversation ten years later when I had a baby and a Spanish-speaking nanny and for a while my daughter spoke only Spanish. I spent frustrating evenings running around the house pointing at different objects while my daughter cried in helpless frustration for her *zapatos* ("slippers" or "shoes").

In the end, Madeleine Albright could not enlighten me about a future career in international relations because she was living with a certain amount of confusion herself. Her family had been Jewish, not Catholic. (A Czech cousin who lived with her family throughout the war in London arrived on a Red Cross rescue train for Jewish children.) They were not the poor immigrant family she sometimes implied. Her father supposedly had received assistance from British Intelligence in making his way from Czechoslovakia to London to the United Nations to Denver. The following year she would leave SAIS for Columbia University when her husband went to work in New York. (While completing her doctorate over the next twelve years,

Albright became a protégé of another Eastern European, Zbigniew Brzezinski, who taught at Columbia, was a founder of the Trilateral Commission, and offered her a spot on the National Security Council staff in 1976 in Jimmy Carter's White House.) Although Madeleine described her life to the Wellesley College alumni bulletin of 1969 as "a Cinderella marriage," she would not be spared many of the upheavals of the era such as divorce, single motherhood, and lack of professional support as an untenured faculty member at Georgetown University.

When her husband of twenty-three years asked for a divorce, she told everyone who would listen how emotionally devastated she was, but she remained clearheaded about the economic realities. Her lawyers asked for, and got, millions in a financial settlement, as well as a farm in Virginia and a house in Georgetown. This foundation of wealth and property, and her skillful use of it, eventually gave her the social capital to become the first woman secretary of state in American history. No matter how brilliant, a woman without tenure, living on an associate professor's salary in a two-bedroom condo, would not have been perceived as a viable appointment to the upper reaches of America's foreign policy establishment. In many ways, Madeleine Albright became the "perfect female gentleman," a phrase coined by Lani Guinier about Yale Law School during the same era. Since no one really knew what women professionals in these fields were supposed to look like, the stunted imaginations of our professors could visualize us only as female gentlemen. We were like immigrants in a foreign land.

It was not long after my conversation with Madeleine Albright that my adviser, one of the cold warriors, called me into his office and asked what my concentration was.

"European studies," I told him.

"Well, then, you must go to Bologna," he said.

"Bologna?" I asked. "But I don't speak Italian." SAIS had a European studies center at the University of Bologna in northern Italy.

"Oh, no one does. You don't need to."

"Why not? It is in Italy?"

"Yes. All the courses are in English."

"I'm taking French. Shouldn't I go to France?" I was missing something.

"Our center for European studies is in Bologna." Looking irritated, he glanced at his watch.

"What about financial aid?" I was out of money. I wasn't seeing a plan to finance this Italian adventure.

"I don't deal with finances. Go see the registrar."

I said I certainly would think about it. I liked the idea of going to Europe, even though, as I mentioned, in those days Europe was much farther away than it is today. I loved the possibility of travel. And by living in a French family, I had actually learned how to speak French, although I did not realize my accent was like that of a six-year-old child.

On the other hand, the issue of what I would do in the world and how I might earn a living was still an unsolved problem. I wasn't sure that going to a city I had never heard of in a country where I didn't know the language and borrowing a lot of money to do it was going to clarify the issue.

It was a beautiful spring day—truly Washington's glorious season, as Dean Thayer had promised me—so, instead of going to the registrar, I decided to take a walk on the other side of Connecticut Avenue and think about my future possibilities. I strolled down side streets lined with elegant town houses, many of which were embassies for African or Latin American countries. I was thinking about Bologna and a novel I was reading by Joseph Heller. Much of *Catch-22* takes place in the air over

Bologna, the Italian city where Yossarian, the book's antihero, tries to drop his bombs as quickly as possible and flee, avoiding antiaircraft fire. It was a book that didn't become a success until years later, but it marked the beginning of a new, deeply subversive attitude toward war.

I was burrowed in thought when a man loomed up in front of me.

"Stop right there," he said, holding up his hand. "Secret Service."

I stopped and looked around. I was standing in front of the embassy of a newly independent African nation. No cars were passing. Then I noticed that Secret Service agents on the opposite side of the street had also stopped traffic. I waited. Soon a black limousine flying the American and presidential flags stopped smoothly in front of the embassy's entry gate. President John F. Kennedy stepped out, tucking his tie into his jacket. Movie star handsome and impeccably tailored, he looked around as though he was expecting a welcoming committee of some kind. But it was just me. As he moved up the walk, he was no more than ten feet away. Since it all seemed remarkably casual, I waved and said, "Hello, Mr. President." He flashed his movie star smile and waved back. Once he was safely inside, the Secret Service agents motioned me forward. The entire episode took only a minute.

Well, that settles it, I thought. Take risks, accept challenges. I recalled the ringing phrases of President Kennedy's speeches—exhorting, inspiring, encouraging. Like everyone else, I had fragments of Kennedy addresses swirling around in my head.

"Let's get America moving."
"The new frontier of which I speak is not a set of promises—it is a set of challenges."

"Ask not what your country can do for you, but what you can do for your country."

Kennedy was an iconic symbol of American energy, progress, vigor. Who was I to resist this omen of the future? Why not go to Italy? Seize the day. I headed back to school to make an appointment with the registrar and set about applying for a student loan, known as a national defense student loan since the *Sputnik* crisis.

I was in a café in Bologna in November 1963 when I heard the news of Kennedy's assassination. Like millions of people around the world, I saw the funeral, the cortege, and the riderless black horse on television. For me, the television was in a little café in my neighborhood on the outskirts of the city. Seeing all the ritual and dignitaries who marched in the funeral procession, I recalled the opening lines from Barbara Tuchman's *Guns of August*. "So gorgeous was the spectacle . . ."

But where were we "on history's clock"? In fact, the sun of the old world was setting. We were about to embark on a revolutionary era.

CHAPTER FIVE

History's Clock

1907

Should you ever come to my house, you will see on the wall of my entry hallway an original sepia photograph from over a hundred years ago. It shows ten young women in identical mutton-sleeve shirtwaist dresses, each with the initials TBBT over her heart. The careful penmanship on the back of the photo identifies the group as the "Swampscott Tom Boys Baseball Team of 1907" and lists the players. Three of the nine players (the tenth was the manager) have the name Nies and were my aunts, my father's sisters. In the top row, second from left is Alice Nies, second base and captain; fourth from left is Claire Nies, center field; bottom row, second from right is May Nies, left field. They were, respectively, seventeen, fourteen, and sixteen years of age.

There are several noteworthy elements about this photo. First, a photo of a woman's sports team from that era is highly unusual. Queen Victoria had been dead for only three years, and cultural belief held that women were biologically delicate and incapable of athletic endeavors. Second, although the majority of women's images from the turn of the century are wedding portraits, my aunts saved no wedding portraits. Claire died on my birthday when I was two; May never married; and Alice married very well, but saved no portraits of herself as a bride.

Alice Nies, second oldest of the nine Nies siblings (my father was three at the time of the photo) organized both the team and the team photograph. Alice, pretty but somber, was also valedictorian of the class of 1907 at Swampscott High School; after graduation she landed a prized job as a secretary at Brophy Brothers Shoe Company, one of Lynn's many shoe factories.

Once known as the "Shoe Capitol of the World" (Brockton, Massachusetts, where the Brophy brothers had a second factory, shared the same motto), Lynn was a thriving center for dozens of huge shoe factories in the early twentieth century. Swampscott, Marblehead, and Salem are towns north of Lynn along the coast. Dating back to the 1700s, they each developed a shoe industry. Families built sheds in their backyards where people, mainly women, cut leather, stitched seams, and glued soles for shoes. A man known as a "factor" transported the pieces of shoes and boots by horse and carriage from stage to stage until the partially finished items of footwear were complete. This piecework system began to change in the 1800s when the factor's job was centralized into a single building—a factory. All the individual piecework was centralized and moved indoors. Many of the new factory workers were women who soon toiled twelve-hour days under rigid and unhealthy working conditions. Although the Lowell textile-mill workers organized the first Factory Girls Association (1836), their first convention was held in Lynn to get the support of the shoe workers.

Unlike some of her classmates, who went to work on the factory floor, Alice had learned the new skills of stenography and typing. Her clerical job was in the main office, and, by 1917, she had moved up to become the personal secretary to James Brophy, the company's founder, owner, and president.

A widower who lived in Jamaica Plain, a suburb of Boston, with two maiden sisters and his only son, Stratton, Mr. Brophy was a wealthy man. Before America's entry into World War I, the shoe business had been in a slump, but with war contracts things picked up and then roared ahead. Soon after April 6, 1917, when the United States joined the war in Europe, the U.S. Army began ordering tens of thousands of boots and shoes for soldiers. While war was extraordinarily good for business, it was not so good for Mr. Brophy's son and heir, who immediately volunteered. Three months later, in August, Stratton was on a troop ship sailing to France as part of the Yankee Division, officially known as the American Expeditionary Force, 26th Division. (The regular army divisions had numbers 1 through 25.) Formed from National Guard units of the six New England states, the Yankee Division was the first such unit to land in France. Stratton served as an ambulance driver, where, as he put it in his letters to his father, he saw some "not so wholesome things."

Although Stratton's letters were necessarily vague about his location—the censor's initials were always on the bottom of the page—the Yankee Division joined the regular army at the western front, the rural region of northern France that the Germans chose as their route to Paris. An area that was the most costly for France to defend, the German strategy was to "bleed France." Stratton saw the massive campaigns of attrition that included the now-forgotten battles of Château-Thierry, the Meuse-Argonne offensive, and the Soissons counteroffensive. The French suffered devastating losses (proportionally greater than any other country) under General Robert Nivelle, who was soon replaced with General Henri-Phillippe Pétain, who relied on the American reinforcements to stop the German advance to Paris at the Marne River. Over eleven thousand men of Stratton's division

were wounded, and close to three thousand died. By the war's
end, over 116,000 American soldiers were buried in Europe. (A
World War I division was made up of sixteen thousand men,
including artillery regiments, machine-gun battalions, and a
series of support units like medical and supply.) The road network in northeastern France was largely made up of unmarked
agricultural roads, few of which were paved, greatly complicating supply lines and medical relief. Stratton was soon transferred
out of the ambulance corps to the communications corps, where
he delivered dispatches to unit headquarters by motorcycle.

"Don't think I am neglecting you," Stratton wrote to his father on November 9, 1917, "but the nature of my work means I
can't write. . . . I am no longer with the Ambulance Corps having been detached to Headquarters as a motorcycle rider carrying dispatches to the different towns around where I am and it
sure is wonderful work." After the horrors of the ambulance
duty, it probably was wonderful. One of his letters described the
French countryside as some of the most beautiful landscape he
had ever seen. The German army had a salient that jutted
sharply into Allied lines, exposing the Germans on three sides.
The western tip of the salient lay at the town of Château-
Thierry on the Marne River. Although his letters could not
mention the towns he traveled to, Stratton carried messages by
motorcycle to the army units stationed around these French
hamlets. "My work is interesting, exciting. . . . When peace has
come, I'd like to come back here and travel my old routes."
Then he added, "I have also seen things of a not so cheerful nature." He mentions fierce weather, endless rain, enduring mud
and more mud, and how it took him three hours to travel fifteen
miles.

His aunts arranged for two of Stratton's letters home to be
published in the *Boston Transcript* under the headline "Over

There." He reported driving at night four miles behind enemy lines without lights, without being able to light a cigarette, his wheels within inches of a deep ditch. He reported that he had become a good mechanic, was able to take a broken motor apart and put it back together, repair an axle, and fix any broken vehicle anywhere. Major Beasley, his former superior, sent James Brophy Sr. a glowing letter about his son.

Brophy Sr. wrote to his son at least three times a week, telling him about Jamaica Plain, about his aunts who were knitting him sweaters, about his dog, Boxer, about golf at the Wollastan golf club, and about the shoe business. "We are getting our production in the factory up to 3600 pairs daily." And later: "It is hard to find help. We have a new foreman in the stitching room." Profits were excellent, even though the costs of materials were high. He mentions grossing over a million dollars in one month.

In later letters, his father worries about Stratton and asks why he hasn't heard from him in almost two months. He mentions Verdun and inquires about the nature of Stratton's "illness" and his hospital stay. Brophy Senior himself has had what he describes as a "health breakdown," and his doctors order him to go to Florida for a month or two to recover. Stratton Brophy was in the army for well over two years, 205 days on the front lines, and he returned with what today we acknowledge as posttraumatic stress. When he returned in 1919 to Jamaica Plain, he was physically whole but emotionally damaged in ways that were not immediately evident.

He took his place in the family business, married my aunt Alice (baseball team captain and valedictorian), and organized a life. For Alice, the marriage was a transformation. She made the leap from her parents' small three-bedroom house that often housed more than thirteen people ("the first girl out of the house was always the best dressed," said my aunt Flo), to a big brick house in Marblehead on Elmwood Road, and a Gatsby-like summer mansion in Wolfeboro, New Hampshire, with turrets, a croquet lawn, and twenty acres of land sloping down to the lake. Soon they had two children. The first, born in 1921, was named James, after Stratton's father, who died soon after his son's return from the war. The second, a girl, Jean, had Down syndrome and eventually was sent away to live with a housekeeper. Alice had two beautiful homes, extravagant clothes, a new Cadillac every year, and when she wanted jewelry, the jeweler came to the house and spread the diamonds out on the dining room table for her to choose from. On the outside looking in, Alice seemed to be living the American Dream.

From the inside, however, the dream was less happy.

Like many veterans of the Great War, whose trauma and posttraumatic stress went unrecognized and untreated, Stratton managed his war memories by self-medication, usually by drinking a bottle of gin a day. Alice took over many of the business decisions, ran the family real estate, took care of two children, helped her own parents and siblings, and kept an upper-class facade intact. One of her helpers was her youngest brother, Raymond, my father. Raymond, everyone said, had a quick intelligence and was very presentable. Still unmarried and with few family responsibilities, he drove his brother-in-law's Chris-Craft motorboat in races on Lake Winnipesaukee, golfed at the Bald Peak Colony Club, and went to work at Brophy Brothers Shoes in Lynn, while he went to school in accounting at night. In 1932, my father, age twenty-eight, accompanied Stratton on a trip to Europe where Stratton attempted to dry out. They also visited some of the lands and cemeteries where Stratton had been a young soldier. The drying-out part didn't work. What remains from that trip is a collection of old postcards from excellent hotels in France and Germany and a photograph of my father and my uncle Stratton, both nattily dressed, strolling on the boulevard at Nice.

The economic depression that began in 1929 was not lifting. Stratton, even though an alcoholic, was his father's son and a shrewd businessman. By 1934, he put Brophy Brothers Shoes on the market and sold it well before all the value had been leeched out of the company. Stratton never had to work another day in his life, nor did any member of his immediate family. My father, however, couldn't find another job. He started a mink farm in Swampscott with his uncle Joe, which they ran until the end of the Depression in 1940.

The same year Stratton sold the family shoe business, his son, young Jimmy Brophy, now thirteen years old, assembled an entire album of published photographs from World War I. The images are harsh and savage: men being gassed at Ypres, decapitated heads and body parts strewn about from crashed airplanes (no parachutes yet), miles of muddy trenches, pieces of bodies on barbed wire, a bombed-out cathedral used as a makeshift hospital. He also selected a picture of a completely denuded French landscape with a caption describing it as "once wooded and lush French countryside," language that Stratton had similarly used in his letters to his father. (Sometimes I wonder if my cousin Jimmy Brophy read the same album of father-to-son war letters that I found decades later.)

The official history of the Yankee Division notes that it "was inactivated in May 1919 [and] reactivated on 16 January 1941." The same belligerents had two decades to produce a new crop of soldiers for Phase 2 of the Great War. In January 1942, only weeks after Japan's aerial attack on Pearl Harbor (December 7, 1941), young Jimmy Brophy volunteered for the air corps. For more than a year Jimmy Brophy wrote home from various air corps training bases in Utah (Salt Lake City), Nevada (Las Vegas), Colorado (Denver and Greeley), Wyoming (Casper), and California. He said he was doing clerical duties and working as a typist. Then, in late 1943, he wrote to his parents saying he had been transferred to the crew of a bomber squadron, and the letter came from a military post office box in Europe. He and his crew left their base in England, flew four and a half hours to targets in Hamburg, Germany, and were never seen again. It was his first, and last, bombing mission. A year later my mother learned that her only brother had died in a battle in Belgium.

Stratton Brophy stopped drinking for a year following Jimmy's disappearance and then in 1946 began drinking more than ever. He slowly drank himself to death. When Alice called the priest for last rites in 1947, Stratton got up from his bed, roared that all priests were bloodsucking leeches, and chased him out of the house. He died without last rites. Alice lived another five years after Stratton's death, much of it in ill health. She saved every letter from every air force veteran or military serviceman who might have ever come in contact with Jimmy Brophy. I think of both Alice and Stratton as elderly when they died, but they were younger than I am now.

This family history was not without consequences. While I was growing up, my father's favorite reading was the memoirs and autobiographies of the generals of World War II. (He had not been drafted because he was thirty-five when I was born and his age and dependents exempted him.) I grew up hearing about military tactics and strategies, battles in North Africa and northern France, the Wiedemeier Reports, the smart generals and the dumb generals. Every Sunday night we watched *Victory at Sea,* a documentary television program about U.S. Navy battles in the Pacific. When I was in the seventh grade in 1952, I wrote a prizewinning essay on General Eisenhower, with the thesis that he would be a good president and not militaristic because he knew the horrors of war.

1964

So eleven years later, when I was twenty-two and a student in Bologna, Italy, my family background in military history did provide some historical resonance to help explain how it happened that I gave a lecture on General Pétain, the French hero of World War I. Unfortunately, Pétain had turned into the head of the collaborationist Vichy government in France and an ally of the German Nazis. The graduate-school class was on contemporary France and was taught by Alfred Grosser, a French professor from the Institut d'Études Politiques in Paris, who also wrote for *Le Monde* and who flew to Bologna once a week to give the class. Grosser had assigned me to give a report on French historian Raymond Aaron's new book, *The Sword and the Shield*.

I began by describing the "victorious" French general of the terrible World War I battle of Verdun, Marshal Pétain. Pétain had been the French general whose overall command included Stratton Brophy's Yankee Division. During the battle of Verdun, the armies of France and Germany sustained losses estimated at more than 1 million men—480,000 French and 450,000 Germans—over half of them fatalities. My task was to explain how it happened that twenty-three years later, in 1941, the old general, the hero of the western front, became a collaborator with the Nazis. The new hero of World War II was General de Gaulle, who left France and went into exile as head of the Free French. The old general functioned as the shield, the new general as the sword. Aaron's argument was that it was impossible to understand contemporary France or the history of the twentieth century or World War II without understanding World War I. France had still not recovered from the first war when the second one began.

That presentation was my single outstanding academic success in Bologna. Professor Grosser, generally not given to praise, told me I should continue to lecture for the rest of the class, a class that contained both French and German students. The subject of Vichy France, was, understandably, not a popular one among French students. For me, however, both the book and my report raised several personal and pertinent questions: Why was I so interested in war? Why was I able to immerse myself in constructing a narrative of two old French generals from wars that began before I was born? The truth was that learning about the realities of these wars illuminated some dark corners in my family history.

In textbooks we learn that wars begin with a declaration of war and end by means of a treaty. They last four or five years, as long as it takes for the belligerent powers to exhaust their manpower and their resources. Technically, World War I lasted four years, 1914 to 1918. But sixty years later I would find a set of postcards from France that Stratton had written home in the 1930s when he made a pilgrimage, with my father along as traveling companion, to all the battlefield sites of World War I.

The reality is that, in families, the casualties of war reverberate through generations. In families, they create structures of trauma. Mine was such a family. The war traumas of an American family, however, were comparatively minor to the war experiences that some of my European classmates talked about. I knew about Bologna from having read the war novel *Catch-22*; but when I sat in outdoor cafés in downtown Bologna and looked up at the building facades, I saw that many were still pockmarked with bullet holes. The immediacy shocked me.

CHAPTER SIX

The Failure Theory of Success

1963

Bologna sits at the edge of the Po Valley, with buildings made of warm pink brick and painted in over a hundred shades from yellow to cadmium red—an artist actually counted and duplicated 768 different hues. I loved Bologna, but by the time I reached the end of my school year at the European center of Johns Hopkins School of Advanced International Studies in Italy, I had stopped playing the role of "the good student," a role I uncritically had played for much of my life.

A series of experiences before I even reached Bologna had cracked open my beliefs in the view of the world that I had been taught. I had bumped up against far more complex arrangements of space and time. I was no longer able to look at foreign countries as compilations of gross national products and per capita incomes. I was no longer able to imagine the life I was being trained for—a bureaucrat in some international or security agency. As Joseph Campbell wrote, "We must be willing to get rid of the life we've planned so as to have the life that is waiting for us." The life I had planned—or at least had acquiesced to—was about to come to a dead stop.

Like a citizen of ancient Rome, I arrived in Italy by sea from Istanbul (formerly Constantinople) gliding past the old Roman fort into the port of Ancona. It was the last week in September, and I was almost a month late for the start of school. By then, I had felt the wind at Troy, seen Soviet-style militarism in Bulgaria, and traveled by bus alone across Turkey. I had seen the fury in the eyes of Muslim women who, swathed head to toe in black, stared murderously at my bare arms in a sleeveless blouse. Even though the temperature was over a hundred degrees, I acknowledged their stares by draping a sweater over my shoulders. Now I knew in my nervous system that culture and politics had a heartbeat.

This new consciousness came about not because of any careful planning on my part. After all, how could I plan to explore a defunct empire I didn't know existed? My countereducation was the outcome of a sequence of forces variously called accident or—depending on your perspective—openness or availability.

The best part of my Washington education had turned out to be the family I lived with as an au pair. They gave me generosity, warmth, interaction with delightful children, and the ability to speak the French language. Parisian-born Michelle had studied at Yale and at the Cordon Bleu in Paris. From her, I learned the techniques of French cuisine and a sense of how to approach a larger world as an explorer rather than a tourist. She and her attorney husband, David, had met at Yale. He spoke fluent French, which he told me he had learned at a summer camp in France. One evening, David asked if I could join them for dinner with his former mentor, the founder of the MacJannet Camp, famous in Europe for providing an American-style camping experience for children of the international elite.

"David tells me you are a graduate of Tufts," said the tall, courtly, cosmopolitan, aristocratic Mr. MacJannet, as we were introduced. He was equally pleased to discover I had experience as a camp counselor and was a Red Cross–certified swimming instructor. By the end of the dinner, Mr. MacJannet was planning my upcoming summer at his camp in Talloires on Lake Annecy. He painted a vivid picture of the camp's location in one of the garden spots of the world, the glorious Lake Annecy, high in the French Alps. Michelle mentioned that it had famous restaurants and that Escoffier had summered in Talloires.

"It will be a perfect transition," he said, "to your year in Bologna." Incomparable scenery, fascinating colleagues, the opportunity to speak French, wonderful restaurants.

"Talloires," David explained, "is the home of Père Bise, a three-star restaurant."

"There are only a handful of three-star restaurants outside of Paris," added Michelle. Unmentioned was the reality that a single meal at Père Bise would cost more than my salary for the entire summer and I was unlikely ever to dine there.

"Orientation starts in the middle of June," Mr. MacJannet told me, "so you must be ready to leave right after your school ends."

Of course, I went.

In the beginning, I was enchanted. Talloires seemed like a magical place. The camp was high in the French Alps, bathed in crystalline alpine light bouncing off the pure glacial waters of Lake Annecy. But at some point in July I finally acknowledged to myself that something was terribly wrong. Like the exquisite bouquet of alpine flowers that I had picked high in the French Alps but that drooped down into a wilted mess as I descended to lower altitudes, the camp looked idyllic but had some real-world conflicts. The simmering struggle between the director and his staff was growing more ugly by the day.

It was this particular director's first season at the camp, and his previous job had been as head of a Palestinian refugee camp in Gaza. He imposed arbitrary rules and expressed little respect for the opinions of his staff. At first, we tried to point out that our campers were the pampered children of international bankers or affluent European families, not desperate refugees who required constant surveillance and discipline. But the director brooked no discussion about his regulations. Soon, staff meetings bogged down in smoldering furies and ominous silences. Behind his back, we called him Queeg, after the paranoid navy captain in the novel *The Caine Mutiny*, whose bizarre behavior and estrangement from reality caused his crew to mutiny.

So one cloudless day in July, when the director called me into his office to discuss an infraction of the rules, I was careful to go into great detail in explaining an incident from the previous night. A camper had had a bad nightmare while I was the on-duty night counselor. By the time I got to her cabin, three other counselors were already there, and, since they seemed to have everything under control, I didn't go inside to add to the confusion. I thought I had covered the event quite rationally, but the director insisted I had never been at the cabin at all and had fallen asleep on duty. If I hadn't been there, I asked calmly, how could I have told you which three counselors were in the cabin? He concluded the meeting by telling me to pack up and leave by the end of the day.

I was stunned.

"But where will I go?"

He shrugged. That was not his problem. It was a distinctly Alice in Wonderland moment for me.

This was not like being fired from a camp in New Hampshire. I was high in the French Alps, with only a vague notion of European geography. I must have looked as though I had been hit by a bus.

The camp bookkeeper grabbed me as I left the director's office. "What happened?"

"I need to see Mr. MacJannet," I choked out.

"He's in Scotland. He won't be back for several weeks," she answered.

I told her the essence of the meeting. "It's crazy," I concluded.

"I know, I know," she said. "Alas, we all know." There was no appeal, but her empathy and her practical assistance helped a lot. She gave me the key to her vacant apartment in Geneva and some money from petty cash and said she would send me my check as soon as she could.

"Where's Geneva?" I asked.

Switzerland! I was reeling. My plan for the summer was in shambles.

By nightfall, I was stepping off a bus in an outlying neighborhood of Geneva, quite alone in a European city unmediated by any club, community, educational institution, athletic event, or church affiliation. I knew not a single soul. I was completely without bureaucratic cover. I always think of that moment of utter disorientation when I imagine what it means for immigrants today who arrive in America without knowing the language or without means of making a legal living.

The first week was more than a little scary. I had never in my life spent so much time alone. I bought a map and a guidebook, located the university and the inexpensive restaurants around it, and started to figure out Geneva's geography. Eventually, after my panic receded, I realized that although this was the first time I had ever needed to decode a foreign city, all those statues of men in buckled shoes looked comfortingly familiar—like the bronze statues that dot New England's town commons. The Geneva statues were not of English Puritans, but of John Calvin, a major figure of the Protestant Reformation and the spiritual father of New England. Born in France as Jean Chauvin, Calvin's idea that material prosperity was the sign of God's favor shaped English and American Puritanism and helped to build America's true religion, capitalism. (As someone once pointed out, Calvinism was the Reformation without the Renaissance.) Geneva stopped seeming so foreign.

I wasn't alone for long. First came the bookkeeper's husband, who, despite being separated from his wife, retained a key to her apartment and insisted that I allow him to show me around Geneva. He began showing up regularly. Then the doorbell rang again. This time it was Jill, the camp nurse. She was British and feisty. She hadn't hesitated to tell the director that his ideas for running the infirmary were insane. For example, she told him that it was unwise to keep all campers' medicines locked up in her infirmary. What if a camper had an asthma attack in the middle of the night and didn't have his medicine at hand? She was on the bus to Geneva by nightfall. Then came Louis, a doctoral student in French from the University of Michigan. I think he might have tactfully corrected some of Queeg's faulty French translations. The little apartment became crowded. The bookkeeper called to say that more fired counselors were on the way. The director was cleaning house, getting rid of all the people who stood up to him. Before the summer was over, the director had fired eight counselors and several of the kitchen staff. (The stresses of that season were such that Mr. MacJannett put the camp up for sale the following summer and told me at a later meeting that the director had been mad as a hatter.)

But by then I was long gone from Geneva. Jill was going back to England, and Louis had friends in Paris to visit, but I still had almost two months before school started in Bologna. It was Jill who suggested I look for a job as a summer au pair. So I made a list of all the churches in Geneva that served the international community and posted an AU PAIR NEEDS JOB notice on their bulletin boards. In the American church, I saw a three-by-five-inch index card that read:

WRITER AND ANTHROPOLOGIST SEEKS SUMMER
RESEARCH ASSISTANT TO WRITE CORRESPONDENCE,
FILE, MAINTAIN LIBRARY, AND TYPE MANUSCRIPT.
EXCHANGE FOR ROOM AND BOARD.

Mrs. Elizabeth Chesley Baity lived with her husband and two sons in a spacious old house on the shore of Lake Geneva in a village just beyond the city limits. I was her second research assistant of the summer.

"The first didn't work out," Mrs. Baity said, "because she couldn't type." Her son later told me that the previous assistant's typing skills might have been affected by her two A.M. bedtimes and subsequent hangovers.

Mrs. Baity got to work early in the morning, and our workday was usually over by one in the afternoon. I had the rest of the day to myself.

"Bologna is a beautiful city," Mrs. Baity said one morning while we sorted the mail. "The University of Bologna is one of the oldest universities in Europe, you know. It began as a medical school in the eleventh century, after the First Crusade. The medieval Europeans had never seen a medical school before they went into the Arab world. I think both the idea for the medical school—be sure to save those stamps—as well as the porticoes came from the Middle East." She spoke of the eleventh century as though it were yesterday. "At that time the Arabs were far more advanced in architecture, mathematics, astronomy, and medicine than Europeans. Petrarch studied in Bologna, you know. And Copernicus." I would soon learn that Mrs. Baity, as I always called her, thought not in terms of centuries but in thousand-year blocks of time.

Mrs. Baity and her husband came from Chapel Hill but had lived in Geneva for years. Her husband worked for the World Health Organization. She was a scholar doing her doctoral dissertation in anthropology for the University of North Carolina. She was the first woman academic I had ever known. It was energizing and exciting to work with her. At the same time, Mrs. Baity, who was a serious scholar and a good teacher—but without a classroom—must have recognized that she had an eager student at hand. One day, she suggested, in an offhand but deliberate way, that I might find the tools of analyzing cultures to be a useful addition to the study of foreign affairs.

She gave me an introduction to her library and suggested a few books I might like to read. Mrs. Baity was fond of the French anthropologists—Claude Lévi-Strauss and Paul Mus, a sociologist. (Mus had been an adviser to the French in Indochina and later advised Frances Fitzgerald in the writing of her Vietnam classic, *Fire in the Lake*.) For good measure, she also gave me an article by Bronislaw Malinowski and Robert Graves's books *The Greek Myths* and *The White Goddess*. I felt I had been given the key to a secret system. My professors in international studies placed emphasis on economic, military, and political systems. Chesley Baity was proposing that knowledge of anthropology and sociology were key to understanding foreign countries, and that I needed to learn something about cultural continuities. Hers was a radical idea. (It still is. It is why America's policies in Iraq repeated the same ignorance of cultural patterns we displayed in Vietnam.)

I spent my mornings typing note cards, writing letters, reading articles in anthropology journals, and trying to decipher her filing system. Not only was her research organization largely incomprehensible, but the departed research assistant had left a steep pile of unmarked documents about Mrs. Baity's subject, a ritual fire walk called the *anastenaria,* in which ancient peoples walked across a bed of glowing coals without burning their bare feet. The ceremonial fire walk spanned Mediterranean cultures and was a ritual test of a person's ability to negotiate between the material and spiritual planes of life. Mrs. Baity said it was still practiced in eastern Turkey and Iraq.*

Far more challenging than the intellectual work, however, was meal preparation. Unlike the sensual taste combinations of Michelle's French cuisine, Mrs. Baity and her husband believed in vegetable juices and bulgur wheat and other mysterious grains I had never heard about. Considerably ahead of their time, the Baitys were health-food advocates. They told me that smoking would ruin my lungs and my health; they introduced me to the concept that white sugar and white flour were empty calories; they said real nutrition resided in foods such as brown rice and whole grains. For the first time, I witnessed a machine turn solid vegetables into juice.

I didn't give up smoking. I never got to like carrot or beet juice. And I was only marginally successful with the filing system. But the typed notes and manuscript pages began to accumulate. The letters I wrote to professors in Bulgaria and Yugoslavia and Turkey eventually produced replies on tissue-light stationery

---

* Not only did it still exist in eastern Turkey in the 1960s, but it somehow jumped to America in the 1980s, when New Age communities reintroduced the firewalk. At a Stone Age site in Ipswich, Massachusetts, stockbrokers, librarians, and shopkeepers walked across glowing coals in their bare feet without getting burned in order to have a transformative spiritual experience.

enclosed in envelopes with stamps so exotic that I was instructed to cut them off and save them in a special envelope.

Everything settled into a predictable routine. I began to relax (always a mistake). Make no plans. Have no expectations, say the Buddhists.

One day, as we were reviewing the schedule for the week, she said, "I have to move up my travel plans."

"Why is that?"

"I need to meet with a key Hittite scholar who will be available only in August. After that, he'll be leaving for Mesopotamia—Iraq—and won't be back for a year."

"Where does he live?" I asked.

"Ankara, Turkey."

Which is how I found myself on the Orient Express, Europe's fabled transcontinental train, traveling deep into what I called Barbara Tuchman country, a land that held the ruins of defunct empires and seemingly lost countries whose names would bracket the twentieth century. Like a space ship, the Orient Express was a world of its own, hurtling through the Balkan states of southeastern Europe, crossing the invisible borders of the Roman, Byzantine, Ottoman, Austro-Hungarian, and Communist empires. It took me into the geography I had read about in Barbara Tuchman's *The Guns of August*—Kosovo, Bosnia, Croatia, Serbia (then called Yugoslavia). The Orient Express, which first began operation in 1883, was still the most important transcontinental European rail route and spanned a century of history and empires. Its elegant dining cars exuded the mystery and glamour described in Agatha Christie's and Graham Greene's novels, but the train was now slower and ran only twice a week. Europe's strict class divisions, however, were still maintained. First-class carriages had velvet upholstery and sleeping cars; fourth class had wooden benches. We traveled in second class in relative comfort but without sleeping accommodations.

After we boarded in Geneva, the train descended from the Alps, through the Simplon tunnel, down into Milan, east to Venice, and then into the Balkans and the territory of the former Austro-Hungarian Empire. When we crossed into Bosnia—I checked the map for the city of Sarajevo, where Archduke Franz Ferdinand and his wife had been assassinated on June 28, 1914—we entered the former Ottoman Empire, where Muslims and Christians had fought for centuries (and would do so again after the communist empire collapsed in 1991). The Balkan wars were the bookends of the twentieth century. On the second day, the train stopped in Sofia, Bulgaria, and one of Mrs. Baity's fire-walk correspondents, a professor at the University of Sofia, met us at the train. Until then, I thought Geneva was a foreign city, but when I disembarked in Sofia, I felt as though I'd stepped into a parallel universe when I got a sample of Soviet architecture and the Soviet military presence there. It is true that ugly political systems produce ugly architecture, but when the professor took us to a café on a hillside overlooking the city, I realized Sofia had once been a beautiful and gracious city that deserved its designation as the Paris of the Balkans.

Back on the Express—which we nearly missed because we misread the signs in the Cyrillic alphabet and boarded the wrong train—I awoke in the middle of the night to find that we had completely stopped. Peering out into deep blackness, I saw not a single light. Where were we? What was happening? Mrs. Baity was sound asleep, reclining in her upholstered seat.

I waited a while and then gave up trying to fall back to sleep. I got up and walked through car after car of sleeping passengers until I came to the last cars of the train. There I found the source of the delay. Bulgarian soldiers were harshly ordering a crowd of

unruly peasant families—women with kerchiefs tied under their
chins, men in rough work clothes, bewildered children clinging
to their mothers' skirts—onto the train. It was an entire village
being relocated, and the villagers had brought clucking chickens
and bleating goats and a lifetime of belongings tied up in blan-
kets and sheets. I had never seen such forlorn people.

"Who are they?" I asked the conductor in French.

"Turks."

"Why are they being put on the train?"

"Bulgarian Turks are no longer allowed to live in Bulgaria.
They are being returned to Turkey."

"How long have they lived here?"

He shrugged. "Since the war." He meant World War I.
"Maybe longer." Suddenly, the Balkan wars did not seem to
belong to the past. I was getting a lesson in Balkan Turmoil 101,
and it was in the present tense.

Mrs. Baity was eccentric, intelligent, energetic, surprisingly
disorganized, and a walking encyclopedia of the ancient world.
Magna Graecia, the eastern Roman Empire, and the cultures of
two thousand years ago were of far more interest to her than the
events of the twentieth century. There was hardly a question I
asked that she couldn't answer. Even though our purpose was to
follow the route of the fire walk, she was examining a much
larger context for her subject. Along the way, she dropped stories about myth and ancient history. For the first time, I heard
about cultures that were organized around agricultural goddesses and kingdoms that had women rulers. In small regional
museums, we looked at decorative symbols of snakes and but-
terflies and double-sided axes associated with female gods. I saw
images of pregnant goddesses and bare-breasted goddesses and
snake-holding goddesses. (The most famous of the snake-wielding
goddesses is actually in the Museum of Fine Arts in Boston.)

She hoped to go to Çatal Huyuk, an ancient city discovered in central Turkey that was organized around a woman-centered religion. "If you ever go to Crete," she told me, "you'll see the palace of Knossos and remnants of the Minoan civilization, a society that was untouched by war for fifteen hundred years. The Minoans had both men and women rulers. Well, think about it," she said when I seemed skeptical. "If your central religious image is a woman giving birth rather than a man dying on a cross, war and death might not be so dominant."

It would be a mistake to say that Mrs. Baity and I got along perfectly. When we agreed that I would accompany her on this trip as her research assistant, my job was to handle all the travel arrangements and logistics so that she would be free to take notes and write up her observations. Somehow, it didn't occur to either of us that not only had I never executed travel arrangements before, I had hardly ever traveled.

This was difficult traveling in a time long before Turkey had a tourist industry. Services were hard to find. Transportation was limited to local bus services. Hardly anyone spoke English. (Turkey had supported Germany in World War II.) Women didn't travel alone. I had trouble finding connecting buses between villages that would keep us on our schedule. Then, after we arrived at our destination, I had to negotiate with local drivers to take us to remote archaeological sites. It was August, and it was hot. I am irritable in the heat. Mrs. Baity liked to give orders and was impatient to see them carried out, but she didn't know how to make any of the arrangements herself.

On the other hand, she snatched suspect salads out from under my fork, insisted that I drink beer if I couldn't get bottled water, and made me eat lots of yogurt. I never got sick. She would eat any local dish as long as it was cooked. She never complained, no matter how difficult the accommodations, no matter how crowded the buses. We had a few days of long, strained silences after hotel rooms with furnacelike heat, no fans, and no cross-ventilation. But I discovered a talent I didn't know I had. I was a very good traveler. I could decipher bus schedules. I learned phrases from a Turkish phrase book. I asked travelers we encountered for recommendations about restaurants and little hotels that were safe. I became a good reader of maps. I recognized that I was seeing things I might never see again with a guide who had rare knowledge.

In Istanbul, the crossroads of the Christian and Islamic worlds, I got a glimmer that my construct of assumed truths was flimsy. Having grown up in the Roman Catholic Church, I had always understood the crusades of medieval Europe to be a great Christian project against a barbarian enemy. How could I have known that the Muslim cities of the Middle East contained a mixed population of Christians, Jews, and Muslims who lived together in relative harmony? Or that the crusading Christians came from medieval towns beset by disease and failing agriculture? Or that the Catholic Church combined the concept of a religious pilgrimage with a military assault to recover the Holy Land and its riches from its Muslim rulers?

In fact, in 1204, the soldiers of the Fourth Crusade, who left from Venice, ended up by sacking and looting Constantinople, a Christian city, and washed it in blood on a scale that shocked Europe, even in an era when sacking and pillaging were daily fare. By savaging the city, the crusaders discredited the pope, ended three centuries of crusades (although not the pope's impulse to retrieve the lands of the Middle East from the theoretical infidels), and opened Europe to the advance of the Islamic armies and the Ottoman Empire.

From Istanbul, Mrs. Baity and I took a boat out to Turkey's Elizabeth Islands, where Sephardic Jews had settled after the

Spanish Inquisition expelled them from Spain in 1492, and then we traveled down to the Dardanelles and the ancient city of Troy. From the port of Izmir, from which thousands of Armenians escaped during the Armenian genocide, we traveled along the coast to Miletus, Didyma, Ephesus, Bodrum, and Kas into another world and another dimension of time. Today I see them as names on a map, but then they were my route into the world of myth, a world so ancient and so overpowering that my underdeveloped imagination simply quit. In the full noonday sun I sat down on the marble steps of the great library at Ephesus, stretched out on my back, and fell into a deep sleep. No one could wake me up.

"What happened to you up there?" Mrs. Baity asked when we were back in Selçuk, the ragged little village, where I had negotiated the cab and guide to take us to the site at Ephesus. She looked worried.

"I don't know. I just became exhausted. I couldn't keep my eyes open. How long was I asleep?"

"Maybe twenty minutes. Maybe a half an hour. I think it took a while for the guide to find me. Has that ever happened before?" She told me later she thought I might have narcolepsy.

"Well, look," I said, trying to explain the confusion I felt. "Here we are in this scabby little Turkish town"—I gestured to encompass our immediate surroundings, which were very third world—"that is supposedly part of our modern civilization. And there"—I pointed up toward the heights of the ancient city of Ephesus—"is a city from thousands of years ago whose people we call primitive, and yet it's made of marble and it's gorgeous."

"Aha," said Mrs. Baity. "Yes!" She didn't look worried anymore. In fact, she had an amused twinkle in her eyes. A little cognitive dissonance was only to the good, as far as she was concerned. "I don't think anyone has ever called the Greeks primitive. The Greeks knew everything. But how we order time and space are fundamental differences between cultures," she said, ordering two more cups of tea. "If we were Chinese, we would be living in the year 4661 rather than 1963. On a Chinese map, Ephesus would be labeled as the capital of Roman Asia, which it was. Before that it was a major city of Greece. It's just part of a different time line. You know, like translating a language. You need a different vocabulary for time." She realized what I didn't: that I needed to recalibrate my sense of time. My mind could not process the idea of walking the streets of a three-thousand-year-old city, so it shut down and went to sleep.

"In Boston, time begins in 1620," I explained lamely. "It's all I've known." I was having a lot of trouble getting my mind around thousand-year increments of time.

"You'll get over it," she answered sympathetically. "Speaking of time, how many days before we get to Ankara?" We had been traveling for close to a month. "I have to get to Ankara by next Friday, or else my professor will have packed up and left."

Friday. Friday was definitely part of my time line. Friday, however, would hold a surprise for me.

In Ankara, I received startling news. A telegram addressed to me from the SAIS director at Bologna had arrived at Mrs. Baity's Geneva home. Her son read it to me over the phone. The telegram said, in effect, "Show up on time, or don't show up at all." The director was denying me permission to take the trip that I was already on. What's more, he gave me a deadline by which I had to arrive, and, if I didn't meet it, I would no longer be considered an enrolled student at Johns Hopkins University. The deadline was September 23, four days away.

Under the duress of the director's telegram I had no choice but to show up at school. Mrs. Baity regretfully understood that she would have to do the last leg of her trip alone. Since at that time air travel was for the business classes and stunningly expensive, early the next morning I boarded a bus in Ankara and began the seventeen-hour journey to Istanbul. The route had many stops in rural villages where women still wore traditional dress—black head scarfs and black veils from head to toe—despite a decree banning head scarfs. (In his efforts to abolish the Ottoman Empire and create a modern Turkish Republic in 1923, Mustafa Kemal Atatürk recognized equal rights of men and women under secular law and proclaimed that any women still covered in black veils would be considered prostitutes. His decrees were only partially successful.) Outside the cities, Turkey was still ruled by ancient tribal customs, and the culture of the sultan and caliph lived on. Mrs. Baity had warned me that under no circumstances should I ever wear slacks or shorts. But even my bare legs below my skirt and bare arms in a sleeveless blouse were an insult to the Muslim concept of womanhood. For the villagers bare flesh and European dress were the costume of prostitution. I was not without sympathy, but there was little I could do to cross the cultural divide. It was on this interminable trip across Turkey that I began to form a view of international affairs that included women.

To avoid the stares of the black-veiled Turkish women, I sat in the back of the bus, engulfed in scorching wind and dust that blasted through wide-open windows. Mercifully, some of the black-robed women who looked at me with hostilty got off at the next village. A few villages later, the driver swung into a deserted town square, shut off the engine, said something to the passengers in Turkish, and then jumped off the bus. Much to my astonishment, my fellow passengers all got up from their seats and, following the driver, disappeared into the village beyond. I didn't dare move. I didn't have the slightest idea of what was going on. I wondered if the angry women on the bus had filed a complaint against me for indecent exposure.

Finally, when no one came back, I moved off the bus into the weak shade of the few trees in the empty square. Soon men with dark eyes in unsmiling faces came out of the village. Silently staring at me, they formed a semicircle around the bench where I sat. Oh no, I silently prayed. Don't let this turn into a primitive village moment. I was recalling the scene in *Zorba the Greek* where villagers in a remote hamlet stoned a young widow to death for adultery. In the manner of an anthropological documentary, I began to narrate the scene: "Stoning is a ritual form of murder in which complicity is shared by all members of the village. . . ." Maybe you have been reading too many anthropology books, I scolded myself.

The bus driver eventually reappeared with all the other passengers trailing along after him. Smiling and chattering, they climbed on board the bus. The driver handed me a drink and a sandwich of roasted lamb on flat bread, good-naturedly refused any payment, and swung into the driver's seat. He started the engine, and, as we headed off in a cloud of dust, one of the new passengers, a Turkish student who knew some English, explained to me that this village was always the lunch stop on the Ankara-to-Istanbul route. On that particular day there had been a local festival going on. "One of the passengers told the villagers there was a Swedish girl on the bus. That's why the men came out to look at you. They had never seen a Swedish girl." I learned later that "Swedish" was code for "easy sex"; some Turkish men had seen Swedish films of the 1960s. Supposedly, it was every Turkish man's dream to meet a Swedish girl.

Soon the bus was humming across the flat, ginger-colored landscape of the endless Anatolian plain. For hours on end, I looked out at golden fields. It was September, and the wheat harvest was still going on. Framed through the open windows, I saw women in black winnowing grain from the chaff by throwing the wheat into the air with small wooden pitchforks. The motion was slow and rhythmic. The wheat paused in the sun for a fraction of a second before it fell to the ground. In that moment of the pause, I finally felt the reality of a thousand years. People had grown and winnowed wheat on that Anatolian plain for eons.

We arrived in Istanbul at one in the morning, and, within ten minutes, the bus station was almost deserted. It quickly had taken on the feeling of a very unsafe place. I saw only one taxi, and it was driven by an unshaven driver who leered at me from behind the wheel of his strange, hybrid American car—another symbol of the American military. (Turkish taxis were assembled and repaired with parts cannibalized from cars bought from American soldiers stationed at military bases in Turkey.) I waved him on and waited for the next taxi, but there was no next taxi. I had come on the last bus.

So I got out my map of Istanbul, looked up the address of the hotel where I had made a reservation, and began walking. About five minutes into my walk, I began hearing footsteps behind me and realized the full idiocy of being alone on the streets of Istanbul in the middle of the night. But there I was. No turning back. I walked faster. The steps walked faster. Then the steps speeded up even more. I started to panic.

As the sound came up close behind me, a cooler part of my brain took over. I turned around and looked the man in the eye. "Fifty dollars," I said in Turkish.

He looked shocked. Angrily muttering something I couldn't understand, he turned and walked off in the opposite direction.

Only a prostitute would be out on the street at night, I thought.

So I might as well behave like one. I made myself walk the rest of the way to the hostel with purposeful strides, as though the streets were mine. No one bothered me after that. But soon there was a new obstacle.

The next day, I found that the Orient Express train had departed that very morning and there wouldn't be another for four days. If I waited, I would miss the deadline the Bologna director had given me in his telegram.

"Your best alternative to Italy," said the clerk at the Thomas Cook Travel Agency, "is by sea."

"Sea?"

"Yes. The boat leaves tomorrow morning, has a daylong stopover in Greece, and arrives in Ancona, Italy the following morning. From there, it's only a three-hour train ride to Bologna. I can apply your train ticket to the boat fare, and you will have a cabin."

"Well, I don't know," I said doubtfully. I was still absorbing the fact that I had missed the train. Once again, I would be going beyond the boundaries of my maps. Where was Greece in relation to Turkey and Italy? I didn't know where Ancona was. But by then I was a much more experienced traveler. Unknown destinations no longer fazed me. After the heat and dust of the Anatolian plain, the thought of an ocean journey sounded appealing. "How long does it take? How much more does it cost?" I would meet my deadline, but just barely.

"You'll be in Bologna in three days."

"It's the best solution," said a man standing nearby. "I too missed the train. I'm in the same boat, as it were."

I laughed.

Hans was short and bald and spoke English with a thick German accent, but after my long trip alone across Turkey, I was grateful to talk to another English-speaking person. He said he worked for the Brookings Institution in Washington and wasn't I lucky to be going to Bologna. What about meeting for dinner? I signed my next to last traveler's check, bought my ticket, and said I would be happy to meet him for dinner at a restaurant near my hotel.

During a pleasant dinner, I told him about my journey with Mrs. Baity across Turkey. "Would you like to see the red-light district of Istanbul?" he asked casually as we walked back to my hotel. "It's quite famous, and it's not far from here. It would round out your Turkish travels."

I mentioned that the boat left early in the morning. It's not very far, he continued. "Well, okay," I said, "if it's close by. And you said it's like Pigalle." Place Pigalle, the red-light district in the Montmartre neighborhood of Paris, was a brightly lit square that attracted a lot of tourists. But the Istanbul red-light district was nothing like Pigalle.

We walked through a labyrinth of side streets and then into a maze of alleys. "Shouldn't we go back?" I asked. Hans pointed to one more side street, the width of a driveway.

This last alley ended in a dead end. At the end of the alley stood two very tall, husky men on either side of a wooden gate. As we got closer, I realized they were in uniform and were U.S. Military Police. They looked like they once might have been football tackles. Without a word, the MPs opened the gate for us and we stepped through—out of the dark quiet of the Istanbul night into a teeming square swarming with men, almost all of them soldiers and sailors in American uniforms. I caught my breath. It had the sound and motion of a buzzing, swarming hive. Surrounding the enclosed square were hotels and brothels with girls who stood in the doorways and beckoned men to come in. As I took in the pimps, loud music, raucous laughter, and the pushing and fighting, I realized that many of the girls

I saw—despite the heavy makeup and tight dresses—were teen-agers. The first girl I could see closely looked like she was about fourteen. In a Muslim country where women are often swathed in yards of fabric, it was shocking to see girls in short, tight European dresses and various stages of undress. I understood why I had been stared at on the bus.

Soon someone in authority saw me and shouted in American English, "Get her out of here." Very quickly, the MPs material-ized on either side of us, clearing a path through the crowd of American uniforms. We were swiftly pushed back toward the gate. Then the gate swung open, and we stepped through. Back into the dark and the silence.

Later, I almost thought I had dreamed it. But I knew I hadn't. I also understood then that teenage prostitution was the unmen-tioned underside of America's military might, not a topic for discussion in the think tanks of international affairs. If Hans thought it might have been an erotic turn-on to induce me to sleep with him, he soon realized his mistake. On the boat the next day he never mentioned it. He struck up a conversation with two German girls who were students and bought us all tickets for the day trip during the stopover in Piraeus. Hans was staying in Greece.

"Where are we going?" I asked suspiciously when he handed me my ticket.

"Delphi. Mount Parnassós, home of the gods. The ancients regarded Delphi as the center of the world. Popes, emperors, and mere kings all came to Delphi to discover their futures." Hans paid for our tickets, paid for our meals, and ordered pho-tographs of all of us at Delphi, one of which I sent home to my parents. It survived many years and many moves.

"You really should get a camera," Hans told me as we re-turned to the ship. I told him I traveled without a camera because

I didn't want the bother. But I also wanted the experience of being wherever I was without the mental reservation of composing a picture. "I will send you some photos to Bologna," he assured me.

The ship sailed overnight to Italy and arrived the next morning in the harbor at Ancona. Just as the Thomas Cook agent promised, I was in Bologna by four in the afternoon and raced to the director's office to verify my presence.

It was September 23, my birthday. I was twenty-two.

My travels had shown me a glimpse of another world. They had not prepared me for sitting in a classroom. In our classes—where time began with World War II and where we discussed economic development, land reform in undeveloped countries, or the communist menace in Southeast Asia—I knew that the winning of peasant hearts and minds was far from simple. The words *rural* and *peasant* were no longer abstractions. I remembered the women on the bus and in the wheat fields. I remembered the teenagers in the red-light district. I was restless and distracted.

At Bologna, the dynamics of the interactions between the European and American students were complex, and they became even more complex after November 22 and the assassination of President Kennedy. None of the European students believed that the assassination was the work of twenty-four-year-old Lee Harvey Oswald. And after Jack Ruby shot that one lone man as he was being transported from one jail to another prison, the Italians started developing their own theories. The Italians in my neighborhood café and the European students saw these events through a very different set of lenses than the Americans. Their collective memory included Borgia popes, Mussolini's rise and demise, as well as Joe Kennedy's ambassadorship to England and his favorable views of Hitler. The Italians shook their heads and muttered Mafioso and nightclub owner Jack Ruby in the same breath.* Oswald was too insignificant, said the European students, to have accomplished such a historic feat. It takes a lot of information and logistics to be in the right place at the right time to kill a president. And why else, they speculated, would Jack Ruby have had to kill him? It was too big, too sudden, too overwhelming.

"Why is power in America any different than it is anywhere else?" asked Maria, a Spanish student who called me "Hoody" because she couldn't pronounce the "J" sound. "All leaders get assassinated because they have powerful enemies. What about Lincoln? McKinley? How is America different?"

The real barrier was American exceptionalism. We Americans insisted that America *was* different—that, unlike Europe, our political system could transfer power without a revolution, a civil war, a hanging, or a kidnapping. American democracy, we insisted, was governed by laws, not bullets. To challenge that hypothesis, the European students asked us about lynchings of Negroes in the American South. Why did the admission of James Meredith, the first black student to enter the all-white University of Mississippi, cause riots, and why did federal troops have to intervene to protect him? A French journalist, after all, had been one of the people shot and killed during the Meredith race riots. The European students asked about the burning and bombing of the interstate buses during the freedom rides. They wanted to know about lunch counter sit-ins, the Ku Klux Klan,

---

* By 2003, the fortieth anniversary of the Kennedy assassination, the majority of the American public no longer believed that Lee Harvey Oswald was the lone assassin. Carlos Marcello—the mob boss of New Orleans and Dallas, and Jack Ruby's employer—was known to harbor a long-standing vendetta against Bobby Kennedy, the president's brother, who had given the orders to deport Marcello aggressively to Guatemala. "Cut the head off, and the tail stops wagging," was a quote attributed to a Marcello associate.

and the March on Washington in August of the previous summer when Martin Luther King had spoken about the inequities of racism in America. They had read Gunnar Myrdal's classic 1944 study of race in America. We hadn't.

The truth was that most American students, like much of America, were ignorant of the realities of the American South. We didn't know about lynchings. We didn't know that when Europeans studied American history, their texts began with American Indians and the violence of the American West rather than the romance of manifest destiny. We knew nothing about CIA interventions in European elections or overthrow of elected governments in Guatemala and Iran.* We mouthed a collection of anticommunist slogans and myths that we had been taught. We did not know that American democracy was far more democratic in theory than in practice. We really did believe America was an exception. As Eleanor Roosevelt wrote about American self-righteousness during the debate on the United Nations Human Rights Charter in 1946: "It is . . . a trait no other nation seems to possess in quite the same degree that we do—namely, a feeling of almost childish injury and resentment unless the world as a whole recognizes how innocent we are of anything but the most harmless and generous intentions."

The Europeans were more politicized, and more left-leaning. They knew about American involvement in elections in Italy and in France after World War II to prevent the Socialists and Communists from gaining more seats in their parliaments. We knew nothing of this. We believed what we had been taught: that communism was monolithic throughout the world and that the motives of the United States were pure.

---

* These widely known interventions by the American CIA were recently compiled by Tim Weiner in *Legacy of Ashes: A History of the CIA* (New York: Doubleday, 2007).

The common assumption among the American students was that the United States was the "indispensable nation," a beacon of liberty shining into the political darkness. That attitude made for considerable friction with the European students. I, however, was less certain than I had been back in the classrooms of Washington and was becoming more uncertain by the day. My uneasy realization of having been lied to was identical to the feelings that were fueling the growing student protest movement within the United States.

The city of Bologna is the capital of the Italian province of Emilia Romagna, and famous for its red-tile roofs, porticoes, and wonderful food. Although the buildings are in warm colors, Bologna's weather in winter frequently includes many of the raw, gray days for which the Po Valley is famous. During some of those battleship gray days, I found myself staring out classroom windows and recalling the Mediterranean sun. I had fallen into a funk. I looked the same—except for a better haircut and new Italian shoes—but I knew I had changed. I couldn't exactly put my finger on what had happened. Why had I lost my ability to concentrate? What had happened while I crossed that Anatolian plain? Why was I so uncomfortable in this environment of international elites? Instead of feeling privileged, I felt alienated. I had excellent professors. I liked my courses. I had a boyfriend whom I liked a lot.

The boyfriend was a surprise. First of all, he was German. And I had watched enough World War II movies and heard enough about the horrors of the war in Germany—"poor Jimmy Brophy, God rest his soul, dying over Hamburg"—that I didn't want to get to know any Germans. I avoided the German students. But this German was a man who could dance. And for that, I had to make an exception.

I have found that it is rare in American life to meet a man

who can dance. Either American men consider it unmanly to dance well or they have spent too much time playing competitive sports to know how to move to music. In Washington I had one male friend who liked to go to Diamond Jim's, a black nightclub up on Sixteenth Street, where we danced to blues and gospel and rock and roll and where, in that more innocent time, we learned moves we had never learned at dancing school. And Michelle of the French American family where I had been an au pair often invited two Cuban brothers who worked at a nightclub on Connecticut Avenue (I think it was called the Junkanoo) to her parties. Dancing with them to Latin rhythms, I realized music was a sea in which I knew how to swim. I might not know all the steps, but I understood the rhythms. As a child, I had aspired to become a ballet dancer and had graduated to toe shoes in my ballet class and could dance on pointe. (Unfortunately, this dream of being a ballet dancer quickly died as it became clear that my plump little body was not going to elongate into the arrowlike shape required of classic ballet.)

So when this tall German student with the funny accent—he pronounced *v* as *w,* so *V*enice became *W*enice—kept asking me to dance at school parties and then waltzed, actually waltzed, me around the floor as expertly as any partner I had ever had, I was astounded. Of course, dancing meant learning his story, and as it turned out his experience was not part of the black-and-white Nazi war movies I had been raised on. He had, as he described it, "one of those typical German childhoods." Born just before the war, his father, who had died when he was three, was soon lost somewhere over Russia. His mother came from Dresden, and he remembered leaving the city in flames just at the beginning of the Allied firebombing (causing over forty thousand civilian deaths). In Berlin (a two-hour train ride from Dresden) he became separated from his relatives and was soon picking up cigarette butts from American soldiers to survive. Eventually he was put in an orphanage or camp for displaced children. But yes, a decade or so later he was sent to dancing school and to England to learn English.

So the German boyfriend demolished one of my closely held prejudices and became one more experience that must have contributed to my sense of displacement, of being in the wrong place at the wrong time.

I felt I was in a bubble. I lived in an artificial environment—studying French, for example, in Italy. My roommates were American, all very nice, but with career inclinations I couldn't relate to. In response, I developed an alternative persona. I was suddenly confronting a part of my psyche that was a stranger to me. I had always been a good student and a scholarship student, doing whatever the educational system required me to do to pass through its successive gates. But this strange new persona had bubbled up within me. She was questioning the value of being a good student. She was angry, and she refused to accommodate. "This is not the right place for you," she whispered. "There is nothing for you to learn here. Stop kidding yourself." I came to call this persona "Clarissa," which means clarity.

Clarissa didn't believe in "niceness." Truth be told, Clarissa was outraged, and expressions of anger were unacceptable in women. So I became depressed. Clarissa thought it was outrageous that all the international companies came to interview male students for employment but refused to see women. She was even angrier that school officials had so little imagination that they didn't question why the administration was all male. This led to larger and more disturbing questions about the dynamics of American foreign policies.

Every evening, Clarissa was reminded of the young girls in Istanbul's red-light district, because at dusk the prostitutes of

Bologna lined up on the sidewalk opposite the school on Via degli Orti, waiting for the commercial traffic to begin. We were told, "Ignore them. Pretend they're not there." Clarissa made it a point always to say "Buona sera" to them. Clarissa thought her questions about the number of women being drawn into prostitution to service American military bases around the globe were not "irrelevant and foolish." She also came to detest two mid-career CIA officers on sabbatical at the school. After many liters of wine at a local trattoria, they told stories about the bar girls in Thailand who could shoot Ping-Pong balls out of their vaginas (great laughter). They described (approvingly) the sexual sophistication of thirteen-year-olds in Bangkok. If the women of a country weren't sexually available, the entire culture of the country seemed to pass them by.

Sex really was an issue. Clarissa did not know about Betty Friedan's *Feminine Mystique,* which had been published that year, but she was a likely recruit for a movement that was not yet on the horizon. It would be called women's liberation.

In my heart of hearts, I knew I would never work in the public information office of the State Department or the World Bank, would never become an intelligence analyst in some government agency. I knew I didn't want to become what I was being trained to be, a functionary in America's national security bureaucracy. The conservatism of outlook and expectations was numbing to me. Through much of that academic year, I indulged my restlessness by hitchhiking to different Italian towns on weekends with a friend from Swampscott who was working in a medical lab in Ferrara. In January, I moved out of the school apartment building to learn Italian and to avoid an American who was more of a stalker than a suitor. My efforts to avoid my predicament by hitchhiking and learning Italian were delaying tactics.

By May, the moment of truth was at hand. I was in crisis. My symptoms: an inability to concentrate, lack of appetite, insomnia. Ostensibly, the crisis was occasioned by my oral exam. Everything hinged on the oral exam. If I didn't pass, I didn't graduate, and two years of effort and considerable financial debt would have come to nothing, even though I had passed all my courses. The oral exam was a test of one's ability to think on one's feet. I had never taken such an exam before. How could I look these professors in the eye and lie? My German boyfriend, who had had to pass oral exams all through his undergraduate years at university, said they were nothing to worry about. I, however, was worried.

My crisis originated in the sense—felt but not articulated—that I was at a crossroads and was about to set off on the wrong path, one that would be very hard to escape once begun. I was in a culture of people who had been building their résumés since prep school. Finding out what you love to do, how to make mistakes, how to follow your passions: these ideas were not part of this culture. This environment was about the culture of power. The closer the exams came—international law, international economics, European politics, international systems, and French—the more hours I spent in the library staring unseeingly at pages in books I could no longer comprehend.

When the day came for the oral exam, my body entered the room, but Clarissa kept my mind outside.

The oral exam was structured so that five or six professors—all male—sat on one side of the table and formally asked questions of the one student sitting on the other side.

"Define *arbitrage*."

"Tell us about the purpose of the International Monetary Fund and the World Bank. What were the key provisions of the Bretton Woods Agreement?"

"Do you think World War I and World War II were two phases of a European civil war?"

"What was Vinegar Joe Stilwell's relationship with Chiang Kai-shek in China?"

To every question, Clarissa—my new persona—answered in a rather flat monotone, "I don't know." Heads turned. Looks were exchanged. I answered this even to questions I did know, simply because I didn't have the energy to summon up an answer. I was becalmed in a flat psychic sea. Such a colossally inarticulate performance meant that there would be no squeaking through. The academic powers had to fail me. I would not graduate.

"What happened to you in there?" asked Professor Sereni, my international law teacher, taking my arm in the corridor afterward. "You are a smart girl." He looked genuinely concerned, a kindness I always remembered. I was as mystified as he was. "I'm so sorry," I said miserably. Never before had I encountered such a complete failure of will.

Now, some forty years later, I can tell you that a failure of will can be a good thing. There is such a thing as a true self, and it will out. Shutting off the voice of the true self creates a deadening quality. I needed to pay attention to what made me come alive. Emotional growth doesn't take place without experiencing the confusion of complex choices. Being a good student is a fatal mind-set for real life.

In short, Clarissa knew that some essential part of me was in jeopardy if I kept on being a good student. A deep part of my psyche was fundamentally at odds with the values of the culture in which I was expected to succeed. The energy required to keep up appearances in such a deeply hostile environment finally broke down, and I literally silenced myself so that I could escape.

"I don't know" was a truthful statement. I was fighting a colonized mind.

So although I didn't know it then, my failure in my oral exam was also a moment of liberation.

It was why, when, years later, Phil Burton asked me how I knew so much about Vietnam and American foreign policy, I told him I had had an alternative education. Observed experience yielded truths I never could have learned in school.

By then, I had discovered the words of theologian, educator, and guide to the civil rights movement Howard Thurman, who understood that purpose and meaning in life often had little to do with a career. "To ask what the world needs is the wrong question," he warned. "Ask what makes you come alive. Then go and do it. Because what the world needs is people who have come alive."

In one sense, however, I was typical. I became one of millions of young people, in America and in Europe, who stopped believing in what their elders were telling them. I dropped out and went to Greece, where I resumed the tour of the ancient Mediterranean world that I had begun with Mrs. Baity. And then to Paris.

PART II

Hidden History

Citizen of the World

Paris, 1964

"Texxhassss," Madame Gillet said one day, reading about the November 1964 election results in the *International Herald Tribune*. She pronounced it with the accent on the second syllable and a hissing *s*. "What kind of state is Texxhassss that your new president is from? Have you ever traveled in that province?" Madame Gillet wore Chanel suits, had perfectly colored and coiffed red hair, and was anxious to learn English because the family-owned perfume company—she sat on the board while her son ran it—wanted to expand into American markets. Once again, I was a spokesperson for the United States, explaining a country that I didn't understand very well myself.

I told her that, alas, I had never been to Texas. The farthest west I had ever been was Pittsburgh during a debate-team competition in college. I had never visited the real West, which began, as far as I knew, on the far shores of the Mississippi. I had never been to California or seen the South. She gave a French shrug, one that suggested Americans in general were unaware of their ignorance of their own country.

"Has your President Johnson ever traveled outside the United States?" she wanted to know. "It is a problem," she observed, "this American provincialism."

"We are a provincial people," Arkansas senator William Fulbright would later remark about America's lack of knowledge of Vietnam. "And no one was more provincial than Lyndon." (Before entering the White House, Johnson had traveled only once outside the country, and that was to Australia during World War II while he was in the navy reserves.)

I was living in a *chambre de bonne,* a maid's room, on the sixth floor of Madame Gillet's apartment building in a fashionable neighborhood not far from the Arc de Triomphe at the Étoile metro stop. The room with its view of the Eiffel Tower was mine in exchange for giving English lessons to Madame. In French apartment buildings the top floors were for servants, while the most desirable floors were on the lower levels, closer to the furnace and dependable heat. So those of us in the servants' quarters had spectacular views but sporadic heat. My room was so narrow I could nearly touch each wall when I stretched out my arms, but I loved the room and the view of Paris rooftops. It was large enough to accommodate five friends from my French class who regularly squeezed into a circle on the floor to play poker.

My immediate neighbors were Algerians, Tunisians, Cambodians, and Vietnamese from France's tattered colonial empire. They were mostly young men, employed as day laborers or hotel service workers, who were sending their earnings back to their families in their *pays d'origine.* Madame Gillet had warned me about *"les noirs"* and told me her previous tutor—also an American—had complained about their loud music. They did play music at high volumes, but it was American jazz and I loved it. The sounds of Sidney Bechet and Charlie Parker filled the sixth-floor corridors. Whenever Dizzy Gillespie or Thelonious Monk played in Paris nightclubs, one of my neighbors left a note on my door, assuming I would want to know that these eminent American ambassadors were in Paris. One day, Omar the Algerian asked me to translate the liner notes on a jazz record. He was learning English by reading record jackets. He asked if I knew that there was no music like American jazz anywhere else in the world. He explained that jazz began in the funeral processions of New Orleans when the musicians had to improvise on their walks to the African American cemeteries, which were located outside the city. He was disappointed I had never been to New Orleans.

Since the top floor had been the servants' sleeping quarters, and servants were assumed to spend most of their time in the downstairs apartments of their employers, we had no showers or bathtubs and only one toilet for the entire floor. (We did have sinks in our rooms.) I negotiated a weekly bath in exchange for an extra English lesson. Once a week, I got up at six in the morning and ran down the back stairwell to take a luxurious bath in Madame Gillet's Italian-tiled bathroom. Occasionally, I met Ngo and his Vietnamese cousin returning from their night shift at a hotel near the Champs-Élysées. Often they climbed the six flights of stairs—the birdcage elevator was frequently out of order—and we exchanged a muffled *"bonjour"* in the still, cold air. I see us now as shadowy figures on that back stairwell, moving imperceptibly in tandem in the chilly light of dawn. As I sank into Madame Gillet's tub and the hot, silky water perfumed by fragrant salts from her perfume company, I was blissfully unaware that Lyndon Baines Johnson, our newly elected president, was preparing to launch Operation Rolling Thunder and bomb Ngo's family's home in Hanoi.

My lessons with Madame Gillet were generally not about politics. During our English conversations, we discussed her friends, French culture, her two marriages, her divorce, her daughter's marriage, her grandchildren. Three or four times a week—between her appointments with the hairdresser, lunch with friends, shopping, business meetings, visits with her grandchildren, and golf—we scheduled lessons. Golf? A Frenchwoman in Paris in 1964 who golfed?

"Why golf?" I asked in astonishment.

"Because Americans are *fou* for golf and we must do business with Americans."

I was soon disabused of my impression of a wealthy, purposeless socialite. Madame Gillet was a businesswoman. She was an active member of the board of directors of the family's perfume company and spoke almost daily with her son, the president. After a few conversations about the perfume business, I realized Madame Gillet was knowledgeable about business law, import-export regulations, tax matters, foreign trade, advertising strategies, marketing, and international politics. When I repeated what I had been told, namely that women couldn't be successful in business, she was astonished. She was too well bred to snort, but her reaction was the equivalent.

"What is so difficult?" she asked incredulously. In France some of the most important people in the fashion and fragrance world have been women. "You have heard of Coco Chanel and Elsa Schiaparelli?" she continued. She thought there was nothing that a man did in business that a woman couldn't learn. I explained to her how the international corporations and banks that came to my school refused to interview women for jobs because women, they said, could not be in business.

She hopped up from her desk and pulled a copy of Simone de Beauvoir's *Le Deuxième Sexe* from her bookshelf. "The limitations," she said, "are constructed by the culture. It has nothing to do with the abilities of women. You can read this in French, no? Then we will discuss." *The Second Sex*, arguably as influential as any book of the twentieth century, was published in France in 1949 and in English in 1953, but it was not widely read in America until the feminist movement of the late 1960s.* It served as the foundation for Betty Friedan's 1963 landmark American bestseller, *The Feminine Mystique.* I was not an alienated housewife in the suburbs, and I hadn't yet read Friedan's book. *The Second Sex,* however, had a great impact on me. I remember writing out a quote from Simone de Beauvoir and tacking it up next to my window with the view of the Eiffel Tower: "Representation of the world, like the world itself, is the work of men; they describe it from their own point of view, which they confuse with absolute truth."

By and large, however, Madame Gillet and I did not start out with intellectual topics as the focus of our conversations. The format for our English lessons was a chapter-by-chapter reading of the latest book by Harold Robbins, *The Carpetbaggers,* a steamy novel that dealt with sex, drugs, Hollywood glamour, and ruthless business dealings. Madame Gillet thought it "typically American" and saw the characters as representative of American culture with its moralistic prudery combined with fascination for celebrity and sex and power. She bought me my own copy of *The Carpetbaggers* so I could keep up, and she used each chapter to address a larger conversation about American values and morals. Gradually our conversations became more complex. Did I think that America was "sexually healthy?" Why does the Catholic Legion of Decency have so much power over American cinema? How do you deal with homosexuality in America? I was mystified.

---

* *The Feminine Mystique,* which owed an enormous debt to *The Second Sex,* brilliantly analyzed the grip of Freud's ideas on the American mind and how Freudian theories had a quasi-religious hold in defining the relentless domesticity of American women's lives in the postwar era. Other treatments of the social construction of womanhood from an American point of view came much later in Elizabeth Janeway's *Man's World, Woman's Place* (1971) and Carolyn Heilbrun's *Reinventing Womanhood* (1979).

I told her I didn't know any homosexuals (although, of course, I did; I just didn't know they were gay). When Edward Albee's popular Broadway play opened in Paris, Madame Gillet asked what I thought about *Who's Afraid of Virginia Woolf?* It took some time for me to translate the equivalencies of *cunt* and *fucking* since *fucking* as a vocabulary word is not the all-purpose adjective, verb, adverb, noun, and general angry expletive in French that it is in English. Madame Gillet felt Albee's play could be interpreted as portraying a destructive homosexual relationship in the form of two heterosexual couples. That reading was about twenty years ahead of my consciousness.

I had to tell her we really didn't acknowledge homosexuality in the United States. Sexual preference was not recognized as a reality. No one I knew had openly homosexual friends (although some of the gay men in my graduate school would eventually enter what the British call "white marriages," arrangements that provided an heir to whom they could pass on trust funds, and that, in general, met social conventions). In American cities, police still conducted raids of gay bars and lesbian social clubs and published the names of all those arrested in the next day's newspaper.* Many states had statutes making homosexuality a crime, and psychiatrists defined homosexuality as a mental illness—even though the research of Alfred Kinsey had estimated that over 5 million men and women in America were gay. Movie stars Rock Hudson (who remained closeted for his entire career and eventually died of AIDS) and Doris Day were America's favorite romantic couple, and in Hollywood movies

---

* The 1969 police raid of the Stonewall Inn, a famous gay bar in New York, launched the gay power movement. For the first time, gays fought back. The night after a plainclothes force raided the bar, the police swept the same area in Greenwich Village and were confronted by four hundred men and women hurling bottles and chanting "gay power." The *New York Times* called it a "rampage."

they slept in twin beds. The Catholic Legion of Decency prohibited even a married couple being shown in a double bed in Hollywood films. I told her how just going to see the French movie *Jules and Jim* had been a great adventure in college because it had received a C for condemned by the Catholic Legion of Decency.

A more interesting theatrical event, from Madame Gillet's point of view, was the movie *Dr. Strangelove, or: How I Learned to Stop Worrying and Love the Bomb,* a black comedy about an "accidental" nuclear attack set in motion by a deranged American general, Jack D. Ripper, and the retaliation by a drunken Soviet premier. Cold war paranoia was still at its peak. I saw it in a Paris movie theater in the winter of 1964 and found it shockingly funny, but no one around us laughed. The movie theater was silent even during the concluding montage of mushroom clouds accompanied by the World War II song "We'll Meet Again." I asked Madame Gillet if she knew why no one laughed. She shrugged and said that perhaps people in Paris remembered that only the Americans had used the atomic bomb and that the Americans had proposed using "tactical" nuclear weapons to help the French avoid defeat at Dien Bien Phu.★

★ The French military returned to French Indochina in 1946 with American support when a nationalist, communist movement for Vietnamese independence was well under way. By 1952, French dead, wounded, missing, and captured from the ensuing war totaled more than ninety thousand. The following year the French army took up what they believed was an "unassailable" defensive position on the Laotian border in a valley eleven miles long and five miles wide. Well known to the Vietnamese, who bought opium there, the valley was called Dien Bien Phu. The North Vietnamese (known as Vietminh) had the advantage of being in the mountains dominating the valley and moved into position thirty-three infantry battalions, six artillery regiments, and an engineering battalion. Surrounded and outgunned, unable even to evacuate their wounded, the French were clearly defeated without outside help. In Washington a tactical study group concluded that three tactical atomic weapons "properly employed" could smash the Vietminh forces. Although tactical nuclear weapons had their advocates, the tactic was turned down, and the French entered negotiations with the Vietminh in Geneva in 1954.

Occasionally, Madame Gillet mentioned her friend Françoise, whose family had owned a rubber plantation in Vietnam during the country's years as a French colony. Françoise, she told me, said the Americans would be making a great mistake if they expanded the war in Vietnam. France had lost the war because they kept trying to force the North Vietnamese into a fixed battle, the only kind the French army knew how to fight. Instead, they confronted guerrillas and terrorists who came out of nowhere and fought with completely different techniques. It was a Frenchman, Roger Trinquier, who wrote the first analysis of counterinsurgencies and asymmetric warfare. Françoise no longer lived in Vietnam. She lived outside of Paris. France, as it turned out, was the right place to learn about a remote country called Vietnam; French was the right language to know.

It was, however, in the world of work that I learned my most memorable life lesson from Madame Gillet. I earned a meager income by working at Academia Gaya, a French version of Berlitz, teaching English to the executives of Minnesota Mining and Metals—"3M" in English; or "Troi Zem," as they called it in French. As Gaya employees, my friend Tricia and I took the metro three nights a week out to a distant suburb and taught several hours of English classes to French executives, whose great dream seemed to be to travel to the snowy land of Minneapolis and the 3M headquarters.

Our employer, Monsieur Gaya, was sometimes referred to as Monsieur Grenouille, or monsieur Frog, because he was short and fat, with little froglike, bulging eyes. He employed dozens of young foreigners to teach their native languages, paid far below minimum wage, and asked us to take on extra training and work without pay. And because we had no alternatives, we did. Every week I faithfully walked the Parisian executives through the Gaya lesson plans for negotiating American supermarkets and drugstores.

(Paris at that time did not have supermarkets and drugstores were still small family-owned pharmacies; Le Drugstore had just opened on the Champs-Élysées with a soda fountain that served an exquisite dish called "*l'hamburgeur Americaine.*")

One night in January, Monsieur Gaya made a surprise visit to each of our Troi Zem classes. When I went to pick up my paycheck the following week, Monsieur Gaya's assistant called me into his office and told me that my services would no longer be needed and added that my friend Tricia and the other American teacher were also being fired. He also said there would be no need to pay me because I was being fired. The truth was that the 3M contract had not been renewed.

When I told Madame Gillet about these unexpected events, she said, "In the life"—she always referred to *the life*—"I have found that if you do not stand up for yourself, no one else will. You must get the pay you earned as well as the severance you are due. Here is what you must do." Her plan took my breath away, but she was adamant.

Even though I was fearful, I did as she instructed and telephoned for an appointment with Monsieur Gaya. As I approached his office, I had to stop because I was overcome with a panic attack. I couldn't get my breath. My anxiety was so acute I thought I wouldn't have the nerve to go through with the plan. Standing up to a male authority figure and arguing with him in a foreign language was beyond my powers. It seemed to me that this confrontation could end only in humiliation—mine. Even so, with feet that felt as though they were encased in concrete, I climbed the long flight of stairs to the Academia Gaya offices.

The assistant who had fired me opened the door to Monsieur Gaya's large office and motioned me forward. Monsieur Gaya, surrounded by his Oriental rugs and highly polished Empire furniture, looked up at me with an expression that suggested

I had introduced a sour odor into the room. "Well. How did you dare to come back after such egregious behavior? You cost us our contract at 3M," he said in French.

I stood there speechless with fear. The egregious behavior was that we teachers had occasionally used French in our classes. But I began to explain in careful French how I had worked for him for the entire fall and winter term at "Troi Zem," and that no one during all that time had complained. Even if he did not agree, I continued, he still owed me for the last two weeks of teaching. Now I added the key sentences that Madame Gillet had told me I must say: "In addition, I am also owed two weeks of severance pay. This, as you know, Monsieur, is in conformity with standard French employment practice—especially since I am working for you without a *carte de travaille,* as are most of your teachers." We were all without work permits. The Portuguese teacher, who had given me a book of poetry by Fernando Pessoa, had left Lisbon because he refused the six-year compulsory military service under the dictator Salazar. He could not go back to Portugal and could not get a French work permit.

Monsieur Gaya's eyes glittered, and his face took on a menacing expression. "You are without a contract," he exploded. "You were fired for good cause. Why should I pay you for incompetent work? I will pay you nothing." He seemed outraged at my very presence.

With a constricted throat, I forced myself to add the next sentence Madame Gillet had insisted I say: "I hope, Monsieur Gaya, it will not be necessary for me to report you to the Labor Ministry for employing people without proper papers."

I saw an instant alteration in his expression. What an empowering moment! Magically, my voice suddenly came clear again, and I added the exact name of the bureau for immigrant workers at the Labor Ministry and assured Monsieur that I would have no reluctance to report him if he didn't pay what he owed.

"You say we still owe you," he said smoothly with a little smile. "How much is that?"

I named a figure and then doubled it. I decided that while I had the advantage, I might as well collect for my friend Tricia, too.

He didn't blink. He pulled a metal box out of his desk drawer and began counting out hundred-franc notes. He yelled to his assistant to bring in more money. When there was a lovely, bulky pile of notes on his desk, he stood and pulled himself to his full height, at least four inches shorter than me. "You are absolutely wrong about my employment practices. However, I expect there will be no further talk of the Labor Ministry," he said, looking at me meaningfully.

I nodded and stuffed the bills in my pocket without counting them. Just before I slipped down the long flight of stairs to the street, I noticed his assistant looking at me with an amused respect.

That night I gave Tricia her share, and we celebrated with one of our most memorable meals in Paris, toasting Monsieur Gaya with every one of the five courses we ordered at a Left Bank restaurant where a prix fixe of fifty francs (ten dollars) bought an astonishingly fine meal with wine.

"You see?" Madame Gillet said when I told her about the confrontation. "In the life you must always stand up for yourself." Madame Gillet knew it was far cheaper for Monsieur Gaya to pay me off than to pay the fines for being caught employing illegal workers. But she also knew I had to confront him with that possibility. Without her excellent information and coaching about the French employment system, I could never have succeeded.

I learned three life lessons from Madame Gillet: obtain the best inside information you can get, stand up for yourself when you are right (sometimes even when you are wrong), and don't

buy perfume on sale. (Perfume mixes with the chemistry of individual skin and, like shoes, must be "tried on." Otherwise, the
buyer ends up with bottles of rarely used perfume.)

Although I had long since left the tourist universe, I couldn't
enter the French economic universe. And without a work permit,
I could only give English lessons or take care of children, both of
which I did, but that earned me a meager living. I lost fifteen
pounds and developed large sores on my skin that, I learned at the
public health clinic, came from inadequate nutrition. (I cooked
an occasional hot meal on a camping burner in my room.) It began to dawn on me that my future in Paris would not be a long
one. With that end in sight, I enrolled in the Cours de Civilisa-
tion Française at the University of Paris, a course of study designed for foreigners. I had been taking art history courses at the
Louvre and at the Musée Jeu de Paume (originally Napoleon III's
tennis court and, from 1950 to 1986, a museum for the French
Impressionists). The courses were free for students, so my writing
and reading skills in French were improved enough that I felt I
could keep up in a university course. We had studied one Impres-
sionist artist each week, viewed only his paintings in the museum,
and on weekends were invited to attend a lecture in situ. The
Claude Monet lecture, for example, took place in front of the cathedral at Rouen, after we had studied all his paintings of the
same cathedral, which had been executed at different times of
day. It was the most exciting art course I ever had. At the University of Paris, I sat in big lecture halls with hundreds of students,
many of whom came from all over the world. Only three years
later, in 1968, many of my Paris classmates would join the French
worker-student movement and set up barricades in the same
streets around the university. (Their banners were similar to those
of the student demonstrators in America: THE STRUGGLE MUST BE
ORGANIZED AT THE GRASS ROOTS.)

The war in Vietnam transformed what might have been known as a civil rights decade in America and a liberal reform era into the radical decade we know as "the sixties." The escalation of the war, the governmental lying that accompanied it, and an untenable American version of reality reverberated around the globe. In Europe, America's war in Vietnam was seen as a raw, ugly imperialism, and antiwar demonstrations in Germany and France fueled those countries' student movements.

Despite all evidence to the contrary, the United States held that communism was monolithic and that communists everywhere wanted world domination. All communist rulers—whether it was Mao Tse-tung in China, Castro in Cuba, or Ho Chi Minh in Vietnam—were viewed as Soviet puppets. The countries of the developing world were perceived as unstable dominoes: if one third world country fell to communism, the rest would follow. "If we don't stop the Reds in South Vietnam," explained President Johnson, "tomorrow they'll be in Hawaii, and next week they will be in San Francisco." Since power requires being able to convince people of your version of reality, American leaders claimed that we had to stand firm in Vietnam in order to show our commitment to other countries throughout the world—the NATO countries and Japan, Korea, Thailand.

In fact, America's version of reality was highly flawed. Few Americans at the time knew how the history of France's involvement in Vietnam had played out, or how few Vietnamese were Catholic other than the ruling elite, or how slim the people's support was for the corrupt and ineffectual government of South Vietnam. To keep all these alternative realities at bay, in March 1965, the United States began Operation Rolling Thunder, the bombing of North Vietnam.

By then I would be back in Bologna.

"Good," said Madame Gillet when I told her I had reapplied

to "the Bologna Johns Hopkins" to retake my exams. "After all, it is only a credential, not an identity. As in France, you must have the credentials."

Before I left the University of Paris I took the exam for foreigners about French philosophy (Descartes, Diderot, and the other encylopedists), literature (Voltaire, Racine, Montaigne, and Hugo), and French history. My language skills became good enough that I was finally able to read and write and think in French. As Rebecca West once observed, the French academic tradition gives students a real sense of the intellectual trunk from which other Western ideas have branched. I learned that Enlightenment ideas about man in nature came from observations of French Jesuits about Native Americans in North America in the 1600s. These ideas were eventually employed to undermine concepts of the divine right of kings in both Europe and America. (Thomas Jefferson, after all, was a Francophile.)

One day, Madame Gillet finished our lesson early and introduced me to her friend Françoise, a petite woman in her sixties with salt-and-pepper hair piled high on her head, whose family had owned a rubber plantation in Vietnam. She had lived much of her life in French Indochina, or *Indochine,* as she called it. It is too bad, she said, what the Americans are doing in Vietnam. She asked if I had read Jean Lacouture (*End of War*) and Philippe de Villiers (*Histoire du Vietnam*). You must, she said, when I answered I had not. "We lost the graduating class of Saint Cyr every year during our war there." (Saint Cyr is the French equivalent of West Point.) When I mentioned North Vietnam, she waved her hand impatiently. "*Toute artificielle.* There is no North and South Vietnam. You stopped the elections in '54 because you were afraid Ho Chi Minh would win."

"I was in the eighth grade in 1954," I told her, "so I personally had nothing to do with it."

She smiled graciously. "I mean 'you Americans.'"

You Americans.

That phrase, so frequently repeated during my three years in Europe, represented questions of history and identity that I had barely begun to deal with.

Hydra, 1964

"You Americans."

"You Yanks," Nigel had said the summer before with an expression I couldn't read. "How can you Americans be so nice but the country be such a bully?"

I had been in Greece the summer of 1964. Before I went to Paris.

"Did you know," said Nigel, speaking to me from behind his newspaper, "you Americans are going to war?"

We were at separate tables in a harbor café on Hydra, an island in the Saronic Gulf, where I had landed after escaping from the Bologna center. His table was covered with British newspapers, most of them several days old. A friend brought them to him from an Athens hotel that catered to British tourists. Nigel was a member of the island's small artists' colony, mostly English and Scandinavians who had "discovered" Hydra a decade earlier during the filming of the Hollywood movie *Boy on a Dolphin*. By the time of my conversation with Nigel, I had been on Hydra for over two months. I had stayed because I was mesmerized by the light and the sun and fascinated by the silence. Hydra had no cars, no motorcycles, no motorized transportation of any kind. When someone called a taxi, a man showed up with a donkey.

"There are only two colors," Henry Miller had written about

Hydra in the 1930s, "blue and white, and the white is white-washed every day. . . . Aesthetically it is perfect." The central town rose like the stepped layers of a wedding cake into the hills around the harbor. Everything, even the cobblestones in the street, was painted a crisp white that was highlighted by peri-winkle blue doors and shutters. The island had a couple of small pebble beaches, a monastery, and not much else. The view from one side of the island was open sea of the Saronic Gulf; on the other, the distant outline of the Peloponnesian coast. It had few trees. To anyone coming in on the ferry from Athens, the island looked like a loaf of baked bread. But Henry Miller was right. Aesthetically it was perfect.

"And where are we doing that?" I asked Nigel, without too much interest in whatever conflict he was talking about. He and his artist friends were the first people I knew who lived by their imaginations and constructed unconventional lives. I gazed out at the sparkling harbor, the sleek yachts anchored beyond the jetty, the puffs of clouds gathering over the Peloponnese, and relaxed in the languid breezes floating off the water. A hint of lemon was in the air. Military events seemed impossibly remote from the blue and white universe of the Greek islands.

"Vietnam," he answered from behind his newspapers.

"Isn't there already a war there?"

"This is different. Up to now, you were just helping an in-competent and corrupt local government. Now you're in on your own hook. Your Congress just passed a bill that gives your president authority to do whatever he wants. We'll see the full bloody mess. Just like the French all over again."

That was how I learned that the U.S. Congress had passed the Tonkin Gulf Resolution on August 7, 1964. Like most Ameri-cans, I knew little of America's adventures in Vietnam. I would have known even less except for Nigel, an Englishman who insisted on talking to me about American politics, mainly because I spoke English and was the only American on the island.

"How can you Americans spend so many years in college and still be so badly educated?" he commented to me one day after I asked to borrow some books from his library about ancient Greece—Edith Hamilton's *The Greek Way*, Mary Renault's *Bull from the Sea*, and a new translation of the *Iliad*. Until I met Mrs. Chesley Baity, I had never read anything about Greek myths or ancient Greece. I knew little about the Greek playwrights or even that their plays were still performed in ancient Greek in the ancient amphitheaters. It was as Stanley Kunitz has written, "The old myths, the old gods, the old heroes have never died. They are only sleeping at the bottom of our minds, waiting for our call."

The stubble-bearded Nigel rarely appeared for breakfast, so his presence on that particular languid August morning was notable. "Nigel, I've never seen you here this early," I commented.

"Early ferry. Editor in Athens for a visit," Nigel mumbled, and continued reading.

Nigel rented a house in the middle of the island and was very generous about loaning his books. We met because, one day on the pebble beach, I saw he was reading an English language newspaper and asked if I could borrow it after he finished. After that, whenever he saw me, he wanted to talk about political events reported in the papers. He was a former journalist writing a novel. About what? I had asked.

"About you Yanks in Iran," he answered. "How that silly Roosevelt son engineered the coup that brought back the Peacock throne of the shah and his secret police. Sort of a political thriller." Nigel was not exactly what Graham Greene might have described as a burnt-out case, but he had a lot of mileage on him.

Nigel's house was the center of frequent parties, and he kept very late hours. I had gone to a few of his parties, casual affairs strung together with ice-cold ouzo, Greek wine, and hashish that someone had brought from London or North Africa. But I was at least a decade or two younger than most of his crowd, wasn't a girlfriend, wasn't a writer or an artist, and wasn't in the film or music business. So I didn't quite fit in. Also, his friends wanted to know if I was the mistress of the man who owned the shop where I worked. After all, they pointed out, I lived in his house and worked in his store. Only locals worked in the shops. There were no labor permits for foreigners. So how else could an American be working in a Greek clothing and gift shop?

My three-hour-a-day job in a tourist shop, the Windmill, was hardly real work. Actually, it was an arrangement more than a real job. I wasn't paid in cash. But Nigel and his friends didn't know that. Nigel was intrigued that I accomplished something that no other foreigner had in the ten years he had been coming to Hydra. Mr. Nikos, an Egyptian Greek who spoke five languages, had hired me because his local Greek salesgirl couldn't speak the tourist languages—French or English or Italian or German (I faked the German). Mr. Nikos had another shop in Athens and came out to Hydra only on the weekends. He traded a room in his house and credit at the local cafés and restaurants for my linguistic skills. No money changed hands. That way, the Greek girl kept her job, Mr. Nikos stayed clear of Labor Department permit violations, and I could go to the beach every day until I heard the whistle of the afternoon tourist boats. I ate grilled fish and fresh salads. I became very tanned, and my hair turned blond. I knew exactly where to go on the island to keep my body at just the right temperature. I soon forgot my failed exams and my messy retreat from Bologna and graduate school.

Nigel's head burrowed deeper into the newspaper. "Listen to

this. The Tonkin Gulf Resolution passed the House of Representatives in forty minutes, with no dissenting votes. The same
resolution earlier passed the Senate, with only two dissenting
votes—Senators Gruening of Alaska and Morse of Oregon."

"You know that camp in the Alps I told you about. There
was a counselor there from Alaska whose name was Gruening. I
wonder if they're related?"

"You Yanks are going to end up just like the French. Only it
will be so much bloodier and last so much longer. You have so
many more resources to send down the rathole."

Nigel was a student of American politics and Americans. He
was intrigued that I was "a failed product of that CIA school,"
as he put it. He believed that the Bologna Center of Johns Hopkins SAIS was a CIA training school. "Bet you didn't learn that
in that CIA school of yours," he might say after telling me
about some earlier CIA operation in the Congo or Guatemala.
Nigel was also not above pimping for some of the wealthy
Greeks he knew who came into Hydra on their yachts. Once
when, on Nigel's urging, I did take a trip on a staggeringly
luxurious yacht, the ship's owner took me aside and sternly told
me that under no circumstances was I to take any more yacht
rides negotiated by Nigel. Nigel, he said, was untrustworthy
and unreliable. If I trusted Nigel's introductions, I might end
up in North Africa, sold into the white-slave trade. He was
quite serious. Until then, I didn't know there really was such a
thing as the white-slave traffic, or that young girls disappeared
all the time. But I didn't take any more yacht rides with
strangers.

The price of borrowing books from Nigel was that I had to
listen to his monologues about how the CIA was the real face of
America in the world. Although he went into great detail about

Iran—he had known Mossadegh, Iran's deposed president—he had many more stories about secret operations and how we placed dictators in power while nattering on about democracy. He described the business interests that were being served under the American guise of democracy and anticommunism—oil, copper, diamonds, energy, investment banking, agribusinesses that dealt in sugar or bananas or coffee.

I called them the "Nigel Seminars," and they covered CIA operations in Greece (1947), Iran (1953), Guatemala (1954), Cuba (1961), the Congo (1961), and various other Latin American countries and Caribbean islands. I thought his stories were far-fetched, although they all turned out to be true. To him, Vietnam was one more bead on the same string.

"Tell me about the Tonkin Gulf," I asked in an uncharacteristic burst of early-morning inquisitiveness. "I assume you've been there." Nigel had been everywhere.

"Karsts," he said from behind the newspaper.

"What?" I didn't think I had heard him correctly.

"The coast of the Gulf of Tonkin," he said putting the newspaper down, "is defined by steep, small hills called 'karsts.' Carved by nature out of limestone. When you see them in ancient scrolls, you know exactly where they were painted. For centuries, Vietnam has always been invaded through the Gulf of Tonkin. They've been fighting the Chinese for a thousand years. They're not going to roll over for you Yanks."

You Yanks. Whether I liked it or not I was a Yank. Neither of us could know that the resolution passed on August 7, 1964, named for a beautiful body of water, would set in motion a war that—like the Trojan War—would go on for ten years, tear apart a generation, and upend America's political and social structures. Eventually, it would occupy me for my entire working life in Washington.

Bologna, 1965

Back in Bologna, I no longer expected that students would participate in any critical analysis of American policies. Critical thinking was not an expectation at SAIS. I understood that I was supposed to learn and repeat the official version of American foreign policy. I accepted that foreign affairs was largely impervious to democratic processes and resided in the hands of a small group of men who upheld institutions of whiteness, masculinity, and nationalism.

But privately, I resisted. I learned to be more comfortable with paradox. In my travels I had received an alternative education. It allowed me to accommodate ambivalence, the need to recite the official ideology of American foreign policy without having to believe it. One day I came upon the phrase *citizen of the world*. While rushing to lunch at the University of Bologna cafeteria and taking a wrong turn, I saw an exhibit about Petrarch, the fourteenth-century poet, historian, humanist, and scholar whom Mrs. Baity had told me about, and who, in fact, had been a student in Bologna in 1320. For most of his life he was a diplomat for the Roman Catholic Church, but he also wrote secular poetry and essays rooted in classical Greek and Roman literature. He stated publicly that one of the great failings of the Church was its refusal to accept classical literature as part of historical wisdom. I decided Petrarch's example of a larger sense of citizenship was as good as any.

As Madame Gillet pointed out, the degree was only a credential, not an identity.

CHAPTER EIGHT

Honest Work Is Hard to Find

1966

My tax return for 1966 shows that I earned a total of $865.97 at two places of employment. The first W-2 form was from Snelling and Snelling ($577.50), an employment agency in Lynn, Massachusetts. It represented nine weeks of temporary summer work as a "placement specialist." My second W-2 was from the Women's International League for Peace and Freedom ($288.47) in Washington, D.C., where I began working the last two weeks of December.

By the time I returned from Europe in June 1966, I had retaken my oral exams, received a master's degree, and begun searching for professional jobs for women that might lead to a career. I was having a hard time finding any jobs for middle-class women, other than positions for nurses, secretaries, or teachers. I was working at an office in downtown Lynn, and I was in culture shock. No Parisian boulevards or Roman ruins here. Lynn in the 1960s was an economically depressed factory city about to be ravaged by urban renewal.

Sheila Broderick, an old friend from previous summer waitress jobs, also worked at the employment agency, and she had suggested that I apply to fill the job of a woman who had just left. Sheila was the first person I ever knew who read the *Wall Street Journal* every day and understood it. Trained as a teacher with a state teaching certificate, she didn't want to be a teacher. She wanted to be in business. Smart, filled with energy, talented with numbers, and possessor of a brilliant wit, she went to the employment agency to inquire about job possibilities other than teaching. The owner of Snelling and Snelling immediately hired her as a full-time employee for women's placements. She, too, was trying to figure out her next step. The point here is that education was not a barrier to entry; prejudice was.

Our office was not far from the Edison Hotel, named for Thomas Alva Edison, whose inventions brought the giant General Electric plant to Lynn in 1892. General Electric was still the city's largest employer. Most of the women's jobs we handled—all advertisements were segregated by male and female positions—were for shipping clerks or low-level clerical workers, jobs whose possibility for advancement was little to none. This also meant that our commissions were much lower than the men's.

Lynn's moribund industrial district was a maze of streets clotted with sooty red-brick shoe factories that had been mostly empty since the shoe industry and ancillary tool-and-die businesses had moved south in pursuit of cheap labor. The buildings were so densely packed together that little sunlight penetrated. Like an Edward Hopper painting, the vacant windows and silent loading docks spoke to a once vital history that had passed on. I worked in an office building not far from the old Nies family employer—Brophy Brothers Shoe Company.

"How do you get into business?" Sheila asked one day when we were having lunch at Anthony's Hawthorne restaurant.

"I'm not sure. Probably go to business school," I suggested. "Although I'm not sure they take women."

"Do we know anyone who goes to business school?"

We did not. It was 1966, and few women went to business school. (Bonnie Howard, who later became one of the early members of NOW and national treasurer of the NOW Legal Defense Fund, was one of the first woman graduates of the University of Michigan business school. She was the only woman in her class, and she recalled that the professor called on her every day, hoping to humiliate her with a question she couldn't answer. He simply didn't believe that women could understand business concepts.) The previous year Harvard Business School had made headlines for graduating its first women—all eight of them. Few noticed that it took another decade before women made up 10 percent of Harvard Business School's graduating class and another twenty before women made up 25 percent.

"Are you still looking at the universities?" Sheila asked.

I had spent the previous month taking the train into Boston and looking for a job in the city. As I had feared, a master's degree in international studies didn't seem to yield much in the way of job possibilities in New England. I did have an MIT professor calling me to see if I would take the job as his secretary. That lack of possibility was why I had taken the interim job at Snelling and Snelling.

"Look," I asked, "does anyone advise a man to take a secretarial job as a good start? What is it a good start *to*?"

Part of my difficulty was gender; part was class. I was beginning to understand the dynamics of privilege. Unlike many of my male graduate-school classmates, I couldn't call up Uncle Pudge at his law firm to arrange an interview, or have my father get in touch with a fellow member of his club to see if he could make a phone call on my behalf. Soon these classmates were jumping to the head of the line for a previously closed management-training waiting list or starting plum internships at consulting firms. Somehow the obstacles I faced never miraculously melted away as they did for these young men. Most of my women classmates ended up in government agencies related to national security. Of my former roommates from Bologna, Anne had taken a job as a historian in the Pentagon; Lois was working for the Defense Intelligence Agency and would move on to the Oak Ridge Nuclear Laboratory. Valerie, Ann, and Marjorie all went to work for the CIA with assignments that, of course, couldn't be disclosed.

"Well, maybe you should go to Washington," Sheila urged. "You might have better contacts there. My father says getting a job is all about contacts. Isn't that where Mac is going?" Sheila had met Mac when he had come to Swampscott for a weekend visit. He was interviewing in both New York and Washington and had job offers in both cities. Although he hadn't decided which job he would take, he encouraged me to try to find a job wherever he accepted a position.

"What's that book you're reading all the time?" Sheila asked one morning as I walked into my cubicle and dropped a book down on the desk before I started making cold calls to various employers to see if they had any job openings we could help them fill. I held it up so she could see the title: *The Kandy-Colored Tangerine-Flake Streamline Baby.*

"Who's it by and what's it about?"

"Tom Wolfe. Not the *You Can't Go Home Again* Thomas Wolfe, a new Tom Wolfe. I'm not sure what it's about, but it's great." At that point, I'd been out of the country for almost three years—more than 10 percent of my life—and in Tom Wolfe I found a guide, someone who could explain the new America to me. And I did need help: the America I returned to in the summer of 1966 was a different country from the one I had left. I read Sheila a couple of excerpts from the title essay about Junior Johnson, a famous driver in North Carolina stock-car races. Sheila was interested because she was going out with someone from North Carolina.

> *We were all in the middle of a wild new thing, the Southern car world, and heading down the road on my way to see a breed such as sports never saw before, Southern stock-car drivers, all lined up in these two-ton mothers that go over 175 m.p.h., Fireball Roberts, Freddie Lorenzen, Ned Jarrett, Richard Petty, and—the hardest of all the hard chargers, one of the fastest automobile drivers in history—yes! Junior Johnson. . . . They run out like ants and pull those barrels and boards and sawhorses out of the way, and then—Ggghhzzzzzzzzzhhhhhgggggzzzzzzzeeeeeong!— gawdam! There he goes again, it was him, Junior Johnson! With a gawdam agent's sir-een and a red light in his grille!*

I didn't know then that Tom Wolfe, by choosing to write about out-of-the-mainstream events he always labeled "a wild new thing," was helping to define an entirely new form of journalism, later to be called the New Journalism, because it infused nonfiction with literary techniques, social analysis, and personal attitude but was grounded in old-fashioned legwork and observation. This kind of writing was an original and dynamic way of capturing the fluidity of a society whose elements were dissolving and reforming in the tumult of the 1960s. Joan Didion would do the same in her reporting about fringe groups in California, as would Hunter S. Thompson in his writing about the Hell's Angels.

That same summer I saw images on the evening news that I had never seen before. Sheila said she had seen the Los Angeles Watts riots televised the previous summer while I was in Italy, but the extensive American news coverage of urban riots was new to me. That summer's race riots began in Newark, New

Jersey, with televised scenes of fires in the streets, stores with smashed plate-glass windows, and looters running off into the darkness. We learned about urban ghettoes, not those where Jews in European cities had lived in the past, but for American blacks living in Milwaukee, Cleveland, Dayton, and San Francisco. Racial anger was ignited in June when James Meredith—the black student whose entry into the all-white University of Mississippi in 1962 had brought the first federal troops into the South since Reconstruction—announced he would lead a "March Against Fear" from Memphis to Jackson, Mississippi's capital, a distance of 225 miles. His purpose was to show that black people could walk the highways of Mississippi without harm. He encouraged black activists to join him. Few did. On June 6, 1966, the second day of his "walk," a white man stepped out of the bushes and shot him. (Meredith lived, but doctors took over one hundred pieces of shot out of his back and legs.)

After the sniper shooting, hundreds of activists rushed to Memphis to continue the march. At different points along the route, the state police, white citizens armed with ax handles, or local police brutally attacked the marchers. President Johnson ignored requests for federal protection. The nonviolent civil rights movement started to change. Younger leaders took over the civil rights organizations and asked white volunteers to leave. Their former slogan, FREEDOM NOW, shifted to BLACK POWER! The black civil rights organizations began their evolution into the militant Black Power groups of the late 1960s.

At the same time, a growing antiwar movement of professors, college students, religious leaders, and women saw the war in Vietnam as immoral. Their demonstrations and marches increased in participants and frequency. Counterculture dropouts rejected the lives of their commuting fathers and their housekeeping mothers who prided themselves on their spotless floors, and organized themselves around drugs and rock and roll and communal living. *Lifestyle,* for example, was a brand-new word.

Although these forces didn't yet seem to have touched Lynn, the energy of change was percolating everywhere. Civil rights leader Martin Luther King named the historical juncture: "We are at a moment when our lives must be placed on the line if our nation is to survive. Every man of humane convictions must decide on the protest that best suits his convictions—but we must all protest." Even though he didn't say "every person," I felt I couldn't remain in Lynn trying to pursue life as usual.

I came to a decision. "When I finish the last chapter of this book," I told Sheila, "I'm going to leave this job. And don't ask where I'm going or what I'm going to do."

Sheila didn't blink. "How many chapters do you have left?"

I'd been reading Wolfe's book on the bus back and forth to work all summer, savoring the language and the sheer exuberance of it. She picked it up and thumbed through to the end. "Well, when I see you reading 'The Big League Complex,' you'd better make a call to Burt." Burt was our boss.

Three weeks later, I was on the phone trying to give my notice, and Burt had just about succeeded in talking me into staying. "Why leave until you have a job to go to?" he asked reasonably. "That doesn't make any sense. I'll give you time off to go to Washington or New York to interview." He was very sympathetic.

"BE FIRM," said the printed note Sheila held up to the glass wall between our cubicles. She could overhear my weakening resolve. Sheila pointed to her message and nodded.

I said, much more firmly this time, "No. I appreciate your flexibility. But if I were in Washington, I think I might have better luck," I told Burt.

"Are you engaged yet?" Burt asked. He, too, had met Mac when he came for a visit.

"Not officially," I said. "Well, sort of." It was true. Social arrangements were fluid. The rise of the counterculture meant that few young people had formal engagements or big diamond rings anymore (at least for anyone under thirty). Men and women lived together without being married. When Mac decided to take a job in Washington and asked if I would come there, too, the assumption was we would live together.

I had met Mac in March 1965, the second day I was back in Bologna to retake my exams.

"I wondered about the person who belonged to all that mail that was clogging the mailbox," he said, as I sorted through a month's pile of letters. We shared the "M/N" mailbox.

Although the director said I didn't have to retake any courses again—since I had passed all of them—he did suggest that I audit the course in international economics; a large part of the oral examination was on economics, and it was not my strongest subject. Mac was known to be a star economics student, so after a few weeks I asked him if he knew anyone who might tutor me.

He suggested himself.

Our friendship began with graphs (I didn't know how to read them), progressed to going to the movies (I loved movies), and then graduated to traveling on weekends. He was a good traveler. We were good travelers together. He wasn't disturbed by roads that didn't end up where they were supposed to or by an unexpected day in an isolated village. He was relaxed and easy to travel with. He was a lot of fun. It was romance lite.

And I needed the reassurance of a new relationship. While I was in Paris, I had realized that although I was crazy about my German boyfriend, I was not crazy about Germany. When he asked me to leave Paris and come live in Germany, I tried to

visualize myself there working on the assembly line in a Volkswagen factory with the immigrant Turks. Since I didn't know
any German, a factory job would be all I could do. I saw myself
living in his town near the Black Forest, where many of the
trees were turning to a rusty brown and dying of some unnamed disease. (This was before we knew about acid rain.)
While I could visualize living in that town and working in the
Volkswagen factory, I couldn't visualize laughing. I knew it
wouldn't work. After I told him I would not be coming to Germany, I felt emotionally adrift and unanchored. It was a decision, in fact, that contributed to making me sick.

As the French winter deepened, I realized why Parisians
spent so much time in cafés. The cafés were heated. I also noticed that my clothes had begun to hang off me, and the bone
structure in my face had become more pronounced, my cheek-
bones higher, my chin more pointed. I was becoming thin,
thin, thin. The truth is you *can* be too thin. I was not eating
enough, and vitamin deficiencies had begun to open up raw
sores on my skin. (Now when I read about the severe skin problems of many superthin models and actresses, I know it is because of nutritional deficiencies that can affect the entire
digestive system.) Soon I was in the French health care system,
waiting for hours on hard wooden benches, holding a numbered
card showing the time of my arrival. Diet, said the young intern
who examined me. No more eggs, he said, and no more French
bread. He gave me a prescription for an ointment. The sores
went away for a while, and then they came back. Vaguely, I
wondered if I had scurvy. Soon I was at the American hospital
in Neuilly, having tests I couldn't afford. The American doctor
asked me if I was under a lot of stress. "No," I told him innocently, hardly realizing just how stressful my life had become.

In May, I successfully retook my exams. Mac and I celebrated.

Mac was planning a vacation trip to the island of Sardinia before starting his fellowship in Rome at the Bank of Italy.

"Why don't you come to Sardinia with me?" he asked. He knew I had already booked a ticket home. My brother had written to me in Paris about troubles in my family and suggested I should come home sooner rather than later. "You can change your return ticket for a few weeks later."

In Sardinia, while drinking wine at a café near an old Saracen tower, he said, "Why not spend a few weeks in Rome?" It seemed both easy and logical. I loved Rome. I could change my ticket again. Rome seemed like the last leg of our trip. A few more weeks wouldn't make a big difference.

In Rome, we rented a room in a large apartment overlooking the Piazza Navona. When I opened the shutters in the morning, I looked out on Neptune's naked backside and heard the bubbling splash of water rushing over Bernini's sculpted rocks. Our landlady was an American expatriate, named Susan Creber, whose husband worked in the film industry. (I know her name and precise address—not because I kept a diary, but because that information is in my FBI file.) Other people who rented rooms there included Leon, a film editor who worked at Cinecittà, Rome's Hollywood and the center of the Italian film industry; a British lighting technician, who lived in both London and Rome and was rarely there; and Susan's husband, who was never there.

One day I told Leon that in Paris I had joined a film society and sat for hours in the basement of Alliance Française to see the legendary Abel Gance film *Napoleon*. It was legendary for several reasons, one of them being that, even though it had been filmed in 1927, some scenes had been hand-colored in technicolor. I had read *Cahiers du Cinema,* a magazine of French film criticism, and learned about Italian neorealism and French New Wave films. Leon and I had interesting conversations about movies, including the "spaghetti westerns" then being made in Italy by Sergio Leone, starring the unknown American actor Clint Eastwood. Leon told me they were actually remakes of famous Japanese films and correctly predicted they would be hugely successful in the United States. Explaining why he worked in Rome rather than in Hollywood, he gave me a quick account of cutthroat Hollywood politics, the anticommunist blacklist, and union requirements (guilds, not unions, he corrected me) and said Cinecittà was so closely linked to the American film industry that most of his work was for American studios.

At the time, I was reading *Il Cinema di Fellini* by Brunello Rondi. I filled the margins with notes and translated Italian words. "Fellini puts notices in the newspaper for open auditions just for faces," Leon told me. "He's always looking for interesting faces. All you have to do is show up and stand in line. I'll tell you when they post an ad." By then, I was working for a friend of his, a woman who ran a temporary secretarial agency, and I had my first job in Rome, typing letters for a film producer.

One day, Leon gave me an ad for a Fellini audition. On my lunch hour I went to the address and stood in line for about an hour. People around me studied my face and shook their heads. *Ma no,* they said. *Troppo Americana.* And by "too American" what they meant was that I had the face of a typical American girl, pretty but not interesting. It was the face of a permanent girl—women who age but don't mature. The faces around me were molded out of different cultural material than mine. (Years later, I thought about Fellini's comment when La Passionaria, the madame of a brothel, was elected to the Italian parliament. She rode to the opening day of parliament down the Corso in an open convertible surrounded by pimps and prostitutes and bouncers from her house. Fellini was reported to have said, "And people think I make this all up.") It was through Fellini's films that I began to understand that much of the functional anarchy in Italian life had its roots in the strategies people pursued to outwit the omnipresent control of the Catholic Church.

Mac went off to the Bank of Italy every day. I went off to type letters first for the film producer, then for the American embassy, and then for an American company called International Standard Engineering Inc. (ISEI), just off the Via Veneto. These were all temporary jobs that I got through the secretarial agency. My plan was to go home in October. Mac and I went to movies and explored Rome and took weekend trips. We had never articulated any plans for a future. The future was the following weekend, the next movie, the next trip. Real life was a place we were still to visit.

By the beginning of October I found I was having inexplicable periods of fatigue, and in the afternoon I wanted to do nothing but put my head down and snooze. As a person of generally high energy, I wondered why I was so tired.

Mac was worried about my naps. How late are you? he asked casually. Two, maybe three weeks, I said, doing a rough calculation in my head. I tended to be very irregular. Every month my period came like a surprise. It was 1965 and birth control was nonexistent in Italy, and still illegal in parts of the United States, like Connecticut. The birth control pill had been invented, but it was marketed as a medicine for menstrual cramps. Its use as a birth control pill was still in the future, and it was only for married women.

A week later I confided in Susan, the landlady, about my predicament, which I still believed to be lateness. She gave me the name of a midwife who lived in an apartment building in a section of Rome I had never been to before, far outside the historic district. The midwife asked how late my period was, shook her head, and then did a quick, matter-of-fact exam. "Mmmmm," she said. "It may be that you are just late, but I'm not sure." She paused. Then she handed me a bottle with a sepia-colored fluid, indicating with her fingers how much should be in the glass. "Make a solution and drink it every day. Once in the morning and once in the evening. It will cause some cramps. If it is just a problem of being late. But," she said, shaking her head, "I think you might be pregnant."

The dreaded word. She saw the anxiety on my face. *"Sposata?"* she asked. "No," I answered, "I am not married." The implications were overwhelming. "Don't wait," she warned me as I paid her, rattling on in Italian, explaining that an abortion is comparatively simple if done early in a pregnancy. The longer one waits, the more complicated it gets.

"Do you?" I looked up, asking if she did abortions.

No, she shook her head definitively. "No. No. No. You will need a doctor." She peered over the banister as I descended the long circular stairway from her apartment, my clicking heels echoing in the well of the marble stairway. "Don't wait," she called again as I paused at the bottom. I saw her face floating in the dark at the top of the spiral staircase.

"Well, we'll get married," Mac said. Married. That was as terrifying in its own way as pregnancy. I took refuge in denial. I insisted I was late. I drank the dreadful tonic the midwife had given me. I got terrible cramps. But no monthly period. The midwife's words—"Don't wait"—echoed in my mind. If she said, "Don't wait," then it must mean that something could be done—even though this was Rome, home of the Vatican and the Catholic Church. Technically, in Italy there was no birth control, no abortion. According to the celibate priests of the

Catholic Church, women's sole purpose on earth was to produce babies. On the other hand, by then I had learned that there was a black market for everything in Italy.

I told Mac I was grateful that he was willing to get married, but I thought having a child should be undertaken by two people who were ready to be parents. We were students in a foreign country with student incomes, renting a room in someone else's apartment, and living in the shadow of the Vatican. Neither of us was ready to be a parent. On the other hand, obtaining an abortion in Rome, within sight of the Vatican, seemed like Prometheus stealing fire from Olympus.

So we made dual plans—to get married if necessary, but also to find an abortion if one was possible. We filled out the papers at Rome's city hall for a marriage license. Then I started asking people I knew for recommendations for a doctor. I hadn't seen all those Fellini movies for nothing. His depictions of Catholicism's pagan roots, and of its priests as magicians of Eucharistic transubstantiation, revealed characters living turbulent and unconventional lives. Even though the Catholic Church was the state religion of Italy, I knew not all Italians held the church in high esteem. One Italian woman I knew from Bologna had told me she never left her children alone with a priest because many priests were known to be pedophiles. I reasoned that, in a city as sensual as Rome, not every baby conceived saw the light of day.

The doctor I eventually found told me exactly the same thing.

He was an upscale obstetrician with offices on a pleasant street not far from a Borromini church, where I sat and contemplated my future in its serene white interior before going on to see him. I was about to put my life into the hands of a complete stranger. I was afraid. But I also knew I was running out of time. What little I knew about pregnancy was that after three months "the procedure," as it was called, got riskier. And I was uncertain how pregnant I was.

The doctor was young, intelligent, and charming, and he went out of his way to assuage my anxiety, an act of generosity for which I was grateful. Ah, he said in Italian, it happens all the time, you know. Women get pregnant by their lovers. They cannot have the baby, so they have the procedure, and then the next night they go off to a party with their husbands. Seeing the surprise on my face, he nodded. "But yes, that is the way it is. It happens in life. Sometimes it is even the priest's girlfriends who come here." At first, I thought I must have misunderstood his Italian.

"How old are you?" he asked.

"Twenty-four."

"Mmm. Have you ever been pregnant before? No. You are well along. We must do this soon."

"How soon?" I asked.

"How about next Wednesday?" Wednesday was only five days away.

"Where?" I asked. "And will there be anesthetic?"

"Here in the office. Don't worry. We will have a very good anesthesiologist," he continued. "He works at one of the best hospitals. We will do it during the lunch hour," the doctor continued cheerfully. Rome's normal lunch hour then was three hours long, from one to four. "The payment will be four hundred dollars in cash. You will pay half in advance and half on the day."

I wasn't sure that Mac could get the money by Wednesday, but I nodded.

"You can have your boyfriend take you home." He said this as a statement.

I nodded.

"Someone has to take you home. You cannot go by your-self."

His ease and professionalism were completely outside the mental framework I had grown up with. Pregnancy was the consequence that changed women's lives forever and made sex-uality so much riskier for women than for men. (In the United States the ongoing debate about the sexual revolution was filled with women's rage because women felt "the revolution" was a male myth; nothing had changed.) Once in my college dorm we had taken up a collection for a classmate who had gotten pregnant. Abortions at home were dangerous because they were often performed by doctors who had lost their licenses, often for alcoholism. Many women died unnecessarily from postabortion hemorrhaging. They were also illegal. Abortion was a criminal act. After my conversation with the doctor, it occurred to me that it was senseless for an abortion to be such a dark and covert event, when it could be an intelligent choice performed in the light of day. My experience was made possible by money. With-out access to four hundred dollars, my life would have been very different. The experience, however, was so intense that, like many couples who go through an illegal abortion, Mac and I did end up getting married, but only much later, when it was a choice, not a necessity.

So in the fall of 1966, I did go to Washington, and I did live with Mac in a cozy little apartment near Dupont Circle. Burt of Snelling and Snelling in Lynn turned out to be the crucial rec-ommendation for the job I eventually found. In addition to be-ing one of the owners of the agency, Burt Bartzoff was also a lobbyist for the local trade association of employment agencies. So months later, when the Women's International League for Peace and Freedom called him as a reference and asked if he could predict whether I would be successful as a lobbyist, he was able to say, with some experience in the field, that he thought I would be terrific.

By the time I applied for the women's peace association job, however, I had spent several months sending out résumés, going for interviews, and following up every lead I was given. I consulted the placement office at SAIS, where Aldous Chapin, the career counselor, looked at his list and said, "I have a job that would be perfect for you." Then he read me the job description and requirements: "Fluent in French, writing and editing skills, knowledge of European politics and institutions." It *was* perfect. My spirits rose. Then, without a shred of awareness, he said, "Oops, we have to send a man there. Sorry." I knew the man he sent. He had little knowledge of French and lasted only six months.

At another interview, the supervisor told me, "I'd love to hire you, but my boss doesn't like women." At another, the hiring manager said he could meet me only after working hours for cocktails. My self-appointed godfather, Ray Rubinow, arranged several introductions for me. I had had one meeting with David Lilienthal, director of the Atoms for Peace program, in which he proclaimed the glorious future of atomic energy in agriculture, medicine, research, to say nothing of nuclear power plants. He was the head of an international engineering and consulting firm that was providing energy consulting to developing countries. I learned that one of his important clients was the Shah of Iran and that he was hoping to build nuclear power plants in Iran. I didn't see myself there.

Then I had an interview with a famous political filmmaker, whose offices were in the newly renovated Old Post Office Building on Pennsylvania Avenue. He was looking for a secretary. I knew it was a way to learn the business, but I resisted because I felt, once placed as a secretary, I would never get out.

(Some women insisted they didn't know how to type in order to escape the secretarial trap.) I had tea with India Edwards, a fund-raiser for the Democratic Party, at the Women's Democratic Club near Dupont Circle. All these meetings were cordial and gracious. The skids, after all, had been greased. And if I had been connected to a family who made significant political contributions, these conversations might have turned into actual job offers. Instead, I began temping as a secretary. I was working in an advertising agency on December 7, 1966, when my boss there said, "It's Pearl Harbor Day. Let's go get bombed." Fortunately, by then, I knew I would be leaving. I had just received a job offer from the women's peace group. It had seemed like a miracle after months of following up what seemed like futile leads.

One day at a party, I struck up a conversation with a retired army officer who had started his own employment agency. After telling him about my work for Snelling and Snelling in Lynn, as one insider to another, I asked if he had any tips for job hunting in Washington. He said the only professional job opening he knew about for a woman was with a women's peace organization. I had never heard of the Women's International League for Peace and Freedom, but I called, sent a résumé, and took the train to their main office in Philadelphia for the interview.

Sitting in WILPF's once elegant, but now shabby brownstone town house on Walnut Street, I had no idea I was about to make an extraordinary connection with the feminist and peace movements from the early years of the twentieth century. These former feminist activists were one strand that would make the still embryonic women's movement successful. Although this once powerful political movement had been silenced, it would form a critical foundation for the success of what was to become known as the women's liberation movement of the 1960s—many of whose politicized participants were already retooling their experience from the civil rights and antiwar movements.

My personal connection with this older generation was Mildred Scott Olmstead, president emerita of WILPF, age seventy-six, and a force never to be discounted. I got to know Mildred because we frequently met on the street as I was walking from the train station to Walnut Street on the day of the monthly board meetings. I was fifty years younger, but I still had to take extra long strides to keep up with her. I took it as a metaphor for my intellectual lag. Mildred Scott Olmstead saw in me a young woman she needed to educate. In fact, one of the goals of the organization was exactly what Mildred was doing—educate young women, build on existing knowledge, pass on stories, and "bridge generational differences," as she put it.

She took every opportunity she could to "give me a little background." At some point during these all-day board meetings, Mildred would take me aside and tell me a little story about the organization's history, about her life, about the choices women of her generation had had to make.

In the beginning, I thought I was working for an organization of elderly Quakers—at twenty-five, I was always the youngest person in the room—and only gradually did I come to learn it was an organization of women from highly diverse backgrounds, including many from the South, both black and white. They came from the first generation of professional women educated in early decades of the century: They included red-diaper babies whose parents had been in the Communist or Socialist parties, civil rights activists from the South, founders of antilynching societies, Quaker activists (not the same as godly Quakers who did not believe in political activism), West Coast Japanese who had been subject to internment camps, and women who were concerned about the militarization of

American foreign policy but had no other forum in which to make an institutional contribution.

The organization's history interested me because it began with a women's peace conference held in 1915, while World War I was already in progress. In 1914, German women concerned about the kaiser's arms buildup and bellicosity, put out a call for a women's peace congress. Their call was picked up and circulated through the suffrage associations in Europe and America, and more than fifteen hundred women from twelve nations responded. (Hungarian-born Rosika Schwimmer, a feminist and peace activist who moved from Hungary to England, was an important organizer.) Originally planned for 1914 in Berlin, when war broke out in August 1914, the leaders moved the location to neutral Holland.

"It's the oldest peace organization in the United States," Mildred told me, "and its leaders include the only two American women ever to have won the Nobel Peace Prize."

"Who were they?" I wanted to know. My studies in international affairs hadn't mentioned any women who won the Nobel Peace Prize.

"Jane Addams and Emily Greene Balch."

Miss Addams, as Mildred always called her, led the American delegation to the three-day International Women's Peace Congress at The Hague in April 1915. Hers was not an easy task. First, the leaders of the conservative wing of the American suffrage movement refused to participate, claiming that a focus on peace would endanger efforts to pass the suffrage amendment. Second, although America was not yet part of the war effort, the British government stopped the American delegation when they landed in England and refused to allow them to depart for Holland. They also denied passports to many members of the British delegation. The Americans were allowed to leave England only twenty-four hours before the congress was to open. None of the French delegates arrived, but the German women did, along with women from twelve other nations.

Nationalism struggled with internationalism. No one wanted war, but every country in Europe believed it was fighting in self-defense. Aletta Jacobs, the leader of the Dutch suffrage movement and the first woman doctor in the Netherlands, opened the unique gathering by saying "[We are] an International Congress of Women assembled to protest against war and to suggest steps which may lead to warfare becoming an impossibility." In other words, the delegates were interested in the causes of war and in exploring alternative means of conflict resolution.

This shift—from a concept of peace as the absence of war to a concept of peace as a positive, dynamic process of international relations—was part of a body of progressive thought that included the need for international law, the right to self-determination, and a recognition of the failures of colonialism. These ideas would be continually elaborated on and revised throughout the century. The attendees were members of feminist or suffrage organizations in their own countries or of the International Suffrage Association. Jane Addams chaired the congress and became the first president of the resulting organization that renamed itself the Women's International League for Peace and Freedom. (Rosika Schwimmer became vice president.)

Mildred said she had been working in a settlement house in Philadelphia when the Women's Peace Congress took place in 1915. She had graduated from Smith three years earlier, with her heart set on going to law school. Her father, a judge, refused to pay for law school because he insisted that "judges would never listen to a woman lawyer." Her position was this: How could laws that discriminated against women ever change if there weren't women lawyers who knew the law? Her father still refused to pay for law school. (In the 1970s and '80s, one of the key projects of the NOW Legal Defense Fund was funding education seminars for male judges so they understood how unfairly legal precedents treated women.) Instead, he offered to pay for social work school, then a new profession for women. After the armistice was signed in November 1918, Mildred volunteered to go to Europe to work for the YMCA relief organization in France.

Her new job in Paris was to organize dances and dinners to keep up morale among the troops waiting to be demobilized, and she did this successfully. But being Mildred, she also wanted to do something more substantial. She organized a Thursday-night lecture series. One of the speakers she invited was Jane Addams, then in Paris as part of a woman's delegation trying to influence the terms of the Versailles treaty. "Miss Addams talked about the causes of war and other methods of settling disputes between nations," she said. "The boys were fascinated." Mildred was fascinated. But Colonel House, President Wilson's peace commissioner in Paris, was not fascinated. He canceled the lecture series on the grounds that it was endangering the peace conference.

Tired of organizing dances and dinners, Mildred volunteered for one of the Quaker relief organizations working in the devastated areas of France and Germany. The idyllic French countryside had been scoured. "I saw what the war had done to civilians," said Mildred. Whole sections of the countryside had been denuded of trees. Agriculture in what once had been flourishing farming communities was nonexistent. Crops had not been planted; animals had been killed to feed soldiers. There was no milk for children. People were starving, and along with famine came disease. The influenza epidemic of 1918 had devastated whole towns and regions. (The influenza epidemic of 1918, which killed an estimated 40 million people worldwide, more than World War I itself, was spread by the international movement of troops.)

"I went to Bavaria in Germany to work with orphans and to help get food. It is almost unbelievable what starvation will do to people." She never forgot what she saw or what the postwar lack of housing and sanitation did to women and children. Long after the soldiers had gone home or been buried, the landscape and families were scarred by what had passed through their lives. The Great War had been "the war to end all wars," but for Mildred, the lesson was that war only breeds more war.

When she returned to the United States, she looked up Jane Addams and joined the peace organization that Addams had established in 1917 as the American branch of the Women's Peace Congress. (It went through several name changes before eventually becoming the Women's International League for Peace and Freedom, a name chosen because it translated well in all languages.) Out of her experiences in Europe came her conviction that she needed to find a way to work against war as a system and against the policies that promote war.

"But I always remained a feminist," Mildred told me, especially after 1920, when the constitutional amendment was passed giving women the vote. "And I always made it a point to dress stylishly"— and she dressed very elegantly—"because the press always described feminists as very unattractive and poor dressers."

I was Mildred's generational outreach project. What made Mildred's story so fascinating to me was that she was a connection to a war that had shaped my family. I had never heard the stories she told about suffrage demonstrations. My history books provided no stories about the suffrage movement, no mention of the political acumen and fund-raising skills that American women had invested in the dozens of campaigns to obtain the basic political right to vote. America's collective memory had erased almost a hundred years of radical political activism on the part of five generations of women; no mention of millions of dollars raised in nickels and pennies to finance 56 campaigns for state referenda, 480 campaigns to urge state legislatures to put woman's suffrage on the ballot, 47 campaigns for state constitutional conventions, 30 campaigns to urge presidential party platforms to include woman's suffrage as a plank, and 19 lobbying efforts with nineteen successive Congresses before the Nineteenth Amendment was proposed in Congress in 1919 (passed in the House by one vote) and ratified in 1920.

I told her that the history I had learned was that women had been "given" the vote after World War I because of their contributions to the war effort.

"Oh no," said Mildred, with a sigh. "It wasn't like that at all. During the war, demonstrators from the Women's Party spent a month in jail for petitioning Woodrow Wilson to support the Nineteenth Amendment."

When she heard I was engaged and getting married, she said, "I hope you're going to keep your own name. I think it's important that women not give up their names." She also advised me to make some changes in the marriage ceremony, like taking out the word *obey*.

Mac thought it was funny that the most radical thinker I knew was a seventy-six-year-old woman, but he agreed to make the changes in the marriage ceremony.

The Good Wife and Other Double Binds

Washington, D.C., 1967 to 1969

In 1967, I became a wife. On October 28, a date that today is celebrated as American Indian Day, I publicly exchanged marriage vows with Mac in a ceremony that was both formal and unconventional. For example, it, in fact, included language from a Native American ceremony ("Living is not all victory—we learn through failure and wrong choices but never surrender to any treachery of the moment").

By then, members of the counterculture—small in number but hugely visible in the media—had made inroads into many social rituals and conventions. The media focused on those young people, called "hippies," who lived in communes, wore hand-painted clothing, advocated altered consciousness through drugs, and frequently quoted Timothy Leary's rallying cry of "Tune in, turn on, drop out." Compared with them, Mac and I seemed to be making a relatively mild break with convention. We planned our own wedding and paid for it ourselves. No more than fifty guests, we agreed; no china or silver pattern; no bridal registry. Gifts from family and invited friends were welcome, but optional.

Since we weren't churchgoers, we didn't even consider having a Catholic ceremony. With Mac's agreement, I asked the lobbyist I knew at the Unitarian Universalist Association to recommend a minister. That was how we ended up at the Cedar Lane Unitarian Church in Bethesda, Maryland, with a minister who didn't seem to mind that neither of us had ever attended the Unitarian Church. He also assured us that my request for a revised ceremony was already part of the Unitarian service. Unlike the Catholic marriage ceremony, his service did not include "obey," as in the traditional "love, cherish, and obey," as part of the woman's vows. And the concluding vow would pronounce us "husband and wife" instead of "man and wife." These small adjustments overturned centuries of civil and religious language that reflected the belief that a man was a full human being while the wife was an appendage. Within a decade, however, a small army of sociologists would be writing books on why these seemingly minor alterations in language were having a revolutionary effect on the institution of marriage and the political status of women.

At a time of psychedelic clothes and Haight-Ashbury styles, I thought the wedding was pretty traditional. My father walked me down the aisle; I wore a white dress (short, with a matching coat); I changed my name. Despite Mildred Scott Olmstead's warning, keeping my own name seemed difficult since I was not an artist or an already famous person. I felt there were only so many conventions I could rethink at one time.

On the other hand, I didn't have a diamond engagement ring, and we bought our wedding bands for ten dollars in an antique store in New Hampshire. There were no formal bridesmaids or ushers. My childhood friend Patty Bresnahan was maid of honor. Mac's brother was his best man. Our parents met for the first time the night before the wedding, a meeting Mac and I delayed because of the absence of common ground between the two families.

Only later, after I had spent more time with Mac's family, did I begin to understand how minimalist and casual the wedding must have seemed to his parents. Their friends in New York banking circles underwrote large formal weddings for their children as a matter of status and style. My father worked as a foreman at the United Shoe Machinery Corporation, and my mother taught piano. It was, after all, a time of rebellion. What I didn't realize at the time was that I was Mac's rebellion.

After we were married, I began to understand the many expectations of wifedom that previously had been invisible to me. By day, I worked in an activist woman's organization with leaders in the civil rights and antiwar movements. At night, I played the role of a traditional Washington wife, which meant that I gave dinner parties, attended administration receptions, and smiled frequently and agreeably. I enjoyed putting on dinner parties; what I didn't enjoy was how women's opinions were dismissed or ignored. In official Washington, men still retired to the study for after-dinner brandy, while women retreated to the powder room (or kitchen, depending on the size of the house) to exchange gossip. Our last names were our husbands'. We wore skirts, never slacks—except on weekends. No one asked me what I did. They didn't have to: I was a wife. Although Mac gave lip service to the idea of opportunities for women, he had no idea how it translated into practical realities. The image of Jackie Kennedy still loomed large—wardrobe, decorating, dinner parties, entertainment. In Washington, women were professional hostesses. Jackie Kennedy made the dinner party into an art form. Attitudes in the old boys' network were not so different from what Todd Gitlin later wrote about the New Left and SDS: "The SDS old guard was essentially a young boys' network. . . . Men sought [women] out, recruited them, took them seriously, honored their intelligence—then subtly demoted them to girlfriends, wives, note-takers, coffee makers. . . . Ambition, expected in a man, looked suspiciously like ball-busting to the male eye."

Looming even larger, however, than my young husband's expectations for his new wife were those of Mac's parents for their daughter-in-law. Mac was then working for the Export-Import Bank, a government bank that guarantees loans to American corporations doing high-risk business in foreign countries. The most risky business abroad at that time was the building of nuclear power plants, and while Mac talked to his father about things like the financing of nuclear power plants outside the United States, I answered his mother's questions about our social life in Washington.

Sometimes I can look back and see myself through her eyes and see how shockingly unsuitable I must have been for the future career she imagined for her son. His parents' overall expectation was that Mac would have a successful career in the WASP financial world and consolidate all their gains in social status and wealth. They had moved out of a Reading, Pennsylvania, railroad family into the upper levels of New York banking circles, which were then dominated by the so-called six Rockefeller banks that rotated around David Rockefeller at Chase Manhattan. Mac's father worked for William Renchard, Princeton '28, the chairman of Chemical Bank of New York (now part of J. P. Morgan Chase). Mac had grown up in an environment where career moves were analyzed and Wall Street information was parsed and judged. He understood the chessboard of advancement—how important social contacts led to upward motion, and how wrong moves sabotaged a promising career. A good marriage brought connections, social background, wealth, and class savvy. I brought none of these. But, on the other hand, Mac claimed he definitely did not want a corporate life.

His mother wanted to get to know me better and asked about my work. Florence looked puzzled when I said I loved my job. *My* job? I saw the question mark in her eyes, but at the time didn't understand it. My married life was supposed to be about Mac's job. She loved being Mrs. Vice President. Florence was not one of those wives Betty Friedan described as unhappy in the suburbs. She belonged to the Ridgewood Country Club and the Ridgewood Garden Club and entertained well and often.

Mac's mother was a product of the postwar period that historians have called the most intensely domestic period in American history. It was a narrow world circumscribed by children, schools, and church—a worldview that the male editors of women's magazines reinforced. As Betty Friedan later wrote, "By the time I started writing for women's magazines, in the 1950s, it was simply taken for granted by editors . . . that women were not interested in politics, life outside the United States, national issues, art, science, ideas, adventure, education, or even their own communities. . . . Politics for women became Mamie's clothes and the Nixons' home life." Many women invested all their expressive energies in their children. My mother-in-law was polite, but she revealed not one glimmer of interest in me or my ideas, talents, or ambitions. (She was equally uninterested in the talents of her other daughter-in-law, who was artistic, and who would eventually start an extremely successful business in the Midwest that employed her husband and two of her children.) I *was* interested in art, politics, national issues, ideas, adventure, education, regions of the United States we knew little about, and even life outside the United States. She was a master of the slow blink when she heard something that didn't intersect with the world she knew. Like when I told her that Mrs. Martin Luther King had spent several hours in our apartment before taking her plane back to Georgia. It was not the kind of social contact she had in mind.

I did not tell her about the conversation nor did she ask. Mrs. King had been a member of WILPF for years, believed in equality for women and blacks, was a peace activist, and frequently came to Washington to speak to peace groups against the war in Vietnam. She talked about the connections between the civil rights struggles in the South and the war in Vietnam, as well as the positive role of women as political activists. While she was in our apartment waiting for her plane—it was March 1968—she telephoned Memphis and afterward spoke about the death threats her husband had received and how the FBI knew about them but did not pass them on. (Martin Luther King was assassinated a week later.) She also gave me a quick lesson in the sexual power relationships in the South between black women and white men and how they shaped southern politics. Mrs. King was much more of a politician and feminist than she had been given credit for.

"Just what is it that you do for that—what is it—peace group?" Florence asked, blinking slowly. She seemed distracted when I answered. She was far more interested in knowing about our social life. This was a connection to a world she knew. "Are you meeting people in Washington? Did you join that tennis club that Mac told me about? And didn't he tell me you went out to the Nitzes' farm one Sunday?"

Florence was always interested in the decor and the refreshments. The Nitze farm was in Port Tobacco, Maryland, and I described its barns, tennis courts, flowered chintz sofas, and rolling lawn down to the Potomac River. She blinked more rapidly and asked questions about what food was served, what the women wore, and how the house was decorated. I could see that she thought we were finally networking at the right level. I answered all her questions, but my memory of the afternoon at the Nitze farm was utterly different from the sunny surfaces I described to her.

The Nitze farm was one of several properties owned by Paul H. Nitze, a looming presence in America's foreign policy establishment, and along with Massachusetts governor Christian Herter, a cofounder of SAIS. (In fact, SAIS recently changed its name to the Paul H. Nitze School of Advanced International Studies, and now describes itself as "the country's leading graduate school of international affairs.") Nitze served seven presidents of both parties, and is best known as the author of the famous National Security Council directive known as NSC-68, which set in motion America's massive expenditures on nuclear weapons. Many people, most recently James Carroll, observed that Paul Nitze "did more to shape American attitudes toward military power and nuclear weapons than any other figure." Nitze believed in the militarization of foreign policy and understood the importance of institution building to execute those policies.

SAIS began in 1944 with fifteen students. A year earlier, both Herter and Nitze were working in wartime Washington during Roosevelt's third administration. Their wives were cousins and the two men shared a house in the city while their spouses summered on Long Island. Herter was a Boston Brahmin who in the 1950s would become Eisenhower's secretary of state. Nitze, a former Wall Street banker with a phenomenally wealthy wife—Phyllis Pratt, a Standard Oil heiress and granddaughter of Rockefeller partner Charles Pratt—moved back and forth between Defense and State. (In 1950, he would take over George Kennan's job as director of the Policy Planning Office at the

State Department.) The two men believed that a new school was needed to prepare a postwar generation of Americans in managing the transition in colonial empires that the exhausted European powers could no longer administer. At the time, there were only three schools of international affairs: the Fletcher School at Tufts (too scholarly), the School of Foreign Service at Georgetown (too small, too Catholic), and the Institute of International Studies in Geneva, Switzerland (too far away). They assembled ten of their best friends, including a representative of the Rockefeller Foundation, set up a foundation to fund the school, a board of trustees to supervise, and the School of Advanced International Studies opened the following year.

Over the next forty years, Nitze would hold a number of subcabinet positions in either Defense or State and always stayed closely linked to SAIS. He also used SAIS as a place to help situate bright young men who came to his attention. Nitze supported the most conservative advocates of nuclear weapons buildup in the military establishment, and in 1957 he helped to establish a prestigious but military-oriented think tank at SAIS, called the Washington Center of Foreign Policy Research (funded by the Rockefeller Foundation). He mentored hundreds of bright young men—no one I talked with could name any women—and placed them in key slots throughout the national security bureaucracy.

His policy objectives were always oriented toward the most advanced weapons systems. In 1969, Nitze founded the Committee to Maintain a Prudent Defense Policy, a lobbying operation created to promote support for antiballistic missile systems (ABM). After the ABM debate was rendered moot because of the ABM Treaty signed by the United States and the Soviet Union, Nitze revived the Committee on the Present Danger, a group of conservatives from various governmental agencies, to educate people on the continuing menace from the Soviet Union. One bright young man who came to his attention was Paul Wolfowitz, who wrote position papers supporting the need for ever-escalating military expenditures in the face of the Soviet danger. His conclusions were subsequently proved to be completely wrong, but at the time they were extremely influential.

By 1993, Nitze sponsored Wolfowitz to be the new dean of SAIS, a post Wolfowitz held until 2001, when he left to become deputy secretary of defense, in charge of Iraq war planning. During Wolfowitz's nine years at SAIS, he helped organize the Project for the New American Century, a neoconservative group many of whose members came from previous Nitze committees and whose foreign policy goal was to sustain "American dominance" as the world's lone superpower. As a defense policy strategist, he consulted for a major defense contractor. And as an educator, Wolfowitz maintained the all-male imbalance that I had encountered thirty-five years earlier. During his tenure as dean, he did increase the school's total number of tenured women professors by 100 percent, in that he appointed *one* tenured woman professor. In 2000, when I telephoned his office to find out if the figure was a mistake, his secretary said it was accurate, and added, "The dean knows it's a problem." The irony of Wolfowitz's lack of support for women professionals was that he would later be forced to resign from his position as president of the World Bank over an ethics controversy that centered on showing favoritism to an Iranian employee of the bank, a woman who was also his girlfriend. He had arranged for her appointment to a special post at the U.S. State Department but at a salary, paid by the World Bank, higher than that of the U.S. secretary of state.

Part of Nitze's influence was based on his ability to create tight personal networks through social events he hosted at his various homes in Washington, Maine, and Maryland. The Maryland home was a farm on the banks of the Potomac on the eastern shore. At the farm, the wives tended to be the children of present or former high-level officials, cabinet officers, or Pentagon brass. The husbands were the ambitious young men that Paul Nitze had selected to be promoted in Washington's foreign policy establishment. The event that stayed in my mind was not the afternoon I described to my mother-in-law, but another one in the summer of 1969.

On that particular Sunday, Mac played tennis and I served hors d'oeuvres. It was sunny and hot. After circulating with a tray full of gin and tonics, I took a glass for myself, sat down at one of the tables next to the tennis courts, put my feet up on an empty chair, and peered out over my sunglasses at the players.

"Good serve," said a voice from the other side of my table. A muscular, military-looking young man had sat down. He had an almost-shaved head and a jaw so angular it could have been measured with a T square. We introduced ourselves. When I heard his last name, I did not ask if he was related to Admiral Elmo Zumwalt—chief of naval operations and former commander of naval forces in Vietnam—because I assumed he was. Why else would he be there?

Young Elmo Zumwalt III made a few comments about Mac's serve, which he thought was very good. We chatted about the weather (a beautiful, clear sunny day), the players (energetic and handsome in brilliant tennis whites), other people on the sidelines (enthusiastic, attentive, knowledgeable), and the referee (not doing a notably good job).

"How do you know the Nitzes?" he asked.

I explained we were friends of friends. "And you?"

"He's a friend of my father's."

"What branch of the navy are you in?"

"Marines," he said. "I'm on my way to Vietnam. I ship out on Wednesday."

We paused. Long silence here. I searched for other topics of conversation. Vietnam was always the uninvited guest at a party.

"Tell me again who you work for," young Zumwalt asked. Earlier in the afternoon, a congressional staffer had pointed at me, saying, "Look out for her. She works for the bomb throwers," referring to the group of antiwar congressmen who employed me. By then it was 1969, and there were more than a half million troops in Vietnam. There were no casual conversations about the war. Elmo couldn't understand how I could criticize the war effort and work for people who were criticizing the war, even going so far as voting against military appropriations. And I couldn't understand why he was so anxious to get to Vietnam to command a Swift boat. He was convinced we finally had enough boots on the ground to turn the war around. I had a terrible premonition that a grim future lay ahead for Elmo III. In fact, more criticism might have helped young Zumwalt's future. After years of painful debilitating illness, death is not always the worst outcome.

Elmo Zumwalt III would be killed, not by the Vietnamese but by the American chemical industry. When he returned from Vietnam, he began to exhibit a cluster of debilitating physical symptoms—chronic fatigue, nerve damage, immune system breakdown. The Veterans Administration characterized these ailments as battle fatigue or psychological exhaustion and denied any responsibility. But young Zumwalt did not get better. Tens of thousands of Vietnam veterans reported similar symptoms, including various cancers, leukemia, and blood diseases. Some of their children were born with crippling birth defects. Eventually,

Zumwalt was diagnosed with lymphatic cancer. Vietnam veterans began to insist that their illnesses were caused by exposure to a chemical substance called Agent Orange (the name came from its packaging in orange barrels).

The Defense Department denied any correlation between Agent Orange, the chemical defoliant that the air force sprayed over the jungles and fields of Vietnam, and the many symptoms the veterans were reporting. In Congress, however, staffers were already aware of the effects of Agent Orange because pregnant Vietnamese women who had been living in areas sprayed with the defoliant were giving birth to severely deformed babies. Adult Vietnamese had the same diseases reported by the veterans. The defoliated areas tended to be along the banks of rivers where the "brown water" navy had been operating, exactly where young Zumwalt was going.

The main ingredient in Agent Orange was dioxin, an agent so toxic it is considered second only to radioactive waste. Dioxin changes the functioning of cells, and no level of human exposure is acceptable. Although tens of thousands of Vietnam veterans had been exposed to Agent Orange and were exhibiting severe symptoms at every level of physical functioning, the Veterans Administration offered little medical care and no explanation. The army, navy, and air force were unanimously vague about these symptoms. As it turned out, each service had been given specific instructions by the Office of Management and Budget to deny any connection between Agent Orange and Vietnam veterans' health. Why? Money. The financial costs of caring for the veterans as well as the potential liability by the corporations making the chemical would have been staggering. Even the son of the youngest rear admiral in American history didn't get special treatment.

How do I know this? The person who eventually exposed the

truth was young Zumwalt's father, Admiral Zumwalt himself.
Two years after his son died, he asked President George H. W.
Bush to appoint him to the U.S. board examining Agent Orange.
He rejected the American research studies and instead published
Swedish reports confirming the chemical content of Agent Orange and the known effects of dioxin exposure on humans. He
made public the administrative order from the Office of Management and Budget that deliberately directed the military services
to avoid responsibility. Zumwalt told an interviewer: "We found
in that report that the Bureau of the Budget had ordered all the
agencies of government in essence not to find a correlation between Agent Orange and health effects stating that it would be
most unfortunate for two reasons: a) the cost of supporting the
veterans and b) the court liability to which corporations would be
exposed." Later, after the 1991 Gulf War, Admiral Zumwalt
again spoke out about the exposure American soldiers might have
had to toxic chemicals. During the bombing of a chemical facility believed to manufacture nerve gas, the American command
had failed to keep track of troop positions, and, unlike British
troops, the American soldiers had never put on protective masks.

The true heroism of the Zumwalts was tested not in battle in
Vietnam but in coming home, when they took on a bureaucracy
that was mired in corruption and that refused to face the consequences of its own actions. Although the full extent of the
Agent Orange story would not be understood until years in the
future, the enthusiasm of young Zumwalt to go off to Vietnam
was my outstanding memory from that sunny Sunday afternoon
at the Nitze farm.

In reflection, it revealed the paradox of the elegant, moneyed
lifestyle that supported sending young men off to war in a dubious
cause. This social arrangement I wouldn't thoroughly understand
until much later.

"You know, I have a little present for you," Florence said, as I finished my description of the floral sofas in the Nitze decor and we completed preparations for the ritual cocktails.

She handed me a copy of *Forum Feasts,* a cookbook put together by the Ridgewood Garden Club and the Junior League. It was filled with recipes for canapés and hors d'oeuvres for cocktail parties, easy casseroles for entertaining, and fun snacks for children. The cover had drawings of two people in Roman togas.

"You could find a nice dish to make to take out to the Nitze farm the next time you are invited," she said. I thanked her and told her I would use it. And I did.

As it turned out, I would be a beneficiary of Mac's tennis networking. Tennis was the sport of choice in Washington in the 1960s, and Mac was a serious competitor. I was a novice. We joined the National Cathedral Tennis Club, where I took lessons. The first thing Mac instructed me to do was buy full tennis whites and tennis sneakers so I at least looked like I belonged on a court. Being agreeable and fairly athletic, I did as I was told. We played polite mixed doubles with other couples; then the men played aggressive singles. Killer tennis, I called it. Surprisingly, it was tennis that got me my next job, the job that people characterized as "the most interesting job in Washington" and that would worry Mac's mother even more than my position with the Women's International League for Peace and Freedom.

One hot summer evening as we were leaving the club's tennis courts, Mac ran into a former classmate from Yale. They exchanged news of their lives since college. Paul Gorman was working on Capitol Hill for a group of liberal congressmen but was leaving his job in a month. Unlike most of Mac's friends, he turned to me and asked what I did. Astonishingly, he had heard of WILPF and nodded approvingly. "That's a great organiza-tion." He thought for a moment. "You should apply for my job," he said. "You have the right background." I was speechless. Getting a job on Capitol Hill was highly desirable, and no woman I knew worked there professionally. "I mean it," he said. "Send me your résumé, and I'll pass it on to the right people." So without any expectation, I sent it off to him and then forgot about it.

Paul Gorman was a seeker. One aspect of the 1960s was that many well-educated young people were finding that replicating their parents' lives of moneymaking, status, and position left them feeling empty. America's materialism and militarism were not satisfying. After working in Congress, Gorman eventually found his way to a former Harvard psychologist named Richard Alpert, known as Ram Dass, a colleague of Timothy Leary's in psychedelic drug research. (The psychedelic drug known as LSD had been developed by the CIA at a medical facility near Stanford as a potential truth serum.) Ram Dass became a spiri-tual guide to an entire generation of seekers by making Eastern religious thought accessible to the West. Gorman collaborated with Ram Dass on several books about the spiritual path in life, including *The Only Dance There Is.*

Months later, long after I had forgotten about meeting Paul Gorman on the tennis courts, I got a phone call from Mary in Congressman Benjamin Rosenthal's office. Mary—formerly President John Kennedy's secretary when he was in the House—asked if I could meet the congressman at a luncheon the next day that was being sponsored by Another Mother for Peace. She told me Paul Gorman had recommended me, and the congressman was interested in meeting me as one of the candidates for Gorman's job.

"Sure," I said. Why not?

LEFT: JN on the *SS Bremen* coming into New York harbor, 1965. (Photograph by the ship photographer)

BELOW: Swampscott Tomboys' baseball team of 1907. Three out of the ten players have the last name "Nies." In 1907, only five years after Queen Victoria died, most formal portraits of women were wedding photos. This unusual team photo had been carefully preserved in my Aunt Alice's attic. First row: Dolly Melanson, third base; Evelyn Connors, shortstop; Fanny Jacinsky, center field; May Nies, left field; Babe Drake, pitcher. Top row: Edith Jones, right field; Alice Nies, second base and captain; Florence Drake, first base; Claire Nies, center field; Alice Horton, catcher.

ABOVE: Brophy summer house on Lake Winnipesaukee in Wolfeboro, New Hampshire. I called it the "Gatsby House" because it burned down in the 1930s but lived on in family memory as a place of dazzling parties and a vanished life of ease.

BELOW: Nies family in summer whites in Wolfeboro, NH. My father is second from left with his brothers and sisters. Stratton Brophy is far right in leather jacket and yachting cap.

ABOVE: "The Shoe," as the United Shoe Machinery Corporation was known, was the largest factory in the U.S. Contrary to its name, it did not make shoes, but manufactured the machinery that made shoes. From 1941 to his retirement in 1970, my father worked at The Shoe as a foreman. Enclosing over one million square feet of factory space, The Shoe went out of business as a result of an antitrust suit and changing patterns of shoe manufacture. It was recently refurbished into a successful office park with thirty-two acres of interior space. (Photograph courtesy of Cummings Properties)

LEFT: Stratton Brophy and father on the boardwalk in Nice, France, 1933.

ABOVE: In 1975, I was appointed to the Lowell Park Commission, charged with creating a national park out of the decrepit mill buildings, deserted warehouses, rusted machinery, and crumbling canals of America's first planned Industrial City. Boott Mill, built in 1835 and named for Kirk Boott, the first mill agent, could have been one of the mills where my grandmother worked. It was one of the first to be restored by the Lowell Heritage Park Commission and today houses a museum with working mill machinery. (Photograph courtesy of the National Park Service)

RIGHT: JN,
age three,
with father.

ABOVE: I arrived on the federal-state Lowell Commission just in time to make the case for highlighting the labor conditions for the thousands of New England farm girls who provided the labor force that made fortunes for Boston's first millionaires. The prevailing view at the time was that the park should showcase the entrepreneurial genius of the founders—the Lowells, Cabots, and Appletons— and their industrial vision. I argued that although Lowell was a unique historical site (the original location of the Industrial Revolution in America), a national park must interpret the choices made between technological creativity and human cost. At the time I did not prevail, but a new generation of women historians eventually did. By 1984, this sculpture by Mico Kaufman was one of several installations to recognize the contribution of women workers to Lowell's industrial success. (Photograph courtesy of the National Park Service)

ABOVE: JN at Delphi, the beginning of what would be a long voyage hitchhiking around the ancient Mediterranean world.

RIGHT: JN, wedding picture.

ABOVE: Meeting of the Lowell Heritage Commission. JN in trenchcoat.

LEFT: Outside the carriage house at Tregaron. JN in Marimekko dress.

Hitchhiking on the road.

"Are you one of the Hollywood people?" asked a tall man smoking a cigar as I walked through the door of a small private dining room in the Capitol. "I'm Ben Rosenthal."

I burst out laughing. "I'm flattered that you'd think I came from Hollywood. I actually came from across the street. I'm the person you're supposed to meet regarding Paul Gorman's job."

"You?" Rosenthal look incredulous. "You? The new Paul Gorman?" I didn't realize then that the number of women in professional jobs on Capitol Hill could be counted on one hand. Rosenthal put out his cigar, pulled out a chair for me at the table, motioned me to sit down, and leaned in.

"What do you know about this group from Hollywood?" Rosenthal asked, lowering his voice. "Who are these mothers? And how come most of them happen to be movie stars?" In an instant, I had been placed in the position of the staff person whispering in the ear of the politician. And Rosenthal, an astute and shrewd student of media, understood that something far more significant than a lobbying lunch was going on. Hollywood meant publicity. Publicity meant money. "And is that Paul Newman over there with Joanne?" It was.

Until the 1960s, movie stars were products of the studio system and were not allowed to speak out on political issues. Even if they were so inclined, their public activities were supposed to be in the support of patriotic causes, like selling war bonds or entertaining U.S. troops stationed abroad. A star's fame and name recognition was not a commodity—today we would call it a brand—that could be translated into something more substantial in the public world. It had been only a decade since significant numbers of Hollywood writers and actors had been ruined by congressional investigations of their political affiliations. So when Paul Newman and Joanne Woodward and Rod Serling and a host of other movie and television stars came to

Congress under the banner of Another Mother for Peace, it was one of the first times that a new generation of stars banded together to use their publicity machine in a political cause. Unlike the Hollywood Ten demonstrations in the 1950s, which took place only after the House Un-American Activities Committee had subpoenaed Hollywood scriptwriters and producers based on flimsy evidence that they were members of the Communist Party, these movie stars took over a hearing room and criticized the government and the conduct of an American war in progress. Congressman Rosenthal immediately understood the significance of a women's antiwar organization that included movie stars among its members.

"I was told that it began only a year ago," I told Rosenthal, "in the Los Angeles living room of Barbara Avedon. She's a television writer. I think it was an offshoot of Women Strike for Peace in Los Angeles, but her group wanted to aim for a more mainstream audience as well as a lot of people in the film community." The group picked up membership through the public relations networks of its movie-star members and excellent graphics. Their antiwar logo—a sunflower with the words WAR IS NOT HEALTHY FOR CHILDREN AND OTHER LIVING THINGS—was appearing on yellow bumper stickers throughout the country. Their leadership and message to women had caught people's imaginations and had raised a lot of money. At the luncheon, I sat between actress Barbara Rush—who said one of her ancestors had been Benjamin Rush, a signer of the Declaration of Independence—and Rosenthal, who said his ancestors had been in a hay wagon escaping the czar's pogroms about the same time. We had a wonderful time.

"How do you get that tan?" Rosenthal asked television star Rod Serling, who had a permanent George Hamilton–quality tan. As we arrived at the hearing room where the press conference was to take place, Rosenthal looked at the television and print reporters who lined the hallway outside the hearing room and seemed to take a new view of the significance of women's antiwar organizations.

Ben Rosenthal said hello to a few reporters he knew, told Barbara Avedon what a great job she was doing, as though he had known about her forever, and shook hands with Paul Newman, getting a laugh when he called him "Senator Newman."

Then he turned to me and said in a low voice, gesturing to the packed hearing room, "Who are all these women? What are all these women's groups?"

It was a good question. I had been trying to figure out the answer myself. There were many women's peace groups represented in the room, including Women Strike for Peace (WSP), WILPF, and others, but because the press ignored women's groups, they didn't have name recognition. I pointed out the few faces that I recognized.

By the time of the luncheon meeting with Another Mother for Peace, many Americans had begun to feel that the war in Vietnam was a quagmire. Even though the press and the Nixon administration insisted the antiwar movement was made up of bearded hippies, college students who were afraid of the draft, and "outside agitators" who were interested in undermining American democracy, the visible participation of white, middle-class women speaking out against the war made a lie of the administration's version of the peace movement.

My first encounter with WSP had been when I first began working for WILPF in 1967. Donna Allen, who was a member of both WILPF and WSP, telephoned and asked me to join a delegation that was going to appear before the Atomic Energy Commission (AEC).

"Don't worry, you don't have to say anything," she reassured me when I protested that I didn't know anything about nuclear policy. "We'll do all the talking. We just need more bodies in the room."

The AEC was the high temple of nuclear theology and I had been schooled in respect for the authority of such institutions. But when I arrived at the AEC offices in Maryland, I was greeted with a scene of thrilling anarchy.

The meeting was held in a large conference room. At one end of a T-shaped conference table were men from the very agencies I had been trained to work for—the Pentagon, the State Department, the Atomic Energy Commission. The military men were in uniforms with their medals on display; their civilian counterparts were in their own uniforms of dark suits, white shirts, and subdued ties.

On each side of the long end of the table were a dozen women whose wardrobes ranged from Miami leisure wear to trim business suits to big floral-print dresses. Large handbags had been thumped down on the shiny conference table like surveyors' stakes—papers were shuffled and passed around. It was a messy chessboard: the men in black all lined up ready to make their moves, the women in wild colors all over the board. They were refusing to play by the game's usual rules.

The defining quality of these meetings with "high government officials," I was to learn, was a combination of spontaneity, preparation, and history. When I did my graduate-school research on the women lobbying for the Test Ban Treaty in 1963, I had little idea about the personalities of these women. I knew only that Women Strike for Peace began in 1961 as a one-day action of women, primarily housewives, who publicly protested by refusing to carry on their domestic roles and demanded passage of the Nuclear Test Ban Treaty. Their November 1 demonstrations in more than fifty cities were so unexpectedly successful that their leaders were immediately called to testify before the HUAC. In the divisive spirit of the time, the HUAC congressmen characterized the leaders of antinuclear WSP as "subversives, communist dupes, or saboteurs."

For the first time, however, the HUAC members confronted an opponent who fought back with both slyness and a sense of theater. Women Strike for Peace brought an anarchic style to those HUAC hearings. While they played to the stereotypical image of white, middle-class garden-club women, they were carefully prepared, articulate, and well represented.

In her elegant British accent, Dagmar Wilson, a children's book illustrator and a leader of the Washington, D.C., branch, emphasized that Women's Strike for Peace did not keep membership lists. "We are a movement," she insisted, "not an organization." Unlike the Old Left and other liberal organizations, whose leadership had fractured over the question of providing names of members who had been communists, the WSP leaders simply declared any previous affiliation to be irrelevant. In so doing, they disarmed the committee of one of its most potent weapons, the requirement to name names or be held in contempt. This idea of a movement rather than an organization would be the model that the New Left would eventually follow, and it would be a defining tactic of sixties political groups.

In the end, Women Strike for Peace dealt a blow to the credibility of the committee. A Herb Block cartoon in the *Washington Post* showed one befuddled HUAC congressman asking another, "Which is it that is un-American, peace or women?" Other newspaper columnists asked, "Just who are we calling Communist spies?" Typical headlines were "Redhunters Decapitated," "Peace Ladies Tangle with Baffled Congress." The result of the hearing was to raise questions in the public mind about the judgment of the congressmen. The WSP organizers brilliantly used the sex stereotypes of domestic culture in the service of radical politics.

So five years later, by the time I joined the WSP delegation at the Atomic Energy Commission, they already had sat at a lot of conference tables in a lot of government agencies. They had an innovative, nonhierarchical political style and a near total belief in the authenticity of grassroots action. (Their organizational style and their belief that leadership potential was within each person would be their most important legacies to the feminist groups that followed them.) Because Washington was the seat of national government and policy, the Washington branch was savvy about how Washington worked.

At the AEC meeting, I was fascinated by Dagmar Wilson's poise, as well as her whimsicality and playfulness. She brought the same creativity and sense of fun to her political work that she did to her children's books. Although Wilson spoke briefly to open the session, the presentation on our side was leaderless, in the sense that a Quaker meeting is leaderless. Anyone spoke as the spirit moved her. The men on the other side of the table, whose lives and careers had been molded by moving through definitive, hierarchical progressions, clearly found this nonlinear style disconcerting. It was like a jazz band meeting a group of symphony musicians. The classical musicians were at a loss without a score; the jazz players were listening to the flow of the meeting and came in when their instrument was called for.

"Why don't you ladies go home and take care of your husbands and children?" said the air force general, his chest full of ribbons, when he was was no longer able to contain his frustration. At the time, the air force manual prohibited an officer in uniform from carrying a child or groceries in case he had to salute a superior officer.

"We are taking care of our children. Right now. At this very moment," said Edith Villastrigo, one of the key women of the Washington branch. "Key woman" was the phrase they used instead of "leader." I stifled a gasp at her words.

"What is your budget for this year?" asked Donna Allen, a PhD economist who wore trim business suits and whose youthful face was framed by prematurely white hair rolled into a Katharine Hepburn hairstyle. The AEC budget was secret. Allen pointed out that all the gentlemen's salaries at the table, generals and civil servants alike, were paid by taxpayer money. There was no such thing as government money, she said, only taxpayers' money. "I believe we are paying for these nuclear tests; we are entitled to know something about them." (The Test Ban Treaty prohibited aboveground nuclear testing, but not underground testing, which was ongoing.) I never forgot her confidence, or the legitimacy of her question.

By then, Women Strike for Peace had turned into a national movement, with over one hundred local branches, ten regional offices, and contacts in peace movements all over the world. And, as a later Freedom of Information request made clear, every one of their branches and meetings had been infiltrated by an informant from the FBI or the CIA. Few WSP women were feminists. They based their standing in the public world on their role as wives and mothers. Theirs was a stance of moral motherhood, whereby they were taking a moral position in defense of children and the future. One of their most important but unrecognized contributions was, as Amy Swerdlow later wrote, that the public participation of "militant, middle class, middle-aged, white women legitimized a radical critique of the Cold War and U. S. militarism."

Another Mother for Peace had evolved out of that critique along with the demonstrations that WSP had organized in Los Angeles. As I told Ben Rosenthal, many women were members of multiple organizations—Women Strike for Peace and WILPF and Another Mother for Peace.

Actress Joanne Woodward opened the press conference by reading a letter from a soldier in Vietnam and held the room transfixed, a single tear rolling down her cheek as she read. If it was acting, it was the best I have ever seen.

Paul Newman spoke briefly about why he felt it was important to support a women's peace organization and why people must speak out against a war that was claiming their sons while the generals were still asking for more troops.

At the time, there were five hundred thousand American troops in Vietnam, and General Westmoreland had asked for two hundred thousand more. The draft had not yet been replaced by the lottery system, so every male between the ages of eighteen and thirty who didn't have a deferment was eligible to be drafted and sent to Vietnam. The urban poor and blacks from the South went to Vietnam in vastly disproportionate numbers. Many middle-class young men hung in for college degrees they didn't necessarily want so they could keep their deferments. (George W. Bush's vice president, Dick Cheney, for example, asked for and received five draft deferments during the Vietnam War while working on a doctorate that he never completed. Later, his famous comment on his lack of military service was, "I had other priorities.") Others without deferments sought asylum in Canada and Sweden. The author Jane Jacobs, a New Yorker, moved her family to Toronto so her sons couldn't be drafted for service in Vietnam. Many mothers in the antiwar movement provided draft counseling or acted as housing coordinators for Canada-bound draft resisters.

As he was leaving, Rosenthal noticed the wedding ring on my finger, asked how long I had been married, and seemed reassured by the answer. "Your husband won't object to your taking a job on Capitol Hill?" he asked.

"I can't imagine why he would," I said. "He's a friend of Paul Gorman's." Of course, I didn't realize that Mac actually *would* object to the long hours, the stress, the commitment.

"I think you should meet with Kastenmeier and one or two of the other congressmen in our group. I'll set it up. Mary will call you."

That was my initial job interview.

In the three months between my meeting with Ben Rosenthal (July) and my follow-up interview with Bob Kastenmeier (October), huge changes were shaking loose bedrock beliefs about American society. Although the Miss America pageant might seem trivial in the context of the events of 1968—the assassinations of Martin Luther King and Senator Robert F. Kennedy, the Soviet invasion of Czechoslovakia, the student uprising in Paris, the police riot at the Chicago Democratic Convention—it wasn't. The demonstrations at the Miss America pageant were provocative, shocking, and raised alarming questions about the fundamental organization of American society. Only the year before, Harvard sociologist David Riesman had predicted, "If anything remains more or less unchanged, it will be the role of women."

American women were supposed to have the easiest and most envied lifestyle in the world. Why were protestors claiming that American women needed liberation? Who were these women?

CHAPTER TEN

The Rise of the Bra Burners

Summer, 1968

The summer of 1968 had been preceded by a violent spring. When Martin Luther King was assassinated in Memphis in April, riots broke out in more than a hundred cities across America, including Washington, D.C. I got used to the smell of tear gas and the sight of tanks on Connecticut Avenue. The summer, which began hopefully, with Lyndon Johnson's promise not to run for reelection, accelerated in violence after the assassination of presidential candidate Robert Kennedy on June 5. By the time the Democratic Party Convention took place on August 26, in Chicago, television cameras showed the world footage of the Chicago police brutally clubbing demonstrators on the streets in front of the convention hall. Inside the hall, Chicago's Mayor Daley gave the finger to Connecticut senator Abe Ribicoff, who took the podium to condemn what was happening in the streets. In Europe, where I was attending a women's peace conference, I saw these televised images of Chicago police violence shown in tandem with scenes from the Soviet invasion of Czechoslovakia, which began the same week.

Far less prominent, but of considerable significance, during that same summer were the announcements by a group called New York Radical Women that they would hold a protest demonstration at the annual Miss America beauty pageant in Atlantic City, on September 7. What's to protest about a beauty contest? I wondered. According to their flyers, they planned to organize "Picket Lines; Guerrilla Theater; Leafleting; Lobbying . . . Male reporters will be refused interviews. . . . Only *newswomen* will be recognized. Join Us on the Boardwalk at Atlantic City."

The Miss America protest marked the first widespread media attention to the publicly invisible, but bubbling women's liberation movement. Unlike any of the other demonstrations taking place throughout the United States, the sole purpose of this protest was to focus on the constructed image of American women. The protestors made no mention of war, civil rights, poverty, tenants' rights, health care, abortion, or any of the dozens of other social protest movements that were appearing on the streets of America (and from which many of the participants came). The intention of the demonstrators was to draw public attention to the lack of freedom for women in America and to emphasize that women must be valued as full human beings apart from their appearance. The organizers came from radical women's groups in Chicago, New York, and Gainesville, Florida.

Planning for the event had begun well over a year in advance. The leaders came from the New Left, disaffected members of SDS, the civil rights movement, and the antiwar movement; they were canny, smart organizers who had experience in both strategy and tactics. They were well trained in guerrilla street theater, media relations, and political action. In some of the newsletters I subscribed to, I had read their analysis of how they believed female beauty was a social construct and how the advertising industry's promotion of rigid ideals of female appearance enslaved women by holding up unattainable standards. What I didn't imagine was what anyone could do about it. And besides, the war in Vietnam and civil rights seemed more important.

The truth was, I loved the Miss America contest and had watched it on television since I was a little girl, as had my friends and millions of other American girls. I had never questioned it. I loved when the winner came walking down the runway in her crown, carrying her roses, and crying—the winners were always crying—with Bert Parks singing the lyrics "There she is, Miss America" in a baritone reminiscent of a kindly, but drunk uncle. We were thrilled with her prizes. We never questioned why the winner was always white, wasp-waisted, and usually blond, although sometimes there were brunettes. It seemed very innocent.

After the 1968 demonstrations, it was no longer possible to view the pageant as quite so innocent. The pageant protest was visual, creative, political, and outrageous. "Peggy Dobbins from New Orleans got arrested for spraying that obnoxious ammonia-smelling hair permanent stuff around the convention hall," recalled Carol Giardina, one of the founders of Gainesville (Florida) Women's Liberation, which, along with Redstockings in New York and Women's Liberation in Chicago, collaborated with New York Radical Women to organize the protest. Inside the hall, audience members were shocked when they smelled what the press called a "stench bomb," but was, in fact, the permanent-wave solution that Peggy Dobbins and other demonstrators had sprayed into the air. Astounded television audiences saw a banner unfurled inside the convention hall that read in huge letters: WOMEN'S LIBERATION.

Although the protestors were affiliated with groups whose

names had yet to appear in any mainstream newspaper, they knew how to challenge the symbols of an advertising age. Their simple analysis was that women's bodies in America had become a highly effective, but dehumanized object used to sell products from automobiles to cosmetics. "Buy two big ones," ran one advertisement for automobile tires that featured a chesty model posed between two automobile tires. "I'm Margie. Fly me," ran the caption underneath a photograph for a model posing as a stewardess for (now defunct) National Airlines.

The organizers understood the mechanics of political action and the need to express their ideas visually so that photographers would cover them. Outside the hall where the pageant was taking place, pedestrians were astonished to see a surreal scene of a sheep wearing a rhinestone tiara being paraded up and down the Atlantic City boardwalk. The photo of the sheep that appeared in many newspapers was a symbol of how women mindlessly followed the false standards of beauty queens. Several demonstrators correctly pointed out that the pageant had never crowned a winner of a dark skin color.

The organizers were well prepared. They obtained permits, trained marshals, rented bullhorns, conceptualized the demonstrations inside and outside the hall. They assigned volunteers to transport the sheep from a farm in rural New Jersey. They honed their message and came up with a strategy for getting their message to the public. Their insistence on speaking only with female members of the media extended to television reporters and *camerawomen*. (Union rules excluded women from many technical jobs in television.) Women from other cities answered the call from New York Radical Women to join them in Atlantic City.

During the five days of the pageant, over two hundred protestors passed out press releases, held impromptu debates on the

boardwalk—especially when passersby called them communists and told them to go back to Russia—and encouraged
spectators to join them in a ritual ceremony against the tyranny
of cosmetics. The irony is that the central dramatic event of the
protest, from which the term *bra burner* emerged, never happened.

One planned event of street theater was to be a bonfire of
bras, girdles, plastic hair rollers, false eyelashes, and makeup
from all the major cosmetic companies. These "instruments of
beauty torture" were to be burned in a giant "Freedom Trash
Can." But the Atlantic City mayor, concerned about fire safety
on the wooden boardwalk, refused to issue a fire permit. Remembering the televised seventeen minutes of mayhem in front
of the Chicago Hilton during the August Democratic Convention, when Chicago police beat demonstrators senseless, the organizers did not want to provoke another police confrontation.
Instead, organizer Robin Morgan proclaimed "a symbolic bra
burning," whereby all the offending cosmetic items were to be
deposited in a giant garbage can. The Freedom Trash Can ceremony took place without incident and without a fire.

Although the *New York Times* correctly reported that no bra
burnings took place, the rest of the media took up the idea of
bra burning as an irresistible symbol of antifemininity. It marked
the first use of the phrase *bra burner* and became the defining
symbolism of women's libbers. "In a breast-obsessed society,"
author Ruth Rosen astutely pointed out, " 'bra-burning' became a symbolic way of sexualizing—and thereby trivializing—
women's struggle." The idea of women who burned their bras
was repeated until it became fact. Soon even the *Times* was referring to *bra burners,* a term that became an urban legend, syn-
onymous with outlaw women, somewhat reminiscent of pagan
witches.

One of the most significant results of the Miss America demonstration was that it effectively ended the all-male newsroom. Because the Miss America demonstrators refused to speak to male reporters, newsroom editors had to pull women off the food and fashion pages—where most women reporters were assigned—and send them to cover the protest. Women's bylines ran over the stories from the pageant—five days of colorful protests. Why shouldn't women reporters have the opportunity to be political reporters as well as society page reporters? the demonstrators asked. Once women reporters began covering hard news events, it marked the beginning of the media coverage of women's political activism. I applauded the media savvy of the Miss America demonstration organizers and their discipline. That the organizers succeeded in breaking into the front pages of the nation's newspapers was a stunning accomplishment.

"You're not one of those bra burners, are you?" Congressman Kastenmeier asked me at the end of the interview. It was the beginning of October when I finally received a call from Mary, in Ben Rosenthal's office, who told me I should make an appointment to see Congressman Kastenmeier. Bob Kastenmeier came from Madison, Wisconsin, and was the senior member of the congressional group for which Paul Gorman had worked. He was also the most intellectual, the most thoughtful, and the most influential. He was also slow to smile when I told him about the Freedom Trash Can at the Miss America pageant and the false story of bra burners.

"But no," I assured him, "I'm not a bra burner." How could I be, sitting there in my pearls, stockings, heels, and a suit that I had bought in Italy? (I bought the suit in Standa, an inexpensive department store, and it was the kind of simple suit that ordinary shop girls wore in Bologna but that looked like couture fashion in Washington.)

As soon as I began working for this ad hoc group of congress-men in January 1969, my perception of reality changed. Con-gressional offices are staffed largely by people in their twenties, and most of the junior staff are without family commitments or children. Hours are long and longer. Workloads are heavy. Most of the senior staffers I worked with were men with wives, and none of them had ever worked with a woman as a peer. They thought working with a woman downgraded the status of their jobs. "There goes the neighborhood," someone commented when I entered a meeting. They expected me to put up with many off-color jokes and comments about my body parts, dress, hemlines, personality, menstrual cycle, and suitability for pro-fessional life. I was supposed to learn how to act like a guy. I started reading the sports pages. I did not, however, learn how to joke about pornography or prostitution. (Dessima Williams, an attractive former ambassador from Grenada, now a professor of sociology, told audiences about arriving in the lobby of a Washington hotel with a female aide when a man rushed up to her and demanded, "But where are the other two? We ordered four." He thought she was one of the hookers they had ordered for the evening. I, too, had similar experiences.)

So, as "the new Paul Gorman," I was viewed as a woman try-ing to do a man's job. I was also viewed as something of a curi-osity. I was expected to take notes (I did), get coffee (I did not), order lunch (sometimes), and put up with a certain amount of abuse if I was too assertive. Since power was conceived as white and male, I was subjected to many sexual stories that usually had women as the brunt of the joke. I began to realize that to sexu-alize a person in a work situation is to trivialize her.

Although the time demands of my days changed, the expec-tations of wifedom did not. If I had to travel, Mac never picked me up at the airport, although he assumed I could always juggle my schedule to pick him up. We argued over who would take the clothes to the dry cleaner, who would do the grocery shopping, who could sew on buttons, who would do the cleaning. He didn't do household chores. And if I couldn't, he told me to hire someone who could.

I hired Rosie, the African American woman who had cleaned the WILPF office. Rosie was also a minister in a storefront church in southeast Washington, and one Sunday, at her invitation, I went to her church service in a poor African American neighborhood. Rosie was my education about race and faith. She also showed me a separate Washington, a ghettoized city still intact after one hundred years of segregation and far removed from the grand avenues and memorials that visitors see. I began to understand that Mac and I were temporary residents in Washington.

In 1969, the U.S. Congress had 11 women representatives out of 435 on the House side and 1 in the Senate. Of the nine black representatives, Shirley Chisholm was the first African American woman ever to sit in Congress; she was elected from Brooklyn, New York, over the Republican candidate, civil rights activist James Farmer. His campaign literature called "for a strong black male image in Washington." Later, she famously said, "When I ran for Congress, I met far more discrimination as a woman than as a black." She was one of a group of forceful women legislators, mostly from the Democratic Party.

Patsy Mink, for example, from Hawaii, was known as a first-class legislator and was unafraid to take a controversial stand. Edith Greene from Oregon had introduced and passed the Equal Pay Act in 1963; ten years later she would sponsor the revisions to the Education Act, which gave women equal educational opportunities by requiring that all high schools and colleges receiving federal funds hire women faculty and provide equal budgets for girls' sports. Martha Griffiths from Michigan put together the coalition that passed Title VII of the Civil Rights Act of 1964, which prohibited discrimination in employment because of "race, color, religion, national origin, or sex." Despite her legislative skill (or perhaps because of it), Griffiths was given the chairmanship of a subcommittee that supervised the hair salons and barbershops in the House. No woman had ever chaired a standing committee in Congress.

Historically, although the majority of congresswomen had arrived as widows of their deceased congressional husbands, they were usually competent and good politicians in their own right. But often they inherited their husbands' staffs and constituencies so that the structures within the House and Senate never changed. Women like Lindy Boggs, wife of Hale Boggs of Louisiana, and Arvonne Fraser, wife of Don Fraser of Minnesota, worked in their husbands' offices, ran campaigns, and were politicians in their own right. But like the four thousand other women who worked on Capitol Hill, they were largely invisible, until—in the case of Lindy Boggs—their husbands unexpectedly died. Arvonne Fraser, who remembered the days of attending white-glove lunches and having to go to the White House to leave a calling card, helped organize a group of activist congressional wives and other professional Washington women called the "Nameless Sisterhood."

The workers who kept the House humming were the secretaries and caseworkers, immensely knowledgeable and capable women, but without the titles or salaries to command respect. Not only did the secretaries have to work one unpaid Saturday a month, they had to arrive at work early every day so that, by the time the male legislative and administrative assistants arrived, the coffee was made and the typewriters were chattering. At that point in 1968 and '69, I was one of only a handful of professional women on Capitol Hill. (I never did a formal survey. I just counted the professional women I met on House staffs, and after a year still hadn't used up all the fingers on one hand.) I got to know only one, Linda Kamm, a lawyer on the House Labor and Education Committee.

In meeting after meeting, I was the only woman at the table. If I expressed my views too forcefully or was too aggressive, the men at the table hadn't the slightest hesitancy to say, "That's it. Kick 'em in the balls." Women were still not considered an important part of national politics as either voters or activists. Women were important as supporters—organizers, volunteers, and canvassers for political campaigns—but they were not considered an organized political force with defined interests. Women had little idea about how many key family issues, like child care, were considered peripheral to the political arena.

My first project on the heels of the departed Paul Gorman was to coordinate an ad hoc congressional hearing on the militarization of U.S. foreign policy and the consequent distortions in domestic affairs. It was to take place in March 1969. As a project it was controversial, fascinating, and historic. (When I later asked Don Edwards what he thought I had contributed to the group, he said, "You were responsible for our reputation—which is a historic one.") In part, the hearing was about secret weapons systems in the works at the Pentagon, so secret that even Congress wasn't supposed to debate them; the corollary was how the domestic agenda suffered when more and more of the federal budget was allocated to military and war. (To illustrate with a contemporary example: while seven hundred billion dollars has already been spent on the Iraq war, with no end in sight, politicians consider the one hundred billion dollars of taxpayer money necessary to put a national health care plan in place to be far too expensive.)

By then the missile race between the two superpowers had morphed to a new level, and even with some adroit lying on the part of American officials and generals in the Pentagon, America's claim of a "missile gap" with the Russians was a clear falsehood. The reality was that the missile stockpile was greatly weighted in the United States' favor. The challenge, however, of holding a congressional hearing on secret weaponry and missiles required that the subject of secrecy itself be made part of the congressional hearings. Who was qualified to discuss secret missile systems?

Spring 1969

As it turned out, quite a few people who had worked in government, or in universities with military research contracts, or in the aerospace or nuclear industries were quite willing to provide their expertise in an alternative forum. By the time the hearing took place in March 1969, the U.S. government—that is, we taxpayers—had decided to expand our missile stockpile to include two fabulously expensive new components. The first was an offensive system called MIRV (multiple independently targetable reentry vehicles) that would allow each of our intercontinental missiles to carry up to ten warheads that could be independently aimed. The second system was defensive, the ABM (antiballistic missile) system that theoretically could shoot down incoming missiles in space. Apart from the question of whether increased militarization contributed to national security, it seemed that these two systems would set off a new escalation of the arms race.

Another question was whether or not these systems really would work, other than as a huge boondoggle for aerospace contractors. How could the defensive missile distinguish between decoys and real missiles? Where could the antiballistic missile be based so that it couldn't be hit first? One scenario had these antiballistic missiles moving around the West by train, mounted on portable launchers. Another placed them in indestructible, hardened bunkers. The legislation to authorize the ABM system was before Congress and was being vigorously lobbied in the Senate.

The invited experts were being asked to address topics such as the reasons for the fake missile gaps manufactured by the Pentagon, the realities of the Soviet threat, the consequent pressures to create an antiballistic missile system, the Soviet response, and the resulting distortions in our domestic economy because of disproportionate military spending. Economists John Kenneth Galbraith and Kenneth Boulding pointed to the enormous military contracts that went to aerospace industries and the ways that their profits skewed the political system. Without a debate about budgetary priorities, the reasoning went, congressional oversight would become irrelevant, if not extinct.

Ironically, on the opposite side of the ABM debate was SAIS founder Paul Nitze, who had set up the Committee to Maintain a Prudent Defense to lobby for the antiballistic missile system. He hired Paul Wolfowitz to write position papers and speeches for Senator Henry Jackson, who was the key advocate for the ABM system in the Senate. (Senator Jackson, who was often referred to as the Boeing senator, came from Washington State, home of Boeing aircraft and aerospace.) Wolfowitz, aided by Richard Perle, researched position papers given to key senators to support the ABM legislation, and Nitze later commented, "The papers they helped us produce ran rings around the misinformed papers produced by polemical and pompous scientists." Although the Senate eventually approved the ABM system in 1969, by one vote, President Nixon signed the Antiballistic

Missile Treaty in 1972, which prevented the construction of such systems by both the United States and the Soviet Union. (The treaty remained in effect from 1972 to 2002, when President George W. Bush refused to renew it. By then, Wolfowitz was undersecretary of defense and the Pentagon was again promoting a new ABM system to be deployed somewhere in Eastern Europe.)

My job was to coordinate the staffs of the original sponsoring congressmen and two senators who convened the hearing, make all the arrangements for the dignitaries who came to testify, help write and edit the congressmen's introductory remarks, edit the report that came out of the conference, send it to all the participants for approvals, coordinate the members of Congress—thirty-six congressmen and seven senators—who eventually signed the report, and provide it to the press with accompanying press releases. I did have occasional help, but the job requirements as a one-person staff for an ad hoc committee hearing meant that I routinely began working sixty-hour weeks.

At that point in my life, I was still fearless. I had grasped that I could do anything at any level as long as I didn't ask for credit or recognition. So I wrote speeches for the congressmen and edited Senator Fulbright's epilogue. I knew the hearings were historic, if only because the standing committees of Congress, all chaired by southerners, refused to discuss these topics in a public hearing. At the same time, I was fully aware of the skills I didn't have. So when one of the outside fund-raisers brought in an editor from a large New York publisher who wanted to publish the entire hearing as a trade book, I knew I was out of my depth. I asked for help. I told Bob Kastenmeier that I would need to work with a professional editor who knew something about publishing.

Enter Erwin Knoll.

Erwin was a former reporter for the *Washington Post,* a friend of Bob Kastenmeier, and the Washington editor for *The Progressive* magazine, a Madison, Wisconsin–based publication of progressive values and leftist politics.

I didn't know much about Wisconsin or the Midwest at the time, so when Kastenmeier first introduced me to Erwin, I expected a midwesterner steeped in Wisconsin dairy politics and Lutheran culture. Erwin was many things, but a midwesterner was not one of them. A New Yorker whose family had fled Nazi Austria in 1937 when he was seven, he was irreverent, politically astute, a walking encyclopedia of history, steeped in the tradition of European political thought, and astonishingly open-minded about working with a woman. (Many women journalists, including Molly Ivins, published some of their first opinion columns in *The Progressive.*) He believed in the First Amendment, nonviolence, a sense of humor, and respect for the English language.

I'm sure Erwin was as surprised by me as I was by him. When he quoted Antonio Gramsci—"We must sustain pessimism of the intellect but optimism of the will"—he was surprised I knew that Gramsci was an Italian socialist. (I learned that from Italian classmates in graduate school, not from my right-wing Catholic family.) Later he confided that he thought I must have been a cheerleader type or the daughter of a wealthy contributor, because that was the only way young women got jobs in political offices. I like history, I told him. Liking history, he said, is not a common American trait. Erwin taught me how to write, how to edit, and how to find my voice.

Although English was his second language—his first language had been German, which he spoke as a child in Vienna—he had studied it like an Oxford don and had a huge vocabulary.

He could quote grammar rules from memory and liked to read dictionaries for pleasure. I can still hear him saying, "Don't use the word *enormity* to mean large" or, on reading a paragraph I thought extremely eloquent and passionate, "This is too much heavy breathing." His hero was I. F. Stone, the brilliant and iconoclastic journalist whose independent newsletter was subscribed to by almost every congressional office (and the White House)—the conservatives to calculate the arguments they would have to rebut, the liberals to gain ammunition.

At the time Madison, Wisconsin, was home to some of the most radical university politics in the country. Many of the student protests against military-related research and recruiting began there. For example, University of Wisconsin students began the first demonstrations against Dow Chemical Company. Dow produced napalm, the petroleum-based bombs that burst into flame on impact. The air force dropped napalm bombs in Vietnam to clear helicopter landing zones. After the famous photograph of naked and hideously burned Vietnamese children running away from a napalm attack appeared in American newspapers, Wisconsin students physically blocked Dow recruiters from interviewing on campus. Anti-Dow demonstrations were taken up on campuses all over the country.

Erwin also told me about a political science professor named Kay Clarenbach, who chaired the Wisconsin State Commission on the Status of Women. She helped to transform a passive data-collecting commission into an active legislative lobbying operation that worked to change laws and policies relating to women. Their group was so successful in Wisconsin that Clarenbach wrote a handbook to show other state commissions how to do the same thing; later she became the first president of the association of all the state commissions on the status of women, a founder of NOW, the NOW Legal Defense Fund, and the National Women's Political Caucus. "Feminism," she said, "is a vision of a different kind of society." Erwin, because of his Wisconsin connection, was one of the few journalists paying attention to the new commissions on the status of women and their successor organization, the National Organization for Women, which soon became known as NOW. Wisconsin's progressive political traditions and strong unions were producing a new kind of political ethos.

Erwin and his family lived in Carrollsburg Square, a real estate development in southwest Washington, where Mac and I had moved after we were married. Mac and I lived in a one-bedroom apartment in the complex with balconies and a swimming pool. Erwin; his wife, Doris; and their two young sons lived in a row of town houses across the street. His house was filled with music and books. To me, Erwin seemed more like a European intellectual than a storytelling Washington political journalist. He was, however, a compulsive storyteller. (He rarely talked about his personal history, but I gathered that many of his Jewish family members had been unable to find sponsors, and had vanished in the concentration camps of Poland and Germany.)

His take on many aspects of American politics was wickedly funny. For example, it was Erwin who told me the story about J. Edgar Hoover starting a file on comedian Groucho Marx because Hoover suspected he was related to Karl Marx. Hoover also opened a file on Erwin. When Erwin found out, he called it "a badge of honor." One day when I confessed to him that I couldn't get final approval on the introduction I had written for the book because all my bosses with approval authority were playing paddleball in the House gym, he waved a hand and said, "Oh, don't worry about it. The less they do on any given day, the better for everyone." He was unflappable and absolutely unfazed by authority.

So a deal was worked out whereby Erwin, as a freelance editor, would help me shape the mass of material from the hearing into a book to be published by Viking Press under the title *American Militarism 1970.* Erwin told me to insist on credit as coeditor. I did. I took the pins out of the bound transcripts of the hearing, made up tentative chapter titles, organized a table of contents, and then shuffled the pages out into piles on my office floor as though I were dealing cards. Then I labeled each pile according to the subject of the discussion and the possible chapter. After sorting and labeling, on my way home I would take one of these sections, now tentatively labeled as a chapter, over to Erwin's town house. His two young sons might be running around and Doris might be playing the piano while we decided if the statements by Herbert York or George Kistiakowsky or George Rathjens—Nitze's "pompous scientists"—belonged in the MIRV section or in the ABM section; if Galbraith's section belonged in the military budget chapter or in the congressional oversight chapter; and if Senator Fulbright's statement should be the introduction or the epilogue. "You'll have to rewrite the introduction to be signed by the congressmen, and Fulbright should go at the end," Erwin directed.

I wrote new introductions, and Erwin edited the transcript materials. A few days later Erwin would call to tell me a section was ready, and I would pick it up on my way to work to bring it back to the office for retyping by one of the secretaries. Then I would send it out to the participants for approval and a signed release. "Always get a release," said Erwin.

Soon every hearing participant was speaking in full sentences and complete paragraphs with fully formed thoughts. The participants sounded eloquent, direct, and convincing. Their remarks were also accessible to someone who knew nothing about missile defense or nuclear strategy. Erwin's editing was so seamless that when I sent the remarks out for approval, many with significant changes, I got phone calls back, saying, "This is terrific. You barely changed a word." Erwin Knoll taught me a lot about writing and politics. He also gave me confidence that I had something to say. One day when I worried that we could never make the publisher's deadline, he answered, "Of course we will. Always meet a deadline. Deadlines are your friend." And we did. Converting a congressional hearing into a commercial trade book was a novel and daunting enterprise.

At the same time, functioning within a work environment that was hostile to women was progressively sapping my spirit. One day I went to the House floor to listen to the debate about military appropriations. The guard who stood at the gallery entrance held up his hand. "You can't go in there," he said loudly, as he vigorously waved my male colleagues through. I showed him my employee identification. "Doesn't make any difference," he said. "You still can't go in there."

"I beg your pardon?" I asked, as I watched my male colleagues take their seats.

"You have to sit in the Ladies' Gallery." He called over another guard and ordered him to escort me to the Ladies' Gallery. I was so outraged I couldn't concentrate on the debate, some of which I had helped write.

The minute I was back in my office, I called up the Speaker's office and asked to speak to the person in charge of the galleries. Fishbait Miller, the doorkeeper of the House, came on the phone. "Little lady," said Fishbait after he heard my complaint, "that's the way it's been since before the Civil War, and that's the way it's going to stay."

With considerable indignation, I reminded him that the House might want to abide by the antidiscrimination laws it had passed for the rest of the nation. I said that Title VII of the Civil

Rights Act of 1964 prohibited discrimination in employment on the basis of race, religion, and sex. I was an employee of the U.S. Congress. "What kind of example are you setting? Do you realize that the Ladies' Gallery is illegal?" He paused and said he would get back to me.

By then I understood the implications of a Ladies' Entrance in a way I hadn't when I stood at the Ladies' Entrance of the Cosmos Club. As long as women stayed behind the scenes in a nonpublic role, it was possible to remain unaware of how unequal the playing field was for women. But once a woman was in the public world, every day brought new awareness of the elaborate structures that kept women and minorities at the margins.

Then one night at a Weight Watchers meeting, I had a revelation.

Tip O'Neill, then majority leader, later to become Speaker of the House, was a member of my Capitol Hill Weight Watchers group ("What do you mean Scotch is not on the diet?"). This was long before gyms or athletics for women, so that when hemlines went up to midthigh, I had my dresses shortened to a relatively conservative above-the-knee length, but still felt compelled to enroll in Weight Watchers to have trimmer legs.

"You're the girl who called Fishbait," he said after I had introduced myself as coming from Massachusetts. "Fishbait spoke with the Speaker, you know." The Speaker was then the elderly John McCormack from Massachusetts, for whom Tip O'Neill was a loyal soldier. "I think the Speaker is going to change the rules for the Ladies' Gallery," he said, looking at me with real curiosity. He must have been wondering, Who are you? Are you a flash in the pan, or are you a harbinger of things to come?

The next day Fishbait himself called to tell me. It was a fact.

"There will be no more Ladies' Galleries. Ladies will be able to sit anywhere." It was then I realized once again the truth of one of Madame Gillet's life lessons: good information and pressure applied at the right points of leverage affect outcomes.

So even though I had assured Bob Kastenmeier that I wasn't a bra burner, the very fact of working in Congress had radicalized me. I was experiencing something similar to what other women must have experienced in other movements for social change, particularly those in the male-dominated New Left and civil rights movements. Like them, I saw the gap between the egalitarian rhetoric and the way women were actually treated. If I tried to point out to colleagues the subservience they automatically expected from women (why should I be the one to make the coffee?), I was told that I should count myself lucky to have the opportunity I did. At the same time, I was learning skills and political savvy. As Alice Echols later pointed out, it was in movements of the left that women "acquired the skills, confidence, and political savvy" necessary to build their own movement. Fighting against one's own oppression, rather than struggling on behalf of other oppressed peoples, is what gave emotional power to the phrase, "the personal is political."

Many of the things that bothered me and that I felt were individual failings turned out to be systemic. My job was to find new ways to magnify the impact of the ad hoc congressional hearings that my ten congressional bosses sponsored and to publicize how war costs escalated, policies shifted, and justifications changed from day to day. I met with rock concert promoters, movie stars, businessmen, Nobel Peace Prize recipients, senators, governors, literary lions, financial angels, university professors, and every variety of activist. I helped coordinate the hearings on Vietnam and military policy, ghostwrote articles and speeches, and provided contact with women's groups, students, and other leaders of the antiwar movement. I edited and managed the publication of books in the congressmen's names.

And yet.

When I arranged for the publication of an excerpt from the military hearing report in the *Washington Post,* the editor, who had gone to graduate school with me, kept Erwin Knoll's name as editor and omitted mine.

When I was going through old files, I found an old memo relating to Paul Gorman's salary and discovered he had been paid a third more than I was.

When I told Mac how tired I was of being hit on, he said I should be flattered that I got so much attention.

When I took an official tour of the Capitol Building that took us into the basement, I saw, tucked away in a corner, a large sculpture of the women suffrage leaders Elizabeth Cady Stanton, Susan B. Anthony, and Lucretia Mott. The guide shrugged and couldn't answer any of my questions about why the statue was hidden in the basement. I called up the Architect of the Capitol and asked why the statue wasn't moved to the Rotunda or Statuary Hall, since there were no statues of women in the Capitol Building.

"The rotunda can't bear the weight," he told me.

I might have been working in politics, but until that moment I was not a politicized woman.

It was only when I began to see myself as part of a larger community of women—and it was a movement that was growing every day—that I saw myself as someone who deserved to take up space and have a voice. And that was the moment I began to change; I saw that I could generate different choices.

PART III

We Live in a World the Sixties Made

CHAPTER ELEVEN

Extraordinary Times

1970

By the fall of 1970 I had had one too many colds.
"According to my records," said Harry Handelsman without looking up, "you have had thirteen colds or sinus infections in the last year." Harry was my doctor, and I was in his office because I couldn't breathe. My sinuses had swollen shut. No nose drops or nasal spray that I could buy from a drugstore had helped. I hadn't slept for two nights. As he inserted cotton swabs dipped in some miraculous substance into my nostrils, he said, "You know, some people are not cut out to handle stress over the long term. Stress would account for this many colds. You might want to think about another job."

"Another job? But I have the most interesting job in Washington." And I felt I was doing important work. How could I give that up? On the other hand, I was ill. I had been working for two years under conditions that had become increasingly stressful, both because of the times and the working conditions.

The expansion of the Vietnam War into Laos and Cambodia had produced a combination of fury, disbelief, and helplessness in the public and within Congress. As with the Iraq war thirty-five years later, America's leaders had little understanding of the country or cultures they were invading and trying to control. President Richard M. Nixon had been elected on the promise of withdrawing American troops from the quagmire of Vietnam, and he was doing so by expanding the war into surrounding countries. Contrary to Prussian strategist Carl von Clausewitz's dictum—"There is a point beyond which perseverance can only be termed desperate folly"—the Pentagon was fighting the war it wanted to fight instead of the war that was there. (A decade later, Barbara Tuchman wrote a book on that very subject, *The March of Folly: From Troy to Vietnam*. If she were alive today, she would extend the time frame to include Iraq, where the identical mind-set seems to be in place.) Theoretically, President Nixon had adopted a policy of "Vietnamization" of the war; that is, South Vietnamese troops were supposed to be taking over the fighting so that American troops could go home. American troops were, in fact, being withdrawn, but only under the umbrella of increased bombing, invasion of neutral countries, and the bombing and mining of Hanoi harbor. These acts intensified antiwar sentiment at home.

Then on April 30, 1970, President Nixon announced in a televised speech that American troops had invaded Cambodia. Within twenty-four hours, massive antiwar protests erupted on college campuses and city squares across the country. In many states National Guard troops had to be called out to quell the demonstrations. On May 4, the Ohio National Guard troops ordered to control a demonstration at Kent State University fired into a crowd and killed four students. The outraged response was national and international.

My working conditions mirrored the turbulence in the country as a whole. Every day brought a new crisis that had to be addressed. In the face of crisis, I focused on the mundane. In the manner of the journals that were published by women's groups, I began keeping a little notebook where I jotted down details about various events that disturbed or interested me. Some were minor. Some were significant. Some were both—that is, they started out as one and turned into the other.

For example, one entry read: "Cafeteria workers strike."

For the most part, African Americans held all the menial jobs in the House and Senate dining rooms and cafeterias and were not paid the minimum wage. They felt, not unreasonably, that they should earn the same minimum wage as restaurant workers in the District of Columbia. So they went on strike. *Strike* was a dirty word. Although I didn't yet fully understand the sociology of how Congress was run as a workplace, I did grasp the plantation spirit. My question was whether or not the strike would spread from the Senate to the House, as had been predicted.

Another entry read: "Fuck problem."

In meetings, male staffers would constantly use the word *fuck* and then look at me, pause, and apologize. As one man told me, the real purpose of the apology was to let me know I was inhibiting the normal flow of all-male discussion. He suggested I needed to remain absolutely unflappable whenever they swore or made jokes about women's anatomies, competencies, and general uselessness.

"Paycheck late."

This entry was frequent and disturbing. I rotated to a different congressman's payroll each month, which allowed my salary to be spread among them. Depending on how efficiently a congressman's office had executed the paperwork, my paycheck often was not delivered on time. My complaints about the erratic paycheck system didn't seem to produce results, and I couldn't think of anyone who could mediate for me. Part of the problem was that

women in politics were viewed as volunteers and all congressional
staffers served solely at the pleasure of the congressmen. There
was no human resources office to go to.

"Why Gorman different?"

Each time my paycheck was late I became more annoyed.
When Bob Kastenmeier took on the coordinating responsibility, I told him that apologies were not paying the rent and skip-
ping a paycheck caused me hardship and bounced checks. His
answer: "Isn't your husband working anymore?" When the responsibility for paying my salary revolved to Ben Rosenthal, I
asked him why there had been so little difficulty in paying Paul
Gorman. Rosenthal said, "Paying a man is a different matter.
There's just not the same sense of urgency for a woman."

"Secretaries v. professionals."

I related best to the secretaries and caseworkers because they
were knowledgeable and usually the only women on staff.
(Later, both John Conyers and Don Edwards promoted women to
professional positions.) On the other hand, I wasn't a secretary and
depended on secretaries to do work for me. I also had to make sure
that men saw me as a professional. The secretaries resented me for
asking them to type documents they thought I should be doing
myself. These were issues I didn't feel I could raise with my bosses
because the perfect staff person was faceless, was competent, an-
ticipated problems, and raised no complicating issues.

"Lansdale phone call."

That was the complicating issue that eventually overtook everything else. The telephone call had taken place in January
1970, only weeks before the start of a second congressional conference that I was organizing on war crimes and national responsibility. At the time, I was working out of the fourth-floor
annex of Congressman Ab Mikva's office.

"This is Ed Lansdale," said a gruff voice on the other end of the telephone line. "Ellsberg worked for me in Vietnam. You might want to know more about what he did there. I can tell you he has no business being a participant in a hearing about war crimes."

"Oh," I said. The hearing was only weeks away.

I particularly remember the moment of his phone call because spread out on the desk before me were photographs of My Lai, a Vietnamese hamlet where U.S. soldiers had shot at close range more than four hundred civilians—women, children, and elderly Vietnamese. A helicopter pilot had taken the photos within days of the massacre in 1968, but they hadn't reached the public until a year later, when journalist Seymour Hersh published them on Dispatch News Service in November 1969. The release of the photographs and the resulting press coverage had been one of the motivating forces behind convening a congressional hearing on war crimes. To hold such a congressional hearing during an ongoing war was precedent setting. I tried to pretend to Lansdale that I was a mere clerk, without decision-making authority, but he persisted.

Lansdale was a famous CIA spy. Graham Greene supposedly used him as the model for Pyle, the deceptively self-effacing but ruthless American in Greene's classic Vietnam novel, *The Quiet American*. Unlike the fictional Pyle, however, who was ultimately betrayed and killed by the Vietnamese, Lansdale lived on to head up new secret or black operations. As head of Operation Mongoose in 1962, he had partnered with the Mafia in an attempt to assassinate Fidel Castro in Cuba after the failed Bay of Pigs. (The CIA provided the exploding fountain pens, poisoned cigars, and other gadgetry, like a clamshell that was rigged to explode during Castro's skin-diving expeditions. The Mafia provided the manpower.) Lansdale's Mongoose operations also included efforts to disrupt the Cuban economy by circulating counterfeit money and by contaminating the Cubans' sugar exports.

"Can you tell me the purpose of this hearing?" Lansdale asked.

I explained that it was a discussion to explore the questions about individual responsibility in time of war when a government undertakes immoral policies and actions. "Those are the issues raised by the legal principles set out during the Nuremberg trials," I added.

"Who's coming?"

"Telford Taylor, the principal prosecutor at the Nuremberg war crimes trials," I answered. "Philip Noel-Baker, a Nobel Peace laureate and member of Parliament. Hannah Arendt, who is a political philosopher. George Wald, a professor of biology at Harvard, who will address environmental issues and—"

"Which committee is responsible for holding this hearing?" Lansdale interrupted.

Lansdale knew a lot about the techniques of manipulating the public mind. A former advertising man, he had been an expert in psychological warfare for the Office of Strategic Services during World War II. He transferred to the CIA after the war with the rank of air force general and was sent to the Philippines as an undercover agent to prop up leader Raymond Magsaysay against communist guerrillas. After his Philippines success, he was transferred to Vietnam in the early 1950s to run the CIA's covert operation there. Lansdale set up the innocuously named Saigon Military Mission and helped to thwart the elections mandated by the Geneva Conventions of 1954. Suddenly there were two Vietnams, North and South, and South Vietnam had an army, a flag, and a president that the United States helped put in place.

By 1966, Lansdale was back in Vietnam, running a new

counterinsurgency mission, this time with Dan Ellsberg as part of his team. Lansdale had been one of the theorists, some say theologians, of counterinsurgency warfare, which eventually mutated into something quite terrible on the ground. Counterinsurgency operations involved systemic nonconventional warfare on many fronts—economic, psychological, political, and military—and included paramilitary raids, sabotage, terrorism, economic disruptions, and election fraud. Lansdale did them all. He believed in the efficacy of the First Team, a small nucleus of bold, brave, brilliant men, led by himself, who could turn around an insurgency.

In his memoir, Lansdale later wrote, "I was lucky in everything except Dan Ellsberg."

Although I was able to remain unflappable on the phone, I was pretty agitated after I hung up. The fact of the phone call troubled me. The very idea that Edward Lansdale knew my name and where I worked was worrisome.

"You're right. It's never a good thing when someone like Lansdale has your phone number," Erwin Knoll said when I told him about the telephone call. Erwin and I were going to edit another book together based on the war crimes hearing, and he was in my office to go over a list of questions for the hearing. I planned to mail them to every participant. "But it sure is interesting," he said with a smile. "What's his bottom line?"

"He wanted the congressmen to withdraw Ellsberg's invitation. He kept saying, 'Ellsberg is not your man. He has no business being at a conference on war crimes.' Coming from someone like Lansdale, I thought that might be construed as a recommendation."

"Not to put too fine a point on it, who is Dan Ellsberg?" asked Erwin. "And why was he invited?" That was a question I wish I had asked myself more carefully.

Dan Ellsberg, at that time a complete unknown, had arrived in my little office in October 1969 after participating in the October 15 moratorium march against the Vietnam War, the largest demonstration ever seen in Washington. (An equally large demonstration had followed in November.) I was working in the annex of Ab Mikva's office, a separate unmarked office on the fourth floor of the Longworth House Office Building. Ab Mikva, a lawyer from Chicago, had been elected to Congress in 1968 and had recently joined my group of antiwar congressmen. I shared the office with two interns from the University of Chicago. On that particular day, neither of them was around when a man with a hoarse voice and intense eyes strolled in waving a piece of paper.

"I'm Dan Ellsberg," he introduced himself when I looked up from my desk.

"How did you find me?" I asked. The office door had no names, only a number, and my name did not appear in any directory. At first I thought Marc Raskin or Dick Barnet, the codirectors of the Institute for Policy Studies, who were providing advice for the war crimes hearing, had sent him over since they had sent over several antiwar professors who had come for the moratorium. But when I later telephoned them, they said they had never heard of him. The piece of paper in Ellsberg's hand was a copy of an antiwar letter that he and five other RAND Corporation employees had published in the Sunday edition of the *Washington Post*. He suggested his experiences in Vietnam might be useful for the hearing I was organizing.

"How did you know about the hearing?" I wanted to know.

He said one of Congressman Mikva's legislative assistants had told him. That particular aide was a former army officer and married to a graduate-school classmate of mine who worked for the CIA, so I was skeptical. Ellsberg described himself as a

Harvard-trained economist, a former Marine who had served in Vietnam, and now an analyst at RAND. (RAND, a contraction of Research and Development, was originally a think tank formed by Douglas Aircraft and the air force in 1948 to plan for the air force's role in future nuclear and nonnuclear national security scenarios.)

"I thought you might need more participants with firsthand experience in Vietnam," he suggested, handing me several copies of the letter from the *Washington Post* as well as another article he had published. "Would you present my credentials to the congressmen?"

I said I would, and I did. They left his participation up to me. So at the beginning of January 1970, I sent Ellsberg a letter of invitation. He seemed to be a minor player on a stage of stars that included Nobel Peace Prize winners, scholars, and internationally famous jurists and philosophers. He was right, however: we had only two other participants with direct military experience in Vietnam.

Soon after Ellsberg's invitation went out, I received the first of several peculiar visits and phone calls. The first was a red-headed woman journalist who had spent time in Vietnam and wanted to tell me what a fervent supporter of the war Ellsberg had been when she knew him in Vietnam. She had added that he was one of a team that shot Vietnamese peasants from a helicopter. Then I received a telephone call from the chief of staff of the Senate Armed Services Committee, a brusque military man who was even more outspoken than Lansdale and strangely knowledgeable about the details of the hearing I was helping to organize. He, too, insisted that Ellsberg was not the right person for this hearing and suggested that the hearing itself was more or less a treasonous act. His call only made me more determined to proceed. Then a well-known and well-informed television

journalist took me out to lunch and asked a lot of nosy but inci-
sive questions. My camouflage was my youth, my earnestness,
and my gender. But I was worried.

"How did you leave it with Lansdale?" Erwin Knoll asked.

"I told him I would bring his concerns before the congressmen and would call him back if he'd give me his number."

Erwin smiled. "What did he say to that?"

" 'I'll call you.' "

Erwin smiled more broadly and lit another of his ever present
cigarettes. "Excellent. He won't call."

"Do you think I should tell Burton or Edwards?" They were
going to be the cochairs of the hearing. On the other hand, I
also realized it was important not to raise any unnecessary
alarms. I was supposed to put out fires, not create them.

Erwin said, "Sit tight."

I did actually tell Don Edwards, who didn't seem overly concerned, but by then we had many more pressing conflicts.

The hearing took place on February 20 and 21, 1970, and was
a historic success, according to front-page stories in the *Washington Post* and the *New York Times*. Again, Erwin and I worked fe-
verishly, under impossible deadlines, to put together a book from
the hearings. By fall, the publisher, Holt, Rinehart & Winston,
had preview copies of *War Crimes and the American Conscience* in
circulation.

"The single best book on Vietnam to date," announced a review in the *Boston Globe*.

"The most important book on Vietnam in print today," said
James Reston Jr. in the *Saturday Review*.

"Possibly the most valuable and important single-volume collection of relevant source material available on this crucial subject,
and should be read soberly by Americans of every shade of conviction," pronounced *Publishers Weekly*.

So why was I in Dr. Harry Handelsman's office unable to breathe? Was it that Ellsberg had threatened to sue the congressmen because of a missing phrase from his remarks that he had not taken the time to edit? Or was it that Mac had come home with a list of questions from the FBI and said I needed to write a letter to the Treasury Department security officers with answers? Or could it be because I hadn't received a paycheck for six weeks?

In the short term, the mundane trumped everything else. The missing paycheck tipped me over the edge. That brought on my thirteenth cold and sent me to Harry Handelsman's office. As soon as I was feeling better, I went back to work, determined to change my working conditions. Maybe I could ask for a raise, I thought, at least to Gorman's salary level of two years ago. Instead, when I got to my desk, I found none of the promised paychecks in my drawer, making it eight weeks without a paycheck. It's very hard to negotiate for something if you can't get someone's attention. So I wrote myself a check from the special account that I kept for the congressmen and then walked into Ab Mikva's office to explain what I was doing in case anyone decided to sue me for embezzlement. I explained that the constant delay of my paycheck was fundamentally unacceptable, and that, unless I was paid by Friday of that week, I would cash the check I had written and be out the door.

Mikva, who was probably the single smartest individual in the group and would later become a federal appeals court judge and legal counsel in the Clinton White House, hustled me over to Rosenthal's office. Rosenthal got on the phone to Phil Burton.

"We've got a crazy lady here. What's happened to her paycheck? She says she hasn't been paid in two months." Then came a long silence while he listened to Burton on the other end of the phone.

In that moment of silence came my "cosmic click" of clarity. Why was I a "crazy lady" for objecting to not being paid? Entire labor movements had been built on less.

That marked the radicalizing moment when I realized that these gregarious, humorous, funny, smart, politically liberal guys were not on my side and never could be. They were as liberal as the political culture would allow, but in cultural terms they were as conservative as any southern congressman. The essential message of the radical wing of the women's movement was that liberal men could not be trusted to support women's rights, because equality for women upset their own domestic arrangements. My congressional employers were genuine friends with one another and as interesting a group of people as I would ever get to work with, but they had a huge cultural blind spot. I finally grasped that a deep, structural, molecular arrangement of culture defined women as secondary. Women were not supposed to have a voice. Women weren't full human beings except as wives and mothers and secretaries and decoration. We were there to serve. We were always "girls" in the same way African American men were "boys," regardless of age. The realities of sex discrimination overwhelmed the substance of what I was working on.

When Rosenthal finally got off the phone, he explained that for the past two months I had rotated to Phil Burton's payroll, but no paychecks had been issued. Phil said it was a slipup by his administrative assistant and was being corrected even as we spoke. I knew better. I didn't know if Phil resented that I had avoided his advances one night when I drove him home—at his request after too many drinks—or if he really was stretching his payroll too thin. He did juggle a number of ad hoc arrangements—all legal, but funded from his congressional payroll: he was helping to carry a defeated congressman on his payroll until he qualified for his pension; he was also helping to staff the fledgling liberal Democratic Study Group.

In any case, it was no longer my problem. I was not a volunteer. With complete clarity I knew I was at the end of working in "the most interesting job in Washington." I saw nothing further to be gained in collaborating in my own exploitation. I asked Mac what he would do if it happened to him.

He said it wouldn't happen. But whatever I wanted to do was fine with him. I cleaned out my desk and wrote a letter of resignation to each of the congressmen, making sure it went through the internal mail so all their receptionists read it first.

Then I signed up for unemployment insurance—nonpayment of wages is a legitimate reason to quit—and enrolled in a painting class at the Corcoran School of Art, one block up from the White House. Immersing myself in the techniques of color field painting, I reacquainted myself with the world of imagination and creativity. My colds and sinus infection cleared up immediately.

Erwin called me up a few weeks later to find out what I was doing and to follow up on a few details related to the war crimes book.

"Why don't you write an article?" he suggested.

"About what?"

"About women on Capitol Hill. Write about your own experience. No one can argue with that. Other people would be interested to know how women staffers are treated. Not everyone is cut out to be a cheerleader."

While I lost myself in painting large abstract paintings in the fashion of Gene Davis, Kenneth Noland, and Morris Lewis of the Washington color school, I occasionally recalled events that happened in the distant land called Capitol Hill, but they seemed hazy. At the Corcoran, I found I was not the only refugee from the political world lost in the metaphysics of color. One of the people in my class was a woman who told me she had worked in the White House. Marjorie began by painting tiny canvases of lemons and ended by cutting yellow Plexiglas sheets into the shape of enormous lemons. I started with small Paul Klee–like canvases of tiny colored squares and was soon building eight-foot-by-four-foot stretchers and painting large maps of solid color like an aerial view of multicolored farmland. Our works were scheduled to be included in the spring student art exhibition.

Meanwhile, Erwin kept calling. "At least write a short piece about the women who went out on strike in August. Didn't you tell me it was the fiftieth anniversary of the passage of the suffrage amendment giving women the vote?"

So I sat down at my typewriter at home and started writing about the women's strike on Capitol Hill that had taken place on August 26, 1970, the fiftieth anniversary of the ratification of the Nineteenth Amendment, which gave women the right to vote. Called Women Strike for Equality, it was one of similar demonstrations that took place all over the country, with parades and marches of thousands of women carrying banners. But in Washington, not much had happened. Women in government jobs didn't strike because government workers aren't allowed to strike. On Capitol Hill, women rarely left their desks. The two singular exceptions were women from Congressman Don Fraser's office (Minnesota) on the House side and Senator Gaylord Nelson's office (Wisconsin) on the Senate side.

The grievances were many: the obligatory one Saturday a month that all women, but no men, on congressional staffs were obliged to work without pay or compensatory time off; the routine custom of assigning all rush projects—clipping, collating, typing, stuffing envelopes—to women, regardless of whatever other job they might be doing; the gender breakdown whereby male college interns were given research and writing jobs, while female interns were assigned typing, filing, and envelope-stuffing chores. Senator Gaylord Nelson of Wisconsin, rightly famous for having invented the powerful idea of Earth Day to promote environmental awareness, seemed unfazed when the fourteen women on his staff publicly announced they would strike for the entire day.

On the House side, several women from Don Fraser's staff joined the strike and organized a teach-in about the Equal Rights Amendment. Teach-ins were a new form of public conversation inspired by debate over the Vietnam War. Val Fleischauer, a caseworker, spoke to a crowd of Capitol Hill staff women about how the Equal Rights Amendment had finally been reported out of the House Judiciary Committee after a mere *twenty-two years*. Congresswoman Martha Griffiths from Michigan had submitted a discharge petition with 218 congressional signatures, which overrode the refusal of the committee chairman to deal with it. The lobbying to gain the petition signatures had been accomplished by the National Organization for Women and a group called the Ad Hoc Committee on the ERA. One of the people behind the scenes was Arvonne Fraser, Congressman Fraser's wife.

"People would like to know about how congressional offices are really run," Erwin urged. "You could call the article something like 'Women's Lib on Capitol Hill.' I'll run it in *The Progressive*."

"Well, I don't know," I paused. "I've never written anything under my own name."

"Then how are you ever going to write a book?"

Here he had a very good point. I was finding the problem of voice complicated. Since I had never published anything under my own name, I didn't have a voice of my own. I was a speech-writer. I only knew how to write in other people's voices. I listened to them speak, asked questions, and tried to enter their heads. Like a playwright, I wrote dialogue for other characters who stepped out on the public stage. Who was this "I," this twenty-nine-year-old unemployed speechwriter who presumed to rewrite history and who had a husband who thought it was a questionable idea? ("A book and fifty cents will get you a cup of coffee," Mac said.) What was her voice? She had stage fright.

I did, however, have a book contract. During one of the war crimes hearings lunch breaks, I had sat next to Aaron Asher, the editor from Viking Press. In the course of our conversation, I told him about my research in the Library of Congress and my discovery of women leaders in the labor movement, the peace movement, the abolitionist movement—all of whom had been omitted from history. "I'd like to write a book," I said, "like the one I want to read—not about a few women leaders in the suffrage and temperance movements like standard history books cover, but about women who led the significant movements that changed America." I told him I had been motivated because I had seen with my own eyes how the women leaders in the peace movement became invisible in the press. And as a result, they would probably be omitted from the history books as well.

"I think that's a great idea," said Asher. "Send me a proposal, and I'll give you a contract."

Erwin had coached me on the process of writing a book proposal and had been very encouraging. Mac, however, was not enthusiastic about my writing either a book or an article for *The Progressive*. "An article like that," he said, "will only make it harder for you to find another job. You won't have any references, and you won't be seen as a team player. And unless you get a doctorate in history, you won't be a historian, and a book

won't lead anywhere." Mac was not unusual. He was a conventional man who had come from a generation of men who did
not support women doing serious work. But I did send the proposal letter to Aaron Asher, got a contract, and arranged for a
desk in the stacks at the Library of Congress to research the
book. Mac seemed relieved that I had stopped working for the
"subversives" in Congress. Neither of us knew I was about to
start writing myself into a new life.

Although I did spend a lot of time reading at my desk on B
deck in the Library of Congress, I also began to ask everyone I
knew for names of women they thought had been leading activists in labor struggles, civil rights, peace, and women's rights
movements. One name led to another. Often, I wrote these
people letters and asked if I could come talk with them. I took
Ben Rosenthal's concept of the White House telephone operator (the White House operator can find anyone anywhere) to a
new level.

One name that intrigued me was that of Dorothy Day of the
Catholic Worker movement. I was intrigued because she had
not been born or raised Catholic but she had succeeded in organizing Catholics into one of the most effective political-
opposition movements in the country. Moreover, she was a
woman who seemed to have been in and out of the most radical
politics of the century. She had been arrested in front of the
White House with the suffragists of the Woman's Party in 1917.
She was a journalist for *The Masses,* a communist newspaper,
and a novelist who hung out with Eugene O'Neill and the artistic avant-garde of Provincetown. And then, in 1933, while
working as a labor journalist for several Catholic magazines,
she cofounded the Catholic Worker movement with an itiner-
ant French anarchist, Peter Maurin, who came from the tradition of the French worker-priests. He had the ideas: she had

the knowledge and know-how. Day hadn't converted to Catholicism until her late twenties. As she told Maurin, "Up until then my religion had been a private affair." She made a successful synthesis of Catholicism and communism and nurtured some of the most radical antiwar activists of the Vietnam era.

The Vietnam conflict produced a core of Catholic radicalism that had never before been seen in this country. Priests wearing white collars demonstrated in front of the Pentagon, poured blood on draft files, and encouraged young men to burn their draft cards. Nuns spoke out against American imperialism in Central and South America. The Berrigan brothers, two former priests, were on the FBI's most-wanted list, and both went to jail repeatedly for civil disobedience. In Catonsville, Maryland, while waiting for the police to arrive after setting Selective Service files on fire with napalm, Philip Berrigan distributed a message explaining their act: "We confront the Roman Catholic Church and other Christian bodies, and the synagogues of America with their silence and cowardice in the face of our country's crimes. We are convinced that the religious bureaucracy in this country is racist, is an accomplice in this war, and is hostile to the poor." His brother Father Daniel Berrigan wrote of the Catonsville incident: "Our apologies, good friends, for the fracture of good order, the burning of paper instead of children. . . ." They both had come out of the Catholic Worker tradition in Minnesota.

Described as the cradle of Catholic radicalism in America, the Catholic Worker movement was founded on principles of nonviolence, helping the poor, and protesting the state's infringement on individual liberties.

So in 1970, without quite knowing what to expect, I wrote to seventy-three-year-old Dorothy Day, asking for an appointment to talk with her. In my letter I mentioned Abigail McCarthy, the former wife of Senator Eugene McCarthy, who, as a college student in Minnesota in 1939, had passed out copies of the *Catholic Worker* newspaper during a labor strike at a Ford Motor plant and later worked at the Catholic Worker house in St. Paul; Jenny Moore, the wife of the Episcopal bishop of Washington, who had stayed in touch with Dorothy since her husband's seminary days, and said their first ministry in Jersey City had been greatly influenced by the Catholic Worker ethos; and Dwight Macdonald, a writer and cultural critic for the *New Yorker* who had written an influential profile of Day, as well as a review of Michael Harrington's book on poverty, *The Other America,* which Harrington wrote while he was an editor of the *Catholic Worker.*

"She was like a wind from another land," Jenny Moore recalled, "very exciting and a little frightening."

So I didn't know what to expect when I went to the communal farm in Tivoli, New York, up on the Hudson River, where I was supposed to meet her. But Dorothy Day wasn't there. (Instead, one of the residents showed me around, introduced me to some of the others, including a woman who said she had been Emma Goldman's secretary.) Next, I took the train down to the Bowery in lower Manhattan and waited for her at the Catholic Worker House on Mott Street, which served both as a soup kitchen and a shelter. While I waited, I saw the reality of the human wreckage of New York—the alcoholics, the mentally disturbed, the mumbling men and women with their shopping bags, the refugees from the single-room-occupancy hotels. In the starkest terms, it was possible for me to see the most elemental needs of society—food, shelter, community—and how monumentally America had failed to provide for so many of its citizens.

By the time she showed up, I had completely revised the

questions I planned to ask. I dropped my queries about the Woman's Party and how she and other demonstrators were arrested in front of the White House in 1917, then spent a month in jail without being charged. Instead, I asked about homelessness and single-room-occupancy hotels and the absence of halfway houses for mental patients. I'm sure that's how she converted so many followers. The realities she presented were impossible to deny.

She explained that real estate developers bought up the old boardinghouses and single-room hotels and that the residents couldn't afford anything more than a room. "This is not temporary. You're going to see a lot more homelessness," she told me.

I asked her about Cardinal Spellman and how he publicly threatened to shut down the Catholic Worker House and the newspaper. Cardinal Spellman had been one of the earliest and most fervent supporters of the Vietnam War, while the Catholic Worker movement had produced the war's most implacable and wily foes. Her newspaper, which cost a penny a copy and went around the world, attacked the war in every issue.

"If the Chancery ordered me tomorrow," she said, "to stop publishing the *Catholic Worker,* I would. Then I would pack everything up, go across the river out of the Cardinal's jurisdiction, and start publishing again." I had to smile at that.

She questioned what my religious upbringing had been. "But you no longer believe or go to the Catholic Church?" she asked.

"Look," I said. "If you hadn't had all that political experience as a young woman, you would never have been able to accomplish what you've done. If you'd been born Catholic and raised in the Church, you'd probably be an obscure nun someplace."

She did laugh at that.

I told her I didn't go to church because I felt that the Catholic Church did not have my best interests, as a woman, at heart. Biology was destiny, as far as the Church of Rome was concerned. As a woman who had had an abortion, I had been automatically excommunicated. I raised the issue of birth control and abortion with her because I knew she had had an abortion when she was a young woman in radical politics. But on those topics the conversation stopped. She stuck to the rigid doctrines of Rome. No contraception; no abortion.

These conversations with real life changed me.

I met other women who were excavating American history. Studying the past has a way of introducing humility, the first step to detachment, because it suggests the continuity of the problems we confront.

"The second wave" was a phrase coined by Martha Lear, wife of television producer Norman Lear, in a *New York Times Magazine* article about the new feminism. She described second wave feminism as directly connected with the first wave of women's suffrage activism, but, unlike the first wave, the grassroots nature of the new movement meant the new feminism lacked an organizational chart and officially elected leaders. At that point in time, roughly from 1965 to 1968, one estimate suggests that there were probably no more than one thousand radical feminists in the entire country, but they had a huge presence and an influence far beyond their numbers. They did most of the intellectual heavy lifting. Armed with the tools they had learned in the civil rights and antiwar movements, they knew how to analyze, argue, debate, write, publish, plan, and execute public actions. They understood the power of polemics, and they had that most valuable of political commodities—fresh ideas.

I tuned into this intellectual ferment through local newsletters, particularly those from a women's commune in Washington that published *Off Our Backs: A Journal of Women's Liberation.* I started sending off checks for tiny amounts of money to get copies of stapled and mimeographed documents like Lucinda Cisler's "Women: A Bibliography," which listed books and articles about women's history, economics, and sociology that I didn't even know existed. These pamphlets raised philosophical questions about the achievements of women and questioned assumptions about women's intellectual, emotional, and moral development. This conversation was a radical departure from the views expressed in the *Ladies' Home Journal* and other mainstream women's magazines, which were largely devoted to women as wives and mothers. (We didn't know then that most of the editors of the women's magazines were men.)

At another level were organizations like NOW, a civil rights organization devoted solely to women. Betty Friedan was NOW's well-known public spokesperson and first president. Many younger women, myself included, associated NOW with women at least ten to fifteen years older than we were. NOW emerged as an independent organization in 1966 after the federal government cut off funds for the Presidential Commission on the Status of Women, which had stayed in existence three years after its original Executive Order cutoff date of October 1963. The administration of Lyndon Johnson announced that the commission had assembled all the necessary data and completed its mission. The federal Commission on the Status of Women, however, had spun off forty state commissions, and most of the state commissioners felt that their real work had just begun.

Their own research had established how American women in every state were backsliding in terms of education, economics, health, and jobs. A woman could go from middle class to welfare in the time it took for a divorce to go through. The women commissioners cut across class and color lines and included university professors, state and national labor union officers, local government officials, business executives, physicians, lawyers, and members of churches and religious organizations. They believed the tasks ahead made the national network of women they had created too important to go out of business. So in October 1966, 300 women—120 of them from the Midwest—gathered in Washington, D.C., and announced the formation of a new woman's civil rights organization called the National Organization for Women.

"Neo-suffragettes" the *Washington Post* called them.

The formation of NOW, however, was a signal that liberal political culture had not addressed the failure in women's equal rights. With its origins connected to a federal bureaucracy and the White House, the goals of NOW seemed impeccable. As Betty Friedan stated, NOW's mission was "full equality for women in equal partnership with men."

The grassroots women's movement had grown beyond anyone's control. On the left were younger women; they had been influenced by the counterculture and "movement politics" and wanted fundamental changes in society. They believed in a more equitable distribution of wealth for everyone rather than obtaining a bigger piece of the pie for individual women. No foundation or government agency was writing policy papers determining what women's goals should be. Within six months of NOW's formation, in 1967, two hundred women from thirty-seven states and Canada met in Chicago for the First National Women's Liberation Conference. They wanted to change every aspect of society that limited women's full rights and freedoms. Uninterested in electoral politics or writing laws or changing the tax structure, they wanted free health clinics, universal child care, jobs at all levels, unfettered access to abortion, and contraception.

In many ways, the argument between the two wings of the 1960s women's movement mirrored the factions of the nineteenth-century suffrage associations. The American Woman Suffrage Association, led by Lucy Stone, wanted to concentrate solely on gaining the vote because they believed attention paid to any other issue took away resources and focus. The National Woman Suffrage Association, led by Susan Anthony and Elizabeth Cady Stanton, wanted to deal with women's right to divorce, property and inheritance rights, access to birth control, and a reinterpretation of the Bible. They saw the woman's vote as merely the first step in gaining equality. The two factions spent a lot of time attacking each other. Although the earlier split in the women's movement, with its resulting organizational factionalism, had a certain continuity with the 1960s, the tumult and chaos of that decade added a new element: a belief in violence as the defining existential act.

Two months after Martin Luther King was shot in Memphis, Tennessee, and three days before Bobby Kennedy was assassinated in California, a disturbed young woman whose only claim to fame was writing the SCUM (Society for Cutting Up Men) manifesto walked into the Factory and shot Andy Warhol and three other people. Frequently homeless, unable to hold a job, Valerie Solanas was one of the ever shifting entourage of artists, musicians, poets, drag queens, and fashion models who circulated around Warhol's Factory, the art studios where he made films and produced his vast output of popular art. Unhappily, Solanas was presented as "an important spokeswoman of the feminist movement" by her attorney, NOW member Florynce Kennedy and the New York NOW president, Ti-Grace Atkinson.

Their incendiary statements to the press fanned the flames of radical rhetoric by presenting Solanas's act as a revolutionary deed, rather than the incoherent act of a deeply disturbed woman.* The sensational trial, which began in 1969, was front-page news across the country, and the press, always attracted to blood, focused on Solanas and her one-woman society as a frightening symbol of the women's liberation movement.

The organizational consequences were immediate. When NOW president Betty Friedan asked Atkinson to stop linking NOW's name with Valerie Solanas, Atkinson resigned, taking many of the New York members with her to start a new radical feminist group called the Feminists. This became one of dozens of feminist cells in Chicago, New York, Boston, and Berkeley, and their attitude toward leadership would have an important consequence on the next stage of the women's movement.

Their members were writing, discussing, analyzing, and publishing articles that were duplicated and widely circulated like *samizdat* in the Soviet Union. I ordered a thirty-page mimeographed document called "Notes from the First Year" from New York Radical Feminists without realizing they were the same women who had organized the Miss America pageant demonstration. I ordered, or friends gave me, mimeographed essays from groups with names like Chicago Women's Liberation, Cell 16, and Redstockings. I read original essays like "The Myth of the Vaginal Orgasm" by Anne Koedt and "The Personal Is Political" by Carol Hanisch. These essays, although

---

* Solanas's sister later wrote that Valerie had been sexually abused by their father during adolescence and had been sent away from home when she became pregnant at the age of fifteen. She had aspirations to be a writer, but she was unable to hold a job or structure a life that made artistic work possible. She was placed in a mental hospital for a year, prescribed antipsychotic drugs, sentenced to three years in prison (Warhol refused to press charges), released in 1972, and died in 1988—a year after Warhol—in a welfare hotel in San Francisco.

later anthologized and made famous, were distributed through an underground network and passed on hand to hand. I found the intellectual energy in these publications extraordinary. These were not works that could be bought in any bookstore or found on the *New York Times* bestseller list.

Although I was part of a women's group, I was not a member of any women's organization. One day, the Italian doctor husband of a graduate school friend asked me if I would speak to a dinner group of doctors. He said they wanted to know more about women's liberation. Massimo knew that I had done a lot of reading on the topic. Innocently enough, I said sure, but I told him that I spoke only for myself. It turned out to be the most hostile audience I have ever encountered.

In the 1960s, when a doctor gave an order, a patient, particularly a woman patient, followed it. Without questions. Reliable information on women's health issues—such as hormone levels in the new birth control pill, pregnancy protocols, sexually transmitted diseases, and forced sterilization—was hard to find. At the time, the medical establishment was all male and as professionally socialized as West Point graduates. The most radical piece of literature I had ordered turned out to be *Our Bodies, Ourselves,* published by the Boston Women's Health Collective. A small booklet about women's health printed on newsprint, it was the first book I had ever read that took on the medical establishment and the politics of health care. Most women had health issues arising from the lack of good medical research on women. The authors had not gone to medical school, but they were smart and good researchers and some of them had backgrounds in science. Their first newsprint edition sold over a quarter of a million copies.

The tone of the all-male doctors in my audience was so hostile that my friend's husband was shocked. When I referred to

Our Bodies, Ourselves, they seemed to think the information in the book was fairy-tale medicine put together by unprofessional women who were without medical background and were essentially no better than witches. If I mentioned the low number of women doctors looking at women's health issues, they said medical school and medical residencies were too rigorous for women and that the quotas on women's seats in medical schools were justified. I still remember how angry they were. (Today over 50 percent of seats in medical schools are held by women.)

Our Bodies, Ourselves became one of America's great publishing success stories and led the way for changing women's medical information around the world. It never went out of print, has sold over 10 million copies, been translated into more than twenty languages, and reprinted in multiple editions. In Catholic countries like Spain, Mexico, and Ireland, translated editions frequently were women's only source of information about sexuality, birth control, and abortion.

While radical feminists stirred the intellectual pot, they lost influence to more mainstream organizations because of their dysfunctional leadership structure. Radical women rebelled against elite, hierarchical models of leadership. Like the New Left, from which many of the younger feminists came, the women in radical groups fought with one another; stole one another's ideas; struggled over money and status; criticized the style, statements, and ideological purity of other leaders; sued one another, split up, and divided into new cells. For example, Lucinda Cisler, who had published a woman's bibliography, sued Robin Morgan over her anthology *Sisterhood Is Powerful* (published in 1970), claiming that it arose out of her bibliography.

Their basic reasoning was that every woman was a leader, on an equal footing with every other woman. This emphasis on shared leadership went back to Women Strike for Peace, which refused to have officers, but designated certain women as "key women." As a practical matter, however, and human nature being what it is, there were always leaders, cliques, and criticism. Internal controversies trumped good analyses of how the real world was operating. As the women's movement became a major media story, those women who understood media relations were constantly quoted in the press. Some of the journalists who had been propelled into the newsrooms to cover the women's liberation story became spokespeople themselves. Gloria Steinem, for example, was a largely unknown journalist in 1970, with no affiliation with any of the well-known women's groups. But she would come out of nowhere to be one of the major spokespeople for the feminist cause and founder and editor of *Ms.* magazine.

In hindsight, the refusal of the radical groups to appoint leaders or spokeswomen to speak to the press turned out to be a significant mistake.

It was in this period of intense media interest, but few spokeswomen, that Erwin Knoll asked me to write the article about women on Capitol Hill.

I told him I would think about it.

Then, one weekend, I sat down and wrote a draft. The next weekend I rewrote it. I thought it was terrible. The third weekend I sent it off to Erwin. It would turn out to be the first article I ever published that I didn't ghostwrite for someone else.

A month later, in January 1971, I finally answered all the FBI questions that Mac had brought home in the fall. I took all my answers from previously published materials, wrote up an innocuous letter, and gave it to Mac to deliver to the security people at the Treasury Department.

And it was about this same time when my colds disappeared.

But they were replaced by what I called my Caravaggio dreams. (And I wasn't smoking any cannabis.) The nature of the dream was always the same. A group of men were sitting around a table talking about me. The scene was lit like a Carravaggio painting. Only half a face was illuminated, say from the nose up, or just one eye, or a pair of hands on the table. The psychological tone was filled with menace. I felt dread. The men were turned toward a person at the head of the table. His face is enveloped in shadow. In the background I hear a mechanical noise, like the inner workings of a clock. I can't decipher what is being said. When I woke up, I could always remember the scene, but I could never describe what had transpired.

"You need a vacation," said Mac, when I told him about the dream.

We rented a house in Jamaica with another couple and planned to go the first week in February. But days before we were to leave, Mac's lawyer friend called to say he and his wife couldn't go. Something about a trial he had to cover. So we were alone on the far side of Jamaica, in a little house that came with a cook, near a beautiful little cove where Errol Flynn used to keep his sailing yacht. I remember the spot because it was there, in the middle of the day, that I became so tired I couldn't move. I remembered that I had been like that before and tried to remember why. It was February, warm and sunny in Jamaica. The water was filled with dazzling colored fish; Mac got stung by a sea anenome and had to go to the doctor. At night we saw swarms of iridescent minnows that lit up the water like fireflies. At first I thought I had recovered my energy, but then at the airport on the way home, I sank into lethargy again.

Erwin published my article in the December 1970 issue of *The Progressive*. He said it was the first time anyone had exposed the institutionalized sexism under which thousands of women were expected to work on Capitol Hill. I felt I was doing my part in the women's movement.

Mac, on the other hand, warned that the article would end my working life on Capitol Hill. It might end my working life altogether, he said. I would never be able to get any recommendations. But he turned out to be wrong.

Surprisingly, the article would get me my next job. One that I loved.

CHAPTER TWELVE

The Ghost of Marjorie Merriweather Post

1971

Mrs. Post, as the tenants of Tregaron still referred to her, was beautiful, extraordinarily rich, and an intelligent marketer of American culture. She was American royalty, and from 1941 to 1952, she had made Tregaron into a showplace for Washington elites and postwar American certainties. At the same time, the media placed her within the myth of America's classless society—a myth I was brought up to believe in and only reluctantly relinquished. *Life* magazine—at a time when *Life* was the national voice—crowned her "America's hostess." (Every woman, after all, could be a hostess.) Alfred Eisenstadt, *Life*'s premier photographer, photographed Mrs. Post in her spacious dining room, wearing a strapless satin evening gown, framed by luxuriant flowers and silver as she checked the place cards at an opulent dining table. This same image of female domestic graciousness was overlaid on Jackie Kennedy when she arrived in Washington, identically photographed in a strapless evening gown and long white gloves as she checked the place cards for a White House dinner. (Previous first ladies had not had the shoulders.)

Although I didn't know anything about Mrs. Post while I was a student, I later learned that she was a brilliant manager of the social aspects of power—the ways in which the rich, the powerful, and the merely ambitious socialize, intermarry, and eventually cohere. As I began to learn the dance of Washington's political-social life, it became clear to me that Mrs. Post had understood that most elusive element of Washington, the cultural dimensions of political power.

As she skillfully sorted the A list from the B list, she knew how to keep permanent Washington happy. She knew how to integrate the new blood from Shaker Heights and Bloomfield Hills with the descendants of Henry Adams and John Hay. Lady Bird Johnson remembered when, as the wife of a then not-very-important congressman from Texas in the 1940s, she attended a sit-down dinner for one hundred guests, at which the place settings were made of gold. Mrs. Post had bought them from impoverished Russian aristocrats in the 1930s in Moscow where her third husband, Joseph Davies, was America's first ambassador to the Soviet Union. Some said Davies was appointed ambassador to Russia because of his friendship with Franklin Delano Roosevelt; others, more knowledgeable, said it was because of Mrs. Post's money.

Her annual spring garden party at Tregaron—when the dogwoods were in full bloom and cascading azaleas formed the backdrop for glittering silver punch bowls mounded high with luscious strawberries—eventually became the most sought-after invitation in Washington. Mrs. Post also understood the cachet of Hollywood and allowed several scenes from the movie version of *Advise and Consent*, a bestselling Washington novel of the cold war, to be shot on the expansive back terrace of Tregaron's white-columned, neo-Georgian mansion. (Her daughter Nardenia developed Hollywood aspirations and became the movie star known as Dina Merrill.) The marriage of Hollywood glamour and mass-media political techniques was still in its early stages.

Although the magnificent hedges of rhododendron still bloomed every spring, by the time Mac and I moved to Tregaron, the Post glamour was a distant memory. Mrs. Post had long since divorced Joe Davies and moved on to a new husband and a new estate. The property had been caught up in inheritance struggles and real estate battles. We rented from a bank that leased out the buildings to pay the real estate taxes. The mansion itself housed an international grade school for the children of foreign diplomats. A Greek economist from the World Bank inhabited the oldest building on the property—the original white farmhouse. A speechwriter for Vice President Agnew lived in the romantic Russian dacha. A married couple, both lawyers for the Labor Department, lived in the gardener's cottage next to a neglected greenhouse of fractured glass. Pat, the Labor Department wife, and I used to take the same yoga class, then an exotic new exercise from the East. During our drives to Chinatown, she told me that previous tenants had included Daniel Patrick Moynihan, who camped out in the farmhouse, and Henry Kissinger, who lived somewhat more elegantly in the dacha. The large carriage house where we lived had three other apartments that housed a caretaker and his family, the daughter of a former Greek ambassador to Washington, and a young man who was refitting a sailboat in one of the former garages. Mac and I were thrilled with the extensive grounds, the high-ceilinged, spacious apartment, and the low rent. The deal was that, if anything broke, you fixed it yourself. But by 1971, Washington had seen so many demonstrations, the smell of tear gas had seeped inside the gates of Tregaron. No one was insulated. Washington social life was chaotic.

By 1971, the New Left had fallen apart. Students for a Democratic Society, the most influential student movement of the decade, had disintegrated, splintering into factions like Progressive Labor, Revolutionary Youth Movement, and the Weathermen. The media paid attention to those who screamed the loudest, used the most vulgar language, and threatened the most violent acts. The Weathermen ended when two of their members blew themselves up in a New York town house trying to assemble a bomb. The nonviolent civil rights movement of the mid-1960s had morphed into an armed Black Power movement whose members had little use for white college students or for women. Black Panthers referred to women's liberation as "pussy power."

On the other hand, as the male left declined, the women's movement gained strength and numbers and legitimacy with every passing week. In Washington in the spring of 1971, I was still going to painting classes, and spending my weekends at a lumberyard buying redwood for stretchers or at Sears buying tools or at a sail maker in Annapolis buying canvas. I was no longer doing small, tidy oil paintings. I was trying to finish a large canvas in time for a student art exhibition at the Corcoran Gallery of Art. (My painting from that exhibition, "Existential Errands," still hangs in my hallway.) I was writing my artist's statement when I received a telephone call from Arvonne Fraser, wife of Congressman Don Fraser.

"How are you keeping busy?" asked Arvonne, who said she had read my article in *The Progressive,* and liked it a lot. In her opinion, she said, such an article was long overdue. Arvonne Fraser was a feminist, a behind-the-scenes activist, and a skillful politician in her own right. I had gotten to know Arvonne a little during social functions, because she was not afraid to share her opinions, and she was enthusiastic about ideas that seemed a little risky. Ben Rosenthal used to tease Don Fraser by beginning a sentence, "With a wife like yours . . ." No one else in the group had a wife quite like Arvonne.

She worked in Fraser's office full time (unpaid) and maintained a great network of contacts from Minnesota and a larger Washington social circle. The House did not have all that many activist wives who were politically visible. As a general rule, women in politics were supposed to take care of everything behind the scenes while men were out front with the microphone and the cameras. "What I have in mind," continued Arvonne, after I told her I was taking painting courses at the Corcoran, "is that you could help out with writing press releases and newsletters and speeches for Fraser," she always called her congressman husband Fraser, "and work on some women's projects with me."

"Arvonne, I'd love to," I began. "But you have to know it's not the best time. I just signed a book contract and—"

"Great. What's the book about?" Arvonne asked enthusiastically.

I told her it was going to be about women radicals in the labor, peace, and abolitionist movements as well as suffrage.

"That's exactly the book I'd like to read. In fact, I'd like to write it. Be sure to look up Charlotte Perkins Gilman." And then she proceeded to tell me about women she knew in the labor movement in Washington, like Esther Peterson from Minnesota.

"You don't plan to work on it full time, do you?" Arvonne was not someone to whom I could explain that I needed to recharge my batteries by going to art school, or that regaining perspective was a necessity, not a self-indulgent whim. *Burnout* (a term borrowed from Graham Greene's novel *A Burnt-Out Case*) is a common Washington condition and describes a state of emotional, intellectual, and psychological depletion. It was only after

I was no longer depleted that I had the energy to realize I had been burnt-out.

"That sounds like a perfect job description for me," I told Arvonne. "And I would love to do it. But there is something else you need to know." I didn't feel I could lie to Arvonne. I paused and took a breath. "I just found out I'm pregnant." It was common then for women to lie about being pregnant because pregnancy was a reason for job dismissal. (Even today, dismissal after an employer finds out a woman is pregnant is frequently the source of sex discrimination suits.) But Arvonne had five children and believed in working mothers, so when she asked me about any concerns I had, I felt she deserved an honest answer.

I had found out that I was pregnant in February, right after we came back from Jamaica. The exhaustion I had experienced in Jamaica was exactly the same as I had experienced in Rome, but I couldn't connect the physical state with having been pregnant. We had discussed starting a family. Mac had asked in December, after I had stopped working and had agreed to answer all J. Edgar Hoover's questions, "Isn't it a good time for you to get off birth control pills and get pregnant?" He pointed out that I would be turning thirty that year and pretty soon I might not be able to get pregnant at all. (In 1970, turning thirty for a woman was like turning forty today.)

So I agreed to stop taking the Pill if he agreed to help with child care. Of course, he answered. From what I had heard from friends, it took about six months after stopping the Pill for a woman to get pregnant. But there I was, a mere eight weeks later—definitely pregnant, said the doctor. I also had qualms about bringing a child into such a troubled world, but I did want to have the baby. Mac was very enthusiastic. (It was only later that I realized his idea of helping with child care was the occasional

Saturday afternoon. The idea that men should share responsibility for parenting was not yet on the table. He expected me to stay home and take care of the baby full time.)

"Wonderful," said Arvonne. "Congratulations again. But being pregnant doesn't affect your brain. How many hours a week can you work?"

"Well, maybe I could work half time. Say twenty hours a week."

"Perfect. When can you start?" Arvonne had the energy of three people and enough charm and humor to talk a dog off a meat wagon.

So two weeks later I was back on the express bus heading to Capitol Hill, happy to have a paycheck to look forward to and the financial control that went with it—I was paying for expenses from my unemployment check—as well as the prospect of interesting new colleagues.

Working in Don Fraser's office was a qualitatively different experience from my previous Capitol Hill job. First of all, the staff was literate. The woman at the desk next to mine, whom I shall call Lisa, read Proust—*Remembrance of Things Past*—on the bus. She and her husband ran an antiques stand at flea markets on weekends.

"Have you read *Three Guineas*?" Arvonne asked, passing by my desk. "Oh, you must," she said when I shook my head. "It's the work of our time. There is no one like Virginia Woolf. Women, war, the military, politics. She understands how it all fits together." I told her I hadn't, but would plan to. In fact, *Three Guineas* was not understood in England when it was published in 1938. It wasn't until the late 1960s in the United States that it found its audience. Arvonne was in the vanguard.

Second, Fraser's office was the first experience I had of

working in a balanced environment—where women and men seemed to have equal status regardless of title. It would take me another twenty-five years to encounter it again. Even though the professional jobs were held by men, women's opinions were taken seriously and listened to. This was because Arvonne's desk was in the outer office with the rest of us, and she, of course, had the congressman's ear.

Because of Arvonne, Fraser's office had a liberated sensibility. I didn't have to spend any part of my day fighting derogatory remarks about women. I realized how much energy I had used up trying to remain urbane, imperturbable, and unflappable. Gradually, I learned that Arvonne was part of the group of underground Washington wives of prominent husbands called the Nameless Sisterhood. The name came from the rule that no one could introduce herself by referring to her husband's title, as in "My husband is . . ."

Their group was part of an invisible strata of Washington women who served as crucial connective tissue between the old feminists, the new women's liberationists, and the women in Congress who knew how to introduce, modify, and pass laws. Arvonne was a member of NOW, and was also vice president and legislative director of the Washington chapter of the Women's Equity Action League (WEAL). Both women's organizations translated many of the ideas of the radical women's groups into concrete legislation and institutional change. Without legal changes, many of the gains achieved by the second wave women's movement would never have been institutionalized. As Kevin Phillips has observed, "The least told story of U.S. history is how the social movements of the 1960s institutionalized themselves."

My contribution to WEAL was to examine how America selects and trains its leadership class. The White House Fellows is a prestigious program that selects promising young Americans with leadership potential and places them in cabinet-level offices and gives them a view of power through White House windows. In the seven years since its inception by President Johnson in 1964, it had included over a hundred men and eight women. Arvonne wrote a letter from the congressman on congressional stationery asking the White House why they didn't select more women as White House Fellows. The response—addressed to Congressman Fraser—came from Grant Kendall, a White House Fellow and the son of Donald Kendall Sr., chairman of Pepsi-Cola and a major fund-raiser for Richard Nixon. Young Kendall explained there were so few women fellows because women applicants were not qualified. "After all," his letter concluded with an ill-advised arrogance in dealing with unknown congressional staff, "we can't make a silk purse out of a sow's ear overnight."

"Women applicants as sows' ears?" Arvonne was practically levitating off the floor. "Can you imagine?" A short woman with so much focused energy that she bounced on the balls of her feet when she walked, she wanted to know what could be done to deal with such a disrespectful and unenlightened attitude.

"Why don't I do some research," I suggested, "to see how many women and African Americans have been admitted in the past seven years, and then we'll draft a response." The program took about twenty fellows a year, at least four of them from the military. I was sure that Kendall Jr. thought he was corresponding directly man to man with Congressman Fraser, never imagining the recipient was the congressman's wife and her staff. Since the White House Fellows program was funded by taxpayer money, I assumed it was subject to the antidiscrimination clause of the Civil Rights Act. I asked the Congressional Reference Service to send me everything there was to know about the White House Fellows program—its budget, numbers of applications, positions given to the fellows, breakdown of women and minorities, who was on the selection boards, and how the selectors were selected. By the time I read all the material I received, I knew I had decoded the way white, male leadership perpetuates itself.

The letter that the congressman sent back to the White House, again on congressional stationery and approved by Don Fraser, became the seed of a project that would last for ten years, spread to more than twenty leadership programs, produce three written reports, and eventually attract funding from the Rockefeller Foundation.

My "aha" moment was this: As long as women or minorities were excluded from all the elite fellowship programs in every profession, they would always be considered "less qualified" than male applicants. This included programs like the Rhodes Scholars (Cecil Rhodes excluded women and never imagined black Africans fell under the category of "civilized men"), Nieman fellowships in Journalism, Guggenheim fellowships in academia, and Woodrow Wilson fellowships in foreign policy. Stating that women had fewer qualifications than men for the same job was always a legitimate reason to reject women. On the other hand, if women were prohibited from applying to be a Rhodes scholar, a Nieman fellow, or a Guggenheim fellow, how could they obtain those credentials to be considered equally qualified? Women would always be considered "sows' ears." I was particularly interested in the foreign policy fellowships whose gates, I knew, were closely watched by a tiny group of men. I thought a little shaking up of the White House fellows program was all to the good.*

---

* In 1971 when the WEAL project first began, there had been a total of 104 fellows, of whom 8 had been women. I found no women on the selection committees. I also found that many Rhodes scholars applied for White House fellows when they returned from England, so there was a kind of all-male applicant feedback loop.

Arvonne and I kept writing letters (on the congressman's stationery, which the congressman signed with a wry smile). As we gathered more information, I wrote press releases. Within a matter of months, we had a full-fledged project whose activities attracted great interest from the press. We learned that women applicants were always asked who would take care of their children and how they would divide their responsibilities among husband, home, and job. These questions were never asked of men who were parents. In fact, the selection committee, all men, had never accepted a woman who was married.

After a friend of Arvonne's gave columnist Jack Anderson a copy of our correspondence with the White House fellows program, he wrote a column about Grant Kendall and his "sow's ear" letter. One of the immediate beneficiaries of our project might have been Colin Powell, then a Vietnam veteran and a lieutenant colonel, who was admitted as a White House fellow in 1972, thus expanding the number of minority recipients. (That experience transformed him from a career soldier into a wily political hand, but not quite wily enough for the Cheney-Rumsfeld-Bush triumvirate.)

The WEAL legislative office, which Arvonne had founded, had a committee made up of many women staffers from Capitol Hill legislative offices. One of them was Linda Kamm, formerly a lawyer on the House Labor Committee. By the time I met her, she was about to go live in London for six months while her

---

When I interviewed the director of the White House fellows program, he told me the selection committee (1) had never taken a married woman, (2) had never even considered a woman with children, (3) had never asked men who took care of their children, and 4) had decided the best way to increase the participation of women in the program was to set up a special program for the *wives of the fellows*. In 1971, only 1 woman out of 17 was chosen. In 1973, 4 out of 18 were women. But by 1975, it had dropped back to 2 women out of 18. In 1975, Serena Stier filed suit in U.S. District Court in D.C., charging that she was asked personal questions not asked of male candidates.

husband did research. I asked her if she could arrange to meet with women in the British Parliament to find out how to change the male-only terms of Cecil Rhodes's will. Women couldn't even apply to be Rhodes scholars, because Rhodes had specified men recipients, and his will had been enacted as an Act of Parliament. In order for women to qualify as Rhodes applicants, the British Parliament would have to pass an act amending the men-only provisions of Cecil Rhodes's will.

Cecil Rhodes was an Englishman who lived most of his life in South Africa and made a fortune in mining and in diamonds (De Beers). When he died in 1902, he was believed to be one of the wealthiest men in the world. He also had annexed huge swaths of land north of South Africa and named it for himself. Today the countries of Zimbabwe and Zambia make up the former Rhodesia. Rhodes pushed Africans off their mineral-rich lands by using guile and ruthlessness. He annexed these countries by raising his own private army and equipping his soldiers with repeating rifles and machine guns and used them against tribal peoples outfitted with spears. He disarmed tribal chiefs who wanted to negotiate by having his doctor provide them with "miracle drugs" like opium and morphine to treat minor diseases such as gout. When he found it necessary to wage a war against white people, the Dutch in the Transvaal region of South Africa, whose farmlands held rich gold deposits, he went to Parliament and had Britain declare war against them. When he died in 1902, the Boer War, a colonial war that Britain ultimately lost, was still raging.

Rhodes never married and had no sons. He was, however, an ardent imperialist who believed that the British Empire was the future of the world. "I contend that we [British] are the finest race in the world," he wrote in his 1877 book *Confession of Faith,* "and that the more of the world we inhabit, the better it is for the human race." So he hit upon the idea of creating sons to carry on his name and spreading the ideas of empire by means of a scholarship for young men to study at Oxford for two years. "My desire," Rhodes wrote of the future bearers of his name, "is that the students who shall be elected to the scholarships shall not be merely bookworms" but should be selected for "his literary and scholastic attainments; his fondness of and success in manly outdoor sports such as cricket, football and the like; his qualities of manhood, truth, courage, devotion to duty, sympathy for the protection of the weak, kindliness, unselfishness and fellowship; his exhibition during school days of moral force of character. . . ." Rhodes had none of these qualities himself: he was nothing of a scholar; he was not athletic; and he had no sympathy for the weak. He was a cruel, driven man who personified the instincts of empire.

America then and now has a number of former Rhodes scholars in high positions: Carl Albert, Speaker of the House of Representatives; John Oakes, editorial page editor of the *New York Times*; J. William Fulbright, chairman of the Senate Foreign Relations Committee; Dean Rusk, former secretary of state and head of the Rockefeller Foundation; former president Bill Clinton.

Rhodes believed in "the recovery of the U.S. as part of the British Empire," and his will specified two American Rhodes scholars from every state. (One of his secretaries speculated that Rhodes was under the impression that there were still only thirteen colonies.) The British liked his idea so much that an Act of Parliament created the Rhodes Trust, which administered the $15 million fortune (over a billion dollars in 2007 currency) he left for the scholarship. Soon the trust went back to Parliament to change the provisions of the will, the first time to revise the number of American scholarships down from one hundred to thirty-two; the second time, to include West Germany among the eligible nations. (The scholarship is open to every country of the British Commonwealth, with the addition of West Germany.) It was not necessary to amend the trust to open it to blacks because he had specified "every civilized man" and a nineteenth-century Englishman didn't imagine that civilization belonged to any but whites.

What happened when I wrote to the Rhodes Trust asking them to open the scholarships to women? They didn't answer. What happened when I wrote asking them to support a woman who had been nominated by the University of Minnesota? They said that the male-only terms of Cecil Rhodes's will made it impossible and such terms could be changed only by an act of Parliament.

Linda Kamm did go visit women members of Parliament and was told that the Rhodes Trust felt that "this women's liberation thing is simply an American fad" and would pass. When the *New York Times* wrote about the woman Rhodes applicant from Minnesota, the reporter dismissed the suit as frivolous, saying, "Cecil Rhodes made his fortune in diamonds . . . they're a girl's best friend in the end."

We continued to send letters, threaten suits to universities to provide equivalent international study opportunities for women students, and write letters to the editor. I even wrote a short article about Cecil Rhodes for a national women's magazine.

As it turned out, history was on our side. In 1972, the first Rhodes scholar in seventy years resigned, citing the discrimination against blacks and the exclusion of women. By then women in Britain had launched their own feminist movement and had introduced Britain's Sex Discrimination Act, which outlawed discrimination based on gender. "Women Get Backing as Rhodes Scholars," reported the *New York Times* in 1975, with no mention of five years of pressure from women's groups, legal

suits, or institutional pressure on the Rhodes Trust and Parliament. (Linda Kamm did find one MP who introduced the first
bill.) No one suggested that change originated in anything but
the enlightened benevolence on the part of the Rhodes Trust. I
call this the "Just-Happened" theory of history.

Another member of Arvonne's legislative committee was Arlene Horowitz, a secretary in Congresswoman Patsy Mink's office. Arlene and I, who were younger than most of the others on
the committee, remarked how older women often seemed to
take credit for our ideas. (Women never got credit for anything,
so within women's organizations, women were hungry for recognition. This reality accounted for much splintering and factionalism. NOW had well-publicized savage leadership battles;
WEAL eventually went out of business entirely because the leadership neglected to recruit members.) We agreed that we would
back each other up to prevent that from happening. She came up
with the idea for a bill called the Women's Educational Equity
Act, which would make federal educational grants available to
women from rural or marginal backgrounds. She helped write
the bill, Patsy Mink introduced it in the House, Walter Mondale
introduced it in the Senate, and it passed. During its life span, the
bill eventually funded a program to provide equal education
(particularly math and science) for girls in rural schools; a math-
tutoring service for older minority women returning to community colleges; and a guide to help teenage handicapped girls.
Ten years later, during the Reagan era, this tiny program was
characterized as "the feminist network feeding at the federal
trough" and was eliminated. Undoubtedly, the money went to
pay for a few new doorknobs on an aircraft carrier.

I expanded the Women in Fellowships Committee to include
new fellowship programs. Arvonne sent me to talk with Eileen
Shanahan about the Nieman fellows in journalism. Shanahan,

then one of the few *New York Times* women reporters, was a financial writer, and her bylined articles about the Treasury Department often appeared on the front page. She told me she was on the selection board for the Nieman fellows but couldn't be one herself. "Why not?" I asked. "After all, the program had been started by a woman," Agnes Nieman (in memory of her husband). Prospective applicants had to be referred by their newspapers, Shanahan explained, and the *Times* wouldn't nominate a woman. Nor would most newspaper editors. She suggested I contact the director of the program and ask him to change all the recruiting literature to refer to prospective applicants as "he or she" instead of "he." That alone might help educate newspaper editors that they should nominate women reporters as well as men. (From 1968 to 1972, out of sixty Nieman fellows, two had been women.)

I did everything she suggested, and the Nieman director, James Thompson, formerly of the State Department and Harvard's History Department, was surprisingly agreeable. They were in the process of changing all their literature, he told me, and would welcome suggestions on how to attract women applicants. The first Nieman cohort to include multiple women reporters was in 1973. The four women reporters included future Pulitzer Prize–winning columnist Ellen Goodman, who broke the mold of only men writing about politics on the op-ed page. She also expanded political topics to include work and family issues and how they influence national policy.

Shanahan also gave me a tip when I told her my troubles about interviewing and getting information from the directors of the elite fellowship programs, many of whom were somewhat patronizing.

"If you ever have to interview someone who really tries to intimidate you," she advised me, "chew gum."

Eileen Shanahan was an insider at the *Times* and behaved like an insider until she found out the disparity between what she was paid and what male reporters were paid. She joined the women's class action suit in 1974 against the *Times* management as one of the seven "named defendants." After the case was settled out of court in 1977, she left the *Times* to take a position as a cabinet press secretary in the administration of President Jimmy Carter.

One afternoon in the summer of 1971, Arvonne invited all the women in the office to go down to a meeting in the Longworth Cafeteria. "You're going to hear from the editors of a new women's magazine that will cover politics," she told us. "We're all going to subscribe, I hope."

An audience of more than a hundred women staffers waited in the cafeteria to meet the editors of a new mass-circulation magazine that would include both politics and a feminist editorial viewpoint. A tall, slim blond in tinted aviator glasses presented a new image of feminist cool. Gloria Steinem was articulate, funny, and glamorous. She seemed like the ideal editor for a new feminist magazine. Smart and chic. When someone asked her what experience she had had in politics, the bottom line seemed to be "not much." She was known mainly as a New York journalist who had written a highly publicized, and funny, account of going undercover to work as a Playboy bunny in New York. (Men saw the new Playboy clubs as an expression of the sexual revolution. Women saw Playboy clubs as an old idea dressed up in a new costume, with rabbit ears and a cotton tail. A college classmate of mine worked as a Playboy bunny for one summer and said there was nothing liberating about it. She later got her doctorate and became a college dean.) Ellen Willis, who would later write for *Ms.* and then leave over its editorial policies, said that she felt about "the sexual revolution what Gandhi reputedly felt about Western civilization: namely, that it would be a good idea."

Gloria Steinem's complete answer, however, was that women were creating new political terrain and experience in "old politics" might not be so valuable. Although I was certain I had never seen her before, her name rang a bell from some past association that I couldn't quite place at the time. But I kept rummaging around in my mental closet for the connection. The advent of *Ms.* magazine, however, was a minor blip in the larger world of journalism.

By then, women were no longer waiting politely for their turn at the microphone. Women were causing uproars in institutions everywhere. Women employees had staged sit-ins at the offices of *Newsweek* and the *Ladies' Home Journal*, demanding better pay and better assignments. At *Time, Life, Fortune,* and *Sports Illustrated*, women filed antidiscrimination suits over inequities in pay, promotions, recognition, treatment, and a hostile work environment. NOW filed suit against thirteen hundred corporations for job discrimination against women. WEAL sued more than one hundred colleges and universities for inequitable admissions, hiring, promotion, and tenure policies for women. The legal basis for NOW's suit was the Equal Pay Act of 1963. Introduced and passed by Edith Green of Oregon, the law simply called for equal pay for equal work done by women. WEAL based its suit on Title VII of the Civil Rights Act of 1964, which outlawed discrimination "on the basis of race, religion, sex or national origin" in any project or institution receiving federal taxpayer monies.

The absence of women in American political life became a highly publicized issue during 1970 Senate hearings on the pharmaceutical industry when Barbara Seaman, an author and medical researcher, testified that estrogen levels were much too high in birth control pills and that women were being used as "guinea pigs" by the drug companies. The all-male Senate committee had her removed from the hearing room. (The Senate had only one woman senator, Margaret Chase Smith, and she was not on that committee.) The same year in Albany, New York, a state legislative panel composed of fourteen men and one nun began holding hearings on abortion law reform. They refused to let women from the feminist group Redstockings testify. Leaders of Redstockings organized their own public meetings and demanded repeal, not reform of abortion laws. In many states abortion was still a criminal act.

By 1971, women's demands for change were widely publicized and covered in the nation's press. The arc of the progressive pendulum was still on its forward stroke. But the institutions of the conservative male establishment were regrouping. Conservatives funded Accuracy in Media (AIM) to act as a watchdog against the "liberal bias" in media; the Catholic Church established the National Right to Life Committee to block liberalization of abortion laws; the Mormon Church organized state committees to block the ratification of the Equal Rights Amendment; and the FBI and the CIA increased their massive infiltration of the women's movement. J. Edgar Hoover, who seemed never to sleep, saw the new women's movement as the new communism. Although the FBI had no female agents (no equal opportunity at the FBI), the bureau recruited thousands of female informants to infiltrate the new women's groups. At the same time, feminist and peace activists were in touch with women in France, Italy, Germany, and Latin America who were organizing demonstrations and women's movements of their own. This made them targets for CIA surveillance. The CIA opened an office directly above the Women Strike for Peace office in Washington, D.C.

On the surface of my life everything was going well. I was

happy to be pregnant. I loved my work. I had a desk in the stacks of the Library of Congress and was making progress with my book. I was meeting interesting and intellectually challenging people. My marriage seemed on solid ground.

One day in July, however, I was to rediscover the truth of the Buddhist saying, "Make no plans; have no expectations."

Mac came home with another bombshell. "I've been offered a new job. With a significant increase in grade and pay," he said.

"Wonderful," I said. "What is it?"

"Financial officer with the Peace Corps."

I was surprised because I knew he thought the Peace Corps was not a place for anyone who wanted a serious career. I had heard him describe people we knew as "Peace Corps types," meaning undisciplined, romantic, without a serious work ethic, and lacking a solid sense of how the real world worked.

"I never heard you say you were impressed with the Peace Corps, but if it's a good opportunity, you should take it."

"I have to make up my mind in twenty-four hours."

"Why the rush?"

"I'd have to start in three weeks. And it's not in Washington."

"Where is it?"

"Nigeria. Lagos."

I was astounded, astonished, and speechless. I was so shocked that I disassociated. My physical person stayed in the room while my mind found a perch on the wall and looked down on these two people as though they were characters in a play. Which in many ways they were, only I was the one without a full script.

"In Lagos? You can't be serious. Shouldn't I have been consulted that you were looking for a job outside the country?"

"It came up unexpectedly."

"I can't write a book in Nigeria. I need a library. What will I do there? There's nothing for me to do there."

"You'll have a baby to look after."

Before the feminist movement, if a man said he needed to move for a job, the wife went along, whether she wanted to or not. But the women's movement was giving women choices. I recalled conversations I had with one of the women in my painting class (the one who worked with lemons) who had been a State Department wife and the stories she told about how wives in embassy communities drank too much because they were bored. She told me she had to hire local people as household staff even though she knew the servants worked for the host governments, went through their mail, and frequently listened in on their telephone conversations. In the end, a lot of the embassy and consulate wives occupied their time shopping for whatever was available at the local markets or military Post Exchange or having affairs with husbands from the other embassies. I knew that Lagos was a complex situation because Nigeria had so much oil that all the big multinational oil companies maintained offices there. I wondered if, in fact, Mac would be really working for the Peace Corps or if this position was a cover for another Treasury Department job.

I was so stunned I had the feeling that I was watching a movie of someone else's life.

"Who came up with this idea?" I suddenly had the image of his Gordon Liddy–like boss in my kitchen refusing to take my outstretched hand, telling me he didn't believe in shaking hands with women. "Isn't this something we should have talked about in advance before you went ahead and interviewed? I had no idea you were even thinking of leaving the Treasury Department."

"Well, it came up suddenly," Mac said lamely.

"Mac, in a few weeks no airline will let me fly. I'll be too pregnant."

He didn't take the Peace Corps job, but that conversation smashed my idea that we had a compatible vision of the future.

After that, I felt my personal life had become a pawn in a game quite beyond my powers to control. On my morning walks around Tregaron, I began to wonder somewhat obsessively about how Mrs. Post had been forced out of her home. If she—with all her money and connections—hadn't been able to hold on to her life, what were my prospects?

It has been my experience that wealthy people can always hire people with taste to buy them valuable objects, but that it takes a special sensibility to know what to do with land. Mrs. Marjorie Merriweather Post had invested in a subtle relationship with the land she owned in Washington. At a time when men generally took walks only if they could shoot something and women weren't expected to own hiking shoes, Mrs. Post had shaped her wild outer acres with a unified vision of a "natural" landscape. The bamboo forest, the Japanese cypress, and the unexpected bridge had the harmony and balance of a Buddhist garden encouraging reflection and—if not enlightenment—at least meditation.

I had a lot to meditate on.

It was said that Mrs. Post used to have her gardener bring twenty orchid plants to bloom before a party so that she could choose the perfect orchid to match her dress color. Pat, one of the tenants in the gardener's cottage, told me that Mrs. Post, as everyone called her, had bought the estate in 1941 (this was true) and had given it to Joe Davies, her third husband, as a wedding present (this was not). The heirs were the children and grandchildren of Joe Davies, and occasionally I would see one of them, particularly Senator Joe Tydings, strolling around the fields.

Despite what I had been told about Davies's integrity and statesmanship, I always wondered what kind of man Joe Davies really was. His reputation was that of a political "fixer" and a close friend of FDR. One afternoon, searching for a suitcase I had stored in the attic above the carriage house, I came across an old carton of books and papers and letters that had belonged to Ambassador Davies, as he liked to be called. I sat down on the bare wood floor next to a window while rays of sun lit up dust particles suspended in the air and read through odd papers and correspondence Davies had written twenty years earlier.

From his letters, it was clear that Ambassador Davies thought of himself as a player, an articulate and persuasive member of the Washington establishment. The box also included several copies of *Mission to Moscow*, a bestselling memoir of his four-year posting in the Soviet Union, which began in 1936. (George Kennan and Averill Harriman, who served under him in the Moscow embassy, dubbed the book "Submission to Moscow" because of Davies's inadequate account of the famines, executions, deportations, and show trials under Stalin's rule.) More interesting to me was an unpublished article he had written and his angry correspondence with the editor of *Foreign Affairs* who had rejected it. Ambassador Davies did not deal well with rejection. Reading his exchange of letters with the editor, I could see why some people called him a foreign policy amateur, a person whose grasp of power was limited and unprofessional, a politician uninformed by a statesman's knowledge of history or diplomacy.

A few years after the *Foreign Affairs* correspondence, Davies became engaged in writing another memoir. According to his editor at Simon & Schuster, Justin Kaplan, the subject of the second memoir seemed to be about dictators Davies had known and loved—Generalissimo Franco in Spain, António Salazar in Portugal, and Joseph Stalin in Russia. Kaplan came to the conclusion that the eighty-one-year-old Davies—who frequently showed up in his office wearing a black homburg, fur-collared black overcoat, and silver-headed walking stick insisting he be addressed as Mr. Ambassador—lived in a world of "extended make-believe." This was a conclusion that Marjorie Post came to considerably earlier, once telling a friend, "Joe should have been an actor. His whole life was an act." The memoir project had been concocted by Davies's daughters to keep their father occupied while they had a court declare him incompetent to handle his own affairs. The memoir was never published, and Davies died in 1958.

But such were the rules of the Washington men's club, where land and titles were the credentials to remaining in the game, not a breath of this reality had yet filtered through the scrim of Davies's reputation and alleged stature. Although Joe Davies might have been judged an amateur in the world of international diplomacy and a flake in the world of letters, he was a total professional, according to the men's club rules of Washington. I became suspicious about how willingly Mrs. Post had departed from Tregaron when she had clearly invested so much of herself in the property. Why else had she duplicated the entire property, right down to the Russian dacha, at Hillwood, the estate she bought and renovated in northwest Washington after the divorce? With a little research, I soon discovered that, when it came time for the divorce in 1955, Mrs. Post learned a few more unpleasant truths about the groom. She was astonished to learn that at the time they purchased Tregaron in 1941, Mr. Davies, if nothing else a shrewd Washington lawyer, had had the deed to the estate registered in his name only, even though Mrs. Post had paid the mortgage for years. As I was also to learn about my husband, the acquisition of power requires a certain mastery of the skills of duplicity. I had a presentiment that, like Mrs. Post, I would be rather rudely and abruptly displaced from Tregaron.

Property is an important component of power, a visible expression of invisible forces. Mrs. Post had inherited one of America's great fortunes, and Joe Davies helped transform it into the prerogatives of power and international politics. In the same way the British trace the bloodlines of the Peerage, Americans trace the inheritors of great fortunes. Newspaper accounts always identified Mrs. Post as the "Post Toasties" heiress from Battle Creek, Michigan, inheritor of the Post Cereal fortune, a company that eventually became General Foods. In addition to being one of the richest women in America, she was very beautiful and very smart. Davies, on the other hand, was a Washington lawyer, a deal maker, a man with unfulfilled political ambitions, and a friend and supporter of President Franklin Roosevelt. An ambitious man and a man knowledgeable in the algebra of power, he had divorced his wife of thirty-three years in order to marry Mrs. Post, whom he met as a client of his law firm.

With this second marriage, he gained both title and property and catapulted himself out of the wealthy upper middle class. Ten months after their wedding in December 1935, he left his Washington law firm for the more exotic stage of the ambassador's residency in Moscow. Some said he got the job because he was competent and loyal; others, more knowing, said it was because of Mrs. Post's contributions—estimates range up to a hundred thousand dollars—to Franklin Roosevelt's 1936 reelection campaign. Marjorie and Mrs. Roosevelt corresponded.

Apparently, it was not his posting of choice. He wanted to be in London or Paris. But 1937 marked the critical preliminaries for World War II, and Europe's old capitals were no place for a rookie diplomat. (Another first-time ambassador, Joe Kennedy Sr., John F. Kennedy's father, would be called home from his post as ambassador to England because of his inconvenient expressions of support for Hitler.) Mrs. Post brought a certain capitalist sensibility to the proletariat aesthetics of the new Soviet Union and used her time as the ambassador's wife to collect spectacular Russian art and antiques (and probably the gold place settings that Lady Bird Johnson remembered in her memoir). Czarist decadence became high art in democratic America. Soon after their return to Washington in 1940, Mrs. Post bought the old Palmerlee estate and set out to become Washington's preeminent hostess.

For some people, Tregaron was still the Palmerlee estate. I learned this from a man who told me that his father used to be Mr. Palmerlee's carriage driver. I found him in my garage one morning showing the waterwheel on the ceiling to his fifty-year-old son.

"I wanted to show my son the farm where I spent my boyhood," he said, when I came into the huge garage that had once housed three carriages. "Mr. Palmerlee?" I asked. "Farm?" We were in the heart of some of the most expensive real estate in Washington.

"Mr. Palmerlee," said the elderly father, "came to Washington with President James Garfield. He bought this farm because it reminded him of his own farm in Ohio and built the big house later." He pointed to the big circular piping on the ceiling. "That's a waterwheel. When I was a boy my job was to scramble up on the roof of the carriage and attach a hose. Oh yes," he said, still with a hint of brogue, "the roads weren't paved y'know, and the carriages got filthy. They had to be washed after every outing."

I was happy to show him what once had been his childhood home—a two-bedroom two-bath apartment with high ceilings and elegant proportions. He asked me about the greenhouse and the Russian dacha and Mrs. Post. "Did you hear that Mrs. Post sometimes used a horse and carriage during the war to save on gasoline?" I had not heard that. As we walked back to their car, he pointed to the white house, where an economist from the World Bank was living. "That's the original farmhouse," he said. "And Alexander Graham Bell lived over there," he said, pointing across the wire fence to the next estate, which housed the embassy of Taiwan.

I had taken up jogging about the time Mac brought the FBI questionnaire into my life, and that was how I discovered all the paths and trails that Mrs. Post had designed for her twenty-two acres of land. My old running route had traced the elongated outer edge on the Rock Creek side, parallel with the tall iron fence that enclosed the outer perimeter of the property. As I stepped into the underbrush, following the memory of a trail that had almost disappeared, I realized that the land itself had imprinted itself on my consciousness. It was in my early-morning runs that I constantly made new discoveries about Mrs. Post's aesthetics. I found a necklace of delicate stone bridges that threaded back and forth across a serpentine creek, a grove of majestic bamboo, an exquisite Japanese cypress tree, plants and grasses I had never seen—in or out of a botanical garden. Watching the bamboo sway in the wind, I sometimes felt as though I was in a foreign country. I wondered if bamboo in Vietnam looked like the little bamboo forest on Tregaron.

I enjoyed the natural environment I was privileged to be living in, but I felt it was temporary. On my morning walks around Tregaron, I thought about little fragments of disconnected events. My mind shuffled and reshuffled these fragments, trying to form a pattern. I thought about my original meeting with Ray Rubinow and how he had "encouraged" me to go to the School for Advanced International Studies, and how I later learned that the foundation he worked for was a CIA funding conduit—concentrating on students in international affairs. I recalled that some of my European classmates in Bologna had insisted that CIA money was involved in supporting student organizations at their universities. The CIA looks for student leaders, they said, because they think whoever is a leader in university politics will eventually become a political leader in their country. They identify and back them early.

I had telephoned Ray Rubinow—my "godfather"—immediately after *Ramparts* magazine came out in 1967 with its exposé of how the Kaplan Foundation, among others, channeled CIA money to fund the National Student Association (NSA). Although NSA was supposedly built on the motto of "a free university in a free society," CIA funding in some years amounted to as much as 80 percent of NSA's entire budget. I had asked him how he justified the CIA's underwriting of domestic institutions, organizations, magazines, publishing houses, newspapers, and other cultural groups in order to influence their policies in a direction favored by the agency. He answered that no strings had been attached to the funding. I had asked if an open society wasn't a key element of a democracy and if the Kaplan Foundation was a government group or a private organization. In other words, did he work for the CIA or for a private foundation that "saved Carnegie Hall and all that?" I never heard from him again.

That was when I remembered where I had first seen Gloria Steinem's name. It was in a *Washington Post* article about NSA leaders who had gone on to head up other CIA-funded student organizations. Steinem had been the codirector of one of the youth organizations that received CIA money through one of the bogus foundations. She had been part of my research about the Kaplan Fund. "Miss Steinem was co-director of the Independent Research Service with Dennis Shaul," Robert Kaiser

had written in the *Washington Post* in 1967. "She strongly defended her actions and had great praise for the CIA agents with
whom she collaborated. 'I found them liberal and farsighted and
open. . . .'" The *New York Times* added that her organization
"received funds from the CIA-connected Independence Foundation of Boston." The larger question was whether or not these
were CIA-designed front organizations. I was curious to know if
she had had all the requisite CIA examinations: the psychological
test in one building; the physical in another; the lie detector test.
(My friends had been driven around to different buildings in
Washington before they got CIA jobs. These positions weren't
the kind of jobs women got from answering a Help Wanted
notice in a newspaper.) While I was in Widener Library in
Cambridge writing my college research paper on the Soviet
secret police, Gloria Steinem was working only a mile away in
Cambridge as codirector of the CIA-funded Independent Research Service, "encouraging" students to attend international
youth festivals. By 1975, as leaders of women's groups became
more sophisticated about the extent of FBI and CIA infiltration,
the issue of authentic leadership in the women's movement became confrontational. Gloria Steinem's CIA past would be analyzed in a different light and the integrity of *Ms.* magazine and
the Ms. Foundation questioned.

Like a journal written in invisible ink, some things in my life
were beginning to come clear.

That April, the Greek economist who worked for the World
Bank invited us to a Greek Easter party that he and his Greek
friends gave every year. Stratis (not his real name) once told me
that, as a student, he had taken an old Jeep and followed Alexander the Great's route from Macedonia in northern Greece all the
way to India. He said they did the Greek Easter celebration the
way it was done in Greece, roasting a whole lamb on a spit,

pouring endless wine from woven basket jugs that never ran dry. But that spring, his regular butcher had gone back to Greece, and he was too late to order another prepared lamb in time for the party. On the Wednesday night before Easter, I heard a lamb bleating in a shed outside the farmhouse. On Thursday and Friday, I checked on the lamb. It was still bleating. On Saturday, a priest and a butcher came. Silence. When I saw the body on the spit, it gave new meaning to the phrase "sacrificial lamb." I vowed I wouldn't eat a morsel. But as the party wound on, I forgot and filled my plate like everyone else. It seemed that every Greek in Washington was there. Music came from a record player turned up to full volume on an extension cord that snaked back to the farmhouse. I had learned Greek dances in the Greek islands years before, and with enough wine and enough encouragement, I, too, joined the lines of dancers. With our arms linked around one another's waists, we moved in a continuously expanding sinuous line around the long field in front of the dacha. It was a Greek Easter but with a Dionysian spirit.

Although such a pagan celebration was not as sedate as Mrs. Post's spring garden parties, I felt that Mrs. Post would have enjoyed that Greek Easter party. She liked dancing. She believed in a good time. Who knows? Maybe her spirit was there.

CHAPTER THIRTEEN

Moral Hazard

June 1971

The class differences between Mac and me often appeared without warning. Our car, for example, was a second-hand convertible that we had bought for several hundred dollars from a woman I worked with. It ran perfectly and hadn't required any maintenance except new tires. We had no monthly car payments, and I could put the top down to transport furniture or paintings. But it was a used Chevrolet without cachet. So one weekend, driving back from a social event in Virginia, Mac swung into a foreign-car dealership, saying, "We need a new car. Let's look at some," and within an hour we drove out as the new owners of a brand-new, fire engine red Alfa Romeo sedan. I hadn't even known it was possible to buy a car on the spot. I had just found out I was pregnant, and while I thought the car would be fun, I also thought it was hardly a car for a new family.

One Sunday a few weeks later—June 13, 1971, to be precise—Mac suggested we take a Sunday drive out to Front Royal. He wanted a destination that entailed a long drive, and seventy-five miles each way seemed like a good trip. We also had a houseguest from Austria, Heinz Opelz, a graduate-school friend who worked in Geneva at the International Atomic Energy Agency, and who was enthusiastic about seeing part of the Appalachian Trail. That lovely June morning I packed a picnic and we set out for the Skyline Drive, the picturesque road that cuts along the ridgeline of the Blue Ridge Mountains. As an afterthought, I put the Sunday *New York Times* in the trunk along with the picnic basket.

Sometime in the early afternoon, after the picnic had been consumed and we were relaxing in a dappled, oak-shaded picnic area looking out over the hazy blue hills of the Shenandoah Valley, Mac and Heinz decided to take a short hike to see if they could intersect with the Appalachian Trail. Heinz was a serious hiker and was intrigued with the idea of a single trail that stretched over a thousand miles from Maine to Georgia. Since I was over five months pregnant by then, I was not so enthusiastic about hiking. I said I would happily stay behind and read the paper.

After they left, I opened the paper on the picnic table and saw a jolting headline:

PENTAGON STUDY TRACES THREE DECADES OF GROWING U.S. INVOLVEMENT

A massive study of how the United States went to war in Indochina, conducted by the Pentagon three years ago, demonstrates that four administrations progressively developed a sense of commitment to a non-Communist Vietnam, a readiness to fight the North to protect the South, and an ultimate frustration with this effort—to a much greater extent than their public statements acknowledged at the time.

The 3,000-page analysis, to which 4,000 pages of official documents are appended, was commissioned by Secretary of Defense Robert S. McNamara and covers the American involvement in Southeast Asia from World War II to mid-1968—the start of the peace talks in Paris after President Lyndon B. Johnson had set a limit on further military commitments and revealed his intention to retire.

Most of the study and many of the appended documents have been obtained by the New York Times *and will be described and presented in a series of articles beginning today. . . .*

The months from the beginning of 1964 to the Tonkin Gulf incident in August were a pivotal period, the study makes clear, and the Times *begins its series with this phase.*

The headline alone was unusual, because the *Times* of that era rarely ran large headlines. I spread the newspaper out over the picnic table, anchored several sections by rocks so it wouldn't blow away, and buried myself reading page after page of excerpts from obscure Pentagon documents. Nothing like this official material had appeared in the public domain before. An article by Neil Sheehan introduced the scope of the materials and explained it was taken from a forty-volume decision-making history of the Vietnam War compiled in the Pentagon.

Within Congress it was fairly well accepted that the Tonkin Gulf incident and the circumstances that authorized the war in Vietnam had never happened. But that was insider information that had never found its way to the public before. The publication of the Pentagon Papers, as they were later called, was rewriting history.

When Mac and Heinz came back from their hike, I was still buried in the newspapers. It was the first time all the doubts about American policy had reached the public in official form. Commissioned by Robert McNamara, who had lost confidence that the war was winnable even while he was responsible as secretary of defense for prosecuting it, the papers described the bureaucratic decision making about why we were still bombing a peasant country half a world away and using more bombs that we had used in all of World War II to carry on a war most insiders knew we could not win. The documents had been provided to the *Times* by an anonymous source.

As we drove through the violet-tinged dusk back toward Washington, we talked about the Pentagon Papers and American foreign policy and who could have been the source of such a significant leak. After describing the huge anti–Vietnam War demonstrations taking place in Europe, Heinz asked me, "Do you have any idea who might be the source?" Heinz was in the passenger seat so he could better see the scenery. I was in the backseat with the newspaper. He turned around from the front seat to look at me.

"My guess is Dan Ellsberg," I suggested, recalling Ellsberg's intensity and his résumé. I hadn't known much about Ellsberg when I invited him to the congressional conference on war crimes and national responsibility but after he caused me so much trouble by threatening to sue the congressmen, I had made it my business to learn a lot more. Ellsberg had a Zelig-like presence during the course of the Vietnam War. He had worked for McNamara as one of the "whiz kids" in the Pentagon when the war was being planned; then in Vietnam under Lansdale, where the war was being executed; finally emerging as a peacenik, albeit with powerful friends, as the war was being lost. Ellsberg's PhD dissertation at Harvard in economics had been in decision-making theory. The essence of the material I had been reading in the *New York Times*, as I interpreted it, was about flawed decision making and the anti-learning mechanisms of bureaucracies. This inability to *learn* (repeated in our current war in Iraq) stemmed from pervasive secrecy, the rapid turnover of personnel in both military and civilian bureaucracies, the lack of institutional memory, the failure to study history, and the unrelenting pressures for optimistic reports. I would add the lack of knowledge of and respect for foreign cultures and religions, and the national propensity to see problems in terms of military rather than political solutions. Except for the last two, these were Ellsberg's themes.

By June 13, 1971, however, I was no longer thinking along the accepted narrative lines of American foreign policy. I had been spending time in the Library of Congress researching my book, and I was trying to figure out who actually made American foreign policy. I was learning that, historically, American women had tried to influence foreign policy, to build respect for international law, to address the sources of poverty and injustice that created the conditions for war. By and large, most had been dismissed as subversives, unpatriotic, or enemies of the state. (Emily Greene Balch, for example, who won the Nobel Peace Prize in 1946, was dismissed from her job as an economics professor at Wellesley in 1918 because of her pacifist activities during World War I.)

It was only three weeks after our trip along Skyline Drive that Mac came home with the news that he wanted us to move to Lagos, Nigeria. I always remembered the moment because I was wearing the same dress in the photo Heinz took of us before he left. It was one of those long Marimekko dresses with huge flowers that were so popular. Although the marriage would last another three years, the moment of the Marimekko photo was the beginning of its end.

That marked the same moment I began reading Virginia Woolf. In life, as in art, transitions are the most difficult. It is the point in time that one element becomes something else, the delicate moment at which an old equilibrium must be abandoned for one that is not yet established.

At first Woolf was too deep for me. She was an artist of the unnamed, the invisible, the silent. I still believed in direct cause and effect, in facts, in the details of observed realities. As Arvonne recommended, I started reading *Three Guineas* during that summer, but I found it difficult. Her ideas about gender and empire were beyond my conceptual abilities at that time. She was writing about the inexorable forward motion of unseen forces. My consciousness was too limited to grasp the level at which Woolf wrote about culture and empire—about symbols and structure.

"So start with her novels," said Arvonne, when I explained this. "Or read *A Room of One's Own*. It's easier. I'll bet some of the women in your consciousness-raising group have read *A Room of One's Own*," she said. "Ask them."

Arvonne was right. Some of them had.

My consciousness-raising group was made up of women I had met in the Library of Congress. Consciousness-raising groups were the mechanism that transformed the women's liberation movement into a mass movement and politicized an entire generation of women. (They were the forerunners of this era's book-reading groups.) Small groups of women meeting in living rooms were utterly different from impersonal political organizations. Their origin supposedly came from Mao Tse-tung's China and the "speak bitterness" groups that Chairman Mao organized to stamp out the authority of the old elite, ruling classes. But one woman in our group, who was Chinese and knowledgeable about China, said such groups were to promote

Mao's Cultural Revolution, and were very different from women's consciousness-raising groups in America. No matter. The idea as it took form in the United States spread like the craze for Beatles music. Women bonded like members of a bomber crew in a World War II movie. Sisterhood *was* powerful.

Most of the women in my consciousness-raising group came from the B deck of the Library of Congress. Our group formed over lunch one day in the Library of Congress cafeteria. We recognized that we all had one thing in common—perilous futures in the public world. In government, academia, business—women were relegated to the margins, always in administrative jobs supporting men. There was no subtlety to that simple fact. Most of the other women I met there were academics without institutional connections. They had excellent credentials but slim possibilities of getting academic jobs other than as visiting lecturers, a semester at a time. Claire Sherman was an art historian and an expert on medieval manuscripts; Ellen Miles was an intern at the National Gallery (now she is the curator of painting at the National Portrait Gallery). Recalling that the first meeting of our group took place in my living room, Miles remembered driving up Tregaron's long driveway, walking through the garage part of the carriage house, and wondering what kind of group ours would be. "You were pregnant," she recalled.

I had learned that getting people together and engaged in conversation is the first step in any political organizing, so hosting the first meeting seemed to be a good step toward positive action. (Besides, everyone always wanted the opportunity to see what lay inside the gates of Tregaron.) We agreed there would be no official leader, but there would be rules. Everything said inside the room would be confidential. We were not to make personal judgments. We would not call on experts or discuss theories in books. Sharing and analyzing our own personal experience was the subject of the meeting. Our purpose was to find wisdom in our common experiences. No topic was off limits. Gradually we added other members and moved on to meetings in other people's living rooms. It brought together women who might never have met socially. The discussions were exhilarating, challenging, and energizing.

Other groups had published guidelines for organizing a consciousness-raising group and we used them. We questioned all assumptions about the organization of women's lives, from the conditions we faced at work to discussing heretofore private issues like doing housework, raising children, and the idea of partnership in marriage. We named the realities of "sexual harassment" and the still unnamed conditions that made up a "hostile work environment." We discussed birth control, the Pill, the side effects from the Pill (hormone levels were too high), the ability to plan pregnancies, the sexual revolution (Hugh Hefner's Playboy Clubs didn't seem very revolutionary to women), money management, male doctors who didn't take our questions seriously, and husbands who refused to do housework because it was unmanly. We questioned why women couldn't have credit cards or mortgages or bank loans, subjects of considerable importance to the single women in the group. When one of the unmarried women bought a car, she had to pay cash because it was hard for a woman to get credit or financing on her own without a male cosigner.

As we told stories about our lives that we believed to be unique, we discovered our experiences had resonance for everyone. It was through analyzing the commonalities in our own personal experiences that we gained an understanding of women's collective experience. Although we were different ages, from different generations, and from different economic backgrounds, all of us understood the experience of being marginalized. Gradually, "I" became "we."

At the time, I was the only one who was pregnant, and I told the group how astounded I was when my obstetrician dismissed my questions by saying, "Oh, you don't need to worry your pretty head about that." I expected to be an informed participant in childbirth while he assumed I would be a passive medical consumer. "After all, it is my body," I repeated. I was speaking in part from the fears of my Catholic girlhood, when a pregnant woman was viewed as renting out her body to the sacred life of the baby. If there was any emergency whereby a choice had to be made between saving the life of the mother or the life of the baby, the baby won.

"Get a medical textbook on obstetrics and gynecology from the library," suggested Ann, who was older and had two children. "Just don't pay too much attention to all the things that can go wrong." Ann worked for the Office of Management and Budget and had brought into the group a friend named Millie, who worked for the CIA. Even though it occurred to several of us that Millie might be reporting the contents of our meetings back to her supervisor, she also told many stories about how the "girls" at the CIA were treated, regardless of age or rank. (Later, when the women of the CIA filed a class-action suit over gender discrimination in promotions and pay, the suit was secret and the women had to use the CIA's law firm, which meant that the plaintiff and defendant were using attorneys from the same firm, which in every other field is considered a conflict of interest.)

That group that formed in my living room in 1971 also attracted a number of women in the arts, reorganized itself several times, and eventually morphed into a working group for Washington Women in the Arts, staying in operation for the next sixteen years.

Fall 1971

Mac's father died in September. I was eight months pregnant when we drove to New Jersey for the funeral. I remember crying uncontrollably and not really knowing why I was crying, except that the circumstances of his death had been very difficult. After the mass I stood with Mac's mother on the steps of the church as she pointed out various dignitaries from New York who had come for the funeral.

"There's Bill Renchard," she said. "He's the chairman of Chemical Bank."

"Oh, yes," I murmured. "I remember him from the retirement party."

Mac's father's retirement party, a year earlier, had been the single most painful social event I had ever attended. That was probably why I was crying.

Mac's father had been a vice president of the Chemical Bank of New York at a critical moment in the bank's history. The *New Yorker* magazine had published a two-part article about one of the first attempted leveraged buyouts of the 1970s, whereby a small high-technology company with a high stock valuation was able to take over a much larger established institution. The buyout in question was New York's venerable Chemical Bank by thirty-four-year-old financial whiz Saul Steinberg. In a preview of the leveraged buyout craze to come, the elevated share price of Steinberg's new technology company—a computer- leasing firm called Leasco—made it possible for him to leverage his share price to buy an old-line,

WASP, traditional bank. By the time Chemical executives figured out the magnitude of the threat, Steinberg owned a large
percentage of their undervalued stock.

Aside from financial considerations, there were a number of
cultural obstacles in the way of Saul Steinberg's offer. First of all,
he was Jewish at a time when commercial banks were owned
and run by WASPS: investment banking was the traditional area
for Jews. Second, his recent messy divorce had ended up in the
tabloids with his first wife accusing him of drug abuse. He also
weighed too much. And he had neither prepped nor gone to an
Ivy League college. He had, though, graduated from Wharton
School of Business, the same school where my father-in-law had
gone. But my father-in-law was an assimilated Irishman.

Chairman Renchard put Mac's father in charge of preventing the takeover. The *New Yorker* writer quoted Bill Renchard
as saying that he had put the strategy for preventing the buyout
in the hands of Joe McFadden. "A nice guy, but not exactly a
pushover either," he commented to the reporter. That simple
declarative sentence masked a tragedy. Just about the same
time as the takeover bid, Mac's father went into the hospital
for exploratory surgery related to a recurrence of throat cancer
that he had suffered decades earlier. It was possible that Mac
and I had not been informed of the seriousness of the surgery,
but when it was over, Mac's father no longer had a jaw or a
mouth. He had to be fed by a tube in his throat. He couldn't
speak. His face ended just below his nose.

Soon after that, Joe McFadden officially retired. His retirement party took place on the top floor of the Chemical Bank
Building on Park Avenue. I heard how Chemical Bank vice
presidents and lawyers took the limousines from the Park Avenue headquarters out to Ridgewood, New Jersey, accompanied
by secretaries and papers and boxes of files. I was told how, under

Mac's father's direction, the hostile takeover was slowed, then halted. Leasco's share price dropped, then fell so precipitously that the buyout was no longer viable. (Steinberg found that his company could no longer afford to buy Chemical Bank. Later Saul Steinberg said, "I always knew there was a club. Only I thought I was part of it.") Other colleagues told war stories from Mac's father's earlier days at the bank. "I remember the day the auditors came and Joe and I had to . . ."

Mac's older brother read his father's heartfelt thank-you speech, everyone applauded, and we were all getting ready to leave. Chairman Renchard came up to my mother-in-law to thank her again and tell her what an extraordinary service Joe had performed for the bank. As I moved away, I heard him say, "Usually we go out to dinner after an event like this, but under the circumstances, it obviously wouldn't be appropriate."

"No, no," said Florence, my mother-in-law. "I think we should go ahead. I know Joe expects it." I couldn't believe what I heard and turned to see the white-faced chairman. He looked stricken. It took him a second or two to compose himself, then he said smoothly, "We hadn't planned on this, so it will take a little while. But of course." He gamely rounded up several vice presidents and their wives and ordered the limousines, and after a twenty-minute wait, off we went to Lutèce, the best French restaurant in New York. I remember thinking, Why is this happening?

When the members of our party made their way into the restaurant, I kept my eyes straight ahead and listened as a wave of silence rolled over the restaurant, soon broken by the sounds of crashing glass, audible gasps, and a cry of "My God!" I didn't even look when I heard a waiter drop an entire tray of food. The shocked response reflected the reaction of everyone who saw Mac's father for the first time after the operation. He was disfigured.

In order to remove all the cancerous tissue, the surgeon connected his upper lip directly to the skin of his neck. I couldn't imagine what had possessed his wife to insist that the dinner take place. The guest of honor, after all, couldn't speak, couldn't eat.

I had no opportunity to say anything to Mac because I was directed to a seat between the chairman and my father-in-law. Waiters immediately took liquor orders, and drinks were in front of us so quickly it seemed magical. Refills appeared when Chairman Renchard raised his hand. The chairman, who was on my right, was telling me about his despair over his daughter's selection of a fiancé. "He's an Italian, of all things," he complained, shaking his head. I asked him if he had ever been to Italy. No. "When we travel," he explained, "we go to England." Meanwhile, the guest of honor, to my left, was writing comments on a notepad and pushing little pieces of paper across the surface of the immaculate white tablecloth. It was Joe McFadden's only way of participating. I took the little squares of paper and tried to send them to the appropriate person at the table without being rude to the chairman, who was clearly not used to having anything but the undivided attention of his audience. The pieces of paper contained sentence fragments, comments relating to conversations that had been launched and were already long downriver.

Now the sommelier was uncorking bottle after bottle of wine, and waiters were gliding out of the kitchen as though they were on roller skates, bringing course after course of exquisitely prepared food. We began to talk about food, great meals that we had had, restaurants we had been to, the merits of Bourgogne wine versus Bordeaux, and how French wines are named for the region where they are produced and not for the grape.

The little notes were like a blizzard now. But everyone had

too much to drink by then to pay attention. No one looked up when I passed the notes down the table. Everyone was deep into the wine and conversations and the luxury of the dining experience at Lutèce. I tried very hard to get drunk, but I seemed to become more and more sober. (That is why I can still remember the dinner in all its detail thirty-five years later.) Joe's eyes darted with a frantic nervousness and perhaps a panic borne of isolation and an inability to make contact with the event, an event that had supposedly been constructed to honor him. He tried to write faster.

I couldn't understand, and said so later to Mac, why his mother would have insisted that such a dinner take place. Why humiliate a proud man just to observe social convention? But there was no discussing it. Mac said it was the way things were done. I asked why such a disfiguring operation had been allowed to take place, since there could never be reconstructive surgery and his life expectancy was less than a year. Mac's father died ten months later. The casket was closed at the wake. But my questions raised much larger questions of values, and by then, I knew that, in our hugely differing responses, we were in trouble.

Six weeks after the funeral, on November 7, 1971, our daughter was born, on Election Day—a good day, I thought, for a child of a political era. I took six weeks off from work—there was no such thing as paid maternity leave at the time—then hired a Guatemalan woman as a nanny for the three days a week that I worked in Congressman Fraser's office, and went back to work. I also returned to reading Virginia Woolf. This time I understood her writing.

Somehow the Fellowship Project and having to learn about the malevolent genius of Cecil Rhodes made me more attuned to the world of war and empire that Virginia Woolf wrote

about. I often think that Rhodes must have been the man Thorstein Veblen had in mind when he proclaimed, "Behind every
great fortune lies a great crime."

By the time I finished the Rhodes scholars project I knew
enough about Cecil Rhodes, Victorian England, and colonial
empires to understand the world of Virginia Woolf. I understood that she was a political thinker as well as a literary genius.
She understood the domestic constructs that support war and
the belief in empire and white, male dominance.

I picked up *Three Guineas* once more, and this time I got it.
She was asking the key questions of our time: How should war
be prevented? Why doesn't the government support education
for women? Why aren't women allowed to engage in professional work?

These are the central questions of modernity and were the
questions of the 1960s women's movement. Although I also
read the great popular books of the period—Betty Friedan's
Feminine Mystique and Kate Millett's *Sexual Politics* and Mari-
lyn French's *The Women's Room* and Germaine Greer's *The
Female Eunuch*—it was Virginia Woolf who really captured
me. She not only dealt with questions about women, she dealt
with war. And the Vietnam War was always with us.

On the bus ride home from work, I stopped taking congressional papers and hearing reports. I read *A Room of One's Own* and
To the Lighthouse and *Mrs. Dalloway*. Virginia Woolf wrote about
shell shock, class, women's second-class status, modern society. I
was fascinated with how skillfully she wrote about women and
war: the domestic arrangements that prop up the public life of
empire, the facades, the hypocrisies that mask devotion to the
ultimate expression of political power—war. I found her lucidity
and her articulated anger stunning. Unlike me, she could say the
unacceptable.

I focused to the point of obsession on the question of Mrs. Ramsay. Why did Mrs. Ramsay die? And what did Mrs. Ramsay die from? Mrs. Ramsay, the heart and central character of the novel *To the Lighthouse,* wove all the other characters together in a community of meaning, a place where they transcended the limitations of their ordinary lives. But Mrs. Ramsay died in a parenthesis, one of the most shocking deaths in literature.

(Mr. Ramsay, stumbling along a passage on a dark morning, stretched his arms out, but Mrs. Ramsay having died rather suddenly the night before, his arms, though stretched out, remained empty.)

Was it possible, I wondered, that Mrs. Ramsay died from being used up by Mr. Ramsay? Mr. Ramsay was uninterested in community, unconcerned about his children except as trophies. He was a man concerned with status, his place in the world, his external achievements. He was the kind of man, in Woolf's words, who "negotiated treaties, controlled finance, ruled India. . . ." He was a man singularly devoid of empathy, and therefore, perhaps, of morality.

My husband, it seemed to me, was becoming a Mr. Ramsay. His boss *was* a Mr. Ramsay. Mac came from a family where convention was all. I knew, deep in my bones, that the life I had constructed was a temporary shelter.

CHAPTER FOURTEEN

Leave the Gun; Take the Cannoli

1974

Job. Marriage. Home. These are the three pillars of adult life, the rituals and institutions upon which we hang our identities. Their loss strips away the person we think we are and leaves us way back inside ourselves, looking out at life as if through a porthole. We see a landscape we don't recognize.

Like the spirit of the sixties itself, by 1974, I felt the vitality of my time in Washington was slipping away. By the middle of 1974 I had lost job, marriage, home.

Just as I wrote myself into the job in Fraser's office, I wrote myself out of it. One day in 1972, going down in the elevator in the Longworth House Office Building, two freshman congresswomen stepped in. One was Louise Day Hicks, an Irish Catholic from south Boston, who was wearing her trademark white gloves. The other was Bella Abzug, a Jewish liberal from Manhattan, who was wearing one of her famous hats. Beyond the fact that they were both women and attorneys and had been elected to Congress in 1970, they had nothing in common politically.

A former Boston School Committee member, Louise Day

Hicks had been elected with the support of the Catholic Church and the Catholic congregations of south Boston, which were actively committed to preventing the racial integration of Boston schools. Bella Abzug was elected to Congress on a feminist and peace platform, and she had a history of working for progressive causes—racial justice, collective bargaining, women's rights, economic fairness, gay rights.

By the time I encountered the two congresswomen in the elevator, I had spent almost two years in the Library of Congress reading the lost history of the women's rights movement in America and had interviewed many women with astonishing life stories. These stories had changed my entire view of politics and American history. I had discovered old documents about women leaders in the abolitionist movements and in the anti-lynching societies in the South, women in the underground railway and civil rights movement, women leaders in labor and child labor movements, women as peace activists and social reformers.

I saw studies by social workers in 1900 that reported that one out of eight women in New York City was engaged in prostitution because of poverty. (So much for the return of family values from the Victorian era, promoted by today's neoconservative women.) I learned that most of the radical thinking about women's role had been formulated by the end of the nineteenth century. Charlotte Perkins Gilman (whose ideas Thorstein Veblen also borrowed) had published articles on almost every social, political, and cultural issue that Gloria Steinem reframed in *Ms.* seventy-five years later. I had come to understand something about the silences of history and why certain events and people are blacked out in order to maintain the official narrative of history. Writing a book had changed me. I had discovered the power of language and history. I had

found my own voice. By the time our elevator reached the bottom floor, I concluded that Bella Abzug was the future; Louise
Day Hicks was the past.

Louise Day Hicks was defeated after one term, and Bella Abzug almost was. Democratic political bosses in New York redis-
tricted Bella Abzug out of her seat and told her to run against a
conservative in Staten Island. She famously answered, "Staten
Island is a great place to take a ferry to, but it's not a place where
I can get elected." Women candidates were always told to run
against conservatives, or run to raise issues, or run to educate
the public and make a good showing. No one, except Eleanor
Roosevelt, told women to run to win. That was, in part, why in
all U.S. history there had been a total of seventy-two women, as
opposed to over eleven thousand men who had served in the
U.S. Congress. All the political machinery favored male candidates.

When Bella Abzug decided to run in a district where she
could win, she broke unspoken rules. By choosing to run in
the Democratic primary in the liberal Upper West Side against
William Fitts Ryan, a longtime, popular liberal and one of my
former bosses, she challenged the tacit understanding that a
Democrat shouldn't challenge someone in a safe seat. To further
complicate an already complex race, Ryan had terminal cancer,
a reality known, but not admitted. Insiders assumed Ryan's
widow would take his seat after his death. "The widow's cloak"
was the only legitimate way women assumed power.

I liked Bill Ryan, and he was always nice to me, but I also
thought there had to be a way for women to get to Congress
without marrying a politician who might have a timely death. (I
also thought Ryan could have resigned due to health reasons.) I
had seen firsthand how little voice women had in policies or the
decisions of government. The overwhelming issue in my life at

that moment was child care, and child care legislation was considered by many in Congress to be one of the most important pieces of social legislation of the decade. When I went with a delegation of women to see Wilbur Mills (the unofficial mayor of the House) to ask if he would consider opening a child care center for women workers, we were laughed out of his office. (I was thrilled when D.C. police later found him drunk in the pool in front of the Jefferson Memorial, along with his companion of the evening, stripper Fanny Fox.) When the House committee was hearing legislation on child care, the entire committee had been immeasurably helped by the expertise of Congresswoman Shirley Chisholm, who had been Supervisor of the Day Care Division for the city of New York before running for Congress. Both houses of Congress had passed a Child Development Bill that would have provided $2 billion to set up model child care centers. President Nixon vetoed it on the grounds that American children needed to be cared for in families, not in government-run day care centers like those in the Soviet Union. (No one looked at day care centers in other industrial democracies, like France, West Germany, Sweden, Denmark, and Norway.)

I had seen and experienced how women—unlike men, who were always rewarded in one way or another for their work in party politics—were expected to find that their labor on behalf of male politicians was its own reward. As Eleanor Roosevelt had observed, women were "frozen out" of real power by a variety of techniques that were an art form unto themselves. Abzug took Eleanor Roosevelt's admonition literally—run to win. She refused to run a political campaign just to raise issues or educate the public. She played the game the way men did. Politics, after all, is about power. I respected that.

I followed Bella Abzug's primary campaign—how the press

called her "predatory" and "power-hungry." She won. Ryan died twelve weeks after the primary. In New York the gossip was, "She killed him." Within Congress, no one said it publicly. Even though she won the primary and the election, the bitter residue of that campaign lasted throughout Abzug's career. One of the great accomplishments of her election was that she had somehow convinced the moral mothers of Women Strike for Peace—who thought politics was a dirty business—to support her campaign. Her stance was that to effect change they needed to elect women themselves instead of continually going to Washington to beg men to pass the laws they wanted. As one of the founders of the National Women's Political Caucus, she also encouraged women to get involved in party politics. She said, and believed, that the age of women stuffing envelopes for male politicians was over.

With the larger historical context that I now had buzzing around my head, I wrote an analysis of the Abzug campaign and sent it to *Ms.* Much to my surprise, Mary Thom, one of the *Ms.* editors for whom I had previously written a short article about Cecil Rhodes, called me back to say they wanted to run the article, but it would have to be longer because Gloria Steinem wanted to make it a cover story. Political articles by women were still something of a novelty, and except for the articles I had written for Erwin Knoll, it was only the second long article I had ever written. I dropped Mac's last name from the byline because I didn't think he should feel any repercussions for anything I wrote. It appeared in February 1973 under my unmarried name, and it was indeed a cover story. That article proved fatal for both my job and my marriage.

Bella Abzug was slow to understand how glacial was the pace of House proceedings or how her impatience and unrealistic expectations made her extremely difficult to work with. At the same time, I had violated a tribal taboo by writing about Bill Ryan. Within a matter of weeks, Arvonne said they were going to have to reorganize the office staff. Don Fraser said he regretted it, but they would need a full-time staff person. But I knew that Don Fraser was a member of the same group of liberal congressmen I had worked for earlier, which had included Bill Ryan. Tribal loyalties meant that the group of congressmen, who should have been Abzug's natural allies within the House, would never accept her—or anyone who defended her.

Bella Abzug was outspoken, brash, fearless, charming, abrasive, insecure, funny, impatient, angry, and very, very smart. (Eddie Hébert from Louisiana said, "She is one of our most brilliant congresswomen.") Like Shirley Chisholm, who was not welcomed by the black caucus, Abzug was not welcomed or accepted by the liberals in the House. I never regretted writing the article. Among her many accomplishments, before she left the House to run for the Senate, she helped to draft the Freedom of Information Act—the very law that eventually enabled me to get my own files out of the FBI.

But by the end of March I was out of a job. I turned my attention to finishing my book and to spending time with my captivating daughter.

In the meantime, Mac was being considered for yet another job, this time as an assistant to George Shultz, who had become secretary of the treasury. I had met several of the Shultz aides after a concert at the Kennedy Center.

Once again I realized I was being looked over. A man who might be going to work for George Shultz needed to have the right wife. "I write a little," I answered when the somewhat humorless aide asked what I did. A wife who was writing magazine articles on a lefty like Bella Abzug and publishing them under her own name in a magazine called *Ms.* was probably not the right wife for someone in the office of the clubbable, avuncular, golf-playing George Shultz.

By the fall of 1973, the level of tension and the lack of communication in our marriage had become unbearable. We began seeing a marriage counselor. Mac said he'd received contact information for Dr. Sandoz★ from someone at the Treasury Department, who had recommended him as "first rate."

We went together for several sessions and then separately. At my first appointment alone, I asked him why he had a newsletter in his waiting room about UFOs.

Dr. Sandoz didn't look like the sort of man who believed in UFOs. "Some of my clients are in the military," he answered, "and work near military testing grounds where civilians report UFOs." I asked if this was Area 51 of the testing grounds north of Las Vegas, then the most famous secret military installation in America.

Dr. Sandoz didn't look like a marriage counselor either. He didn't seem empathic enough to be a therapist, although at the time I had little experience with therapists or what they should look like. He looked hyperalert, with intense eyes. I soon realized he was negotiating the means and methods by which our marriage would be dissolved.

At my next appointment Dr. Sandoz mentioned the CIA, and he inquired whether I had ever asked Mac if he worked for the CIA. I said I had.

"What made you do that?"

I said we had received telephone calls from someone who said Mac really worked in the CIA, not the Treasury Department. "The telephone calls come in the middle of the night. When

---

★ Dr. Sandoz is not his real name.

Mac answers, there would be no one there. When I answer, a male voice says, 'Do you know your husband works for the CIA?'"

"Is that all he said?"

"Yes."

"Did you ask who it was?"

"Of course. He would repeat the question and then hang up."

"Do you think he's having an affair?" asked Dr. Sandoz.

"I have no idea," I answered truthfully. I thought Dr. Sandoz was going to ask me if I thought Mac really did work for the CIA. But he didn't seem to want to follow that line of questioning. Instead, I talked about what I considered the increasing strangeness of Mac's behavior, particularly his lying and his inability to take care of our new baby. The first time I ever left him alone with our daughter, then only a few months old, he accidentally dropped her. The second time, he banged her head on a door frame, again accidentally, with such a thud, she vomited. The next morning, I answered a knock on the door to find our pediatrician, who wanted to inquire if this was a case of child abuse. (I had telephoned the doctor's answering service to find out if we should go to the hospital emergency room.) I didn't dare leave the baby alone with him anymore. Then there was the lying. On a Saturday that I had made a plan to go into the Maryland countryside with another friend who had a new baby, he invited people over for dinner. He promised me that he would take care of everything—buy steaks, cook them, set the table, have the whole meal planned. All I would have to do, he assured me, was put the baby to bed when I got home and sit down to eat. But then when I got home and the guests were about to show up, there were no steaks, no food, no table set. When confronted, he denied that he had ever promised to take care of everything and said it was my fault for spending the afternoon in Maryland.

"Do most of your clients come from the Treasury Department?" I asked Dr. Sandoz.

"No," he answered. "No so many. Many come from the CIA."

"Why would they do that? Come all the way into Pennsylvania Avenue from Langley?" I was confused. Dr. Sandoz's office was on Pennsylvania Avenue, in an office building with a Scandinavian jewelry store on the street level. After every appointment I went in and bought myself a piece of silver jewelry. I still have a favorite silver necklace I bought in that store.

"There's regular bus service between the Federal Triangle and Langley, so it's easy to get here. And not everyone who works for the CIA works at Langley," he answered, looking at me meaningfully. "Many positions in executive offices downtown are filled by CIA officers."

"Oh." I nodded. Oh, I thought. Suddenly, I was very, very cold. So cold I was afraid my teeth would chatter. It had started to happen a lot, this abrupt drop in body temperature. I was so cold I began talking about Greece, and the warmth of the sun in Crete.

"What were you doing in Greece?" asked Dr. Sandoz reasonably.

I was traveling with five Greek architectural students, hitchhiking among the islands of the Cyclades on fishing boats. I had no camera, but I saw sights I have never forgotten, colors and scenes that had the quality of a dream, more real than real life—dolphins swimming up to the lights on the stern and dancing in the beams of light.

We traveled at night because the fishermen fished at night. The boats were small, so we split up and two of us went on each boat. We stopped at different islands—Paros, Naxos, each with its own myth or legend. Stories, I began to realize, were a way of linking geography, of connecting disparate points and creating coherent worlds. But we drew from very different cultural traditions, the Greek students and I. Greeks know the characters of Homer's epic poems the way Americans know baseball heroes.

When we reached Crete, we split up; they went back to Athens to start school. I began hitchhiking with an American soldier who was staying at the same student hostel I was and wanted to go up in the mountains to Zeus's cave.

The soldier and I hitchhiked as far as we could and then finally took a local bus up to the village closest to the cave of Zeus. The mountains were in fog. We could see nothing of the famous valley. At the cave, the guides spoke only Italian or German. Although the American soldier was stationed in Italy, he didn't know any Italian. So I provided a sketchy translation of the story of Zeus's birth as I interpreted it, similar to the birth of Christ.★ The visit to Zeus's cave had been rather disappointing, although my Greek friends had promised if I traveled to Zeus's cave I would get a glimpse of my future.

After lunch in the sleepy village we boarded the bus and headed back down toward the port of Agios Nikolaos, where I planned to get the ferry to Rhodes. The trip down, however, revealed a completely transformed landscape. The fog had

---

★ Zeus's mother, Rhea, wife of Chronos (the word for *time* in Greek) and a Great Goddess herself, had to flee her kingdom because she feared for her unborn child. One of the priests had told Chronos that one of his children would usurp him, so Chronos had eaten all their children. The pregnant Rhea traveled the Mediterranean but, fearing the wrath of Chronos, no one would take her in when she was ready to give birth. So Zeus was born in a cave. A Cretan shepherd found the baby and raised him. As Zeus grew up, he discovered his godlike powers. He returned to the kingdom and killed Chronos, disgorged all his siblings from Chronos's gut, and parceled out their dominions over land, sea, heaven, and earth. These twelve siblings were the Olympians, the new gods of Homer's Greece, who lasted another two thousand years until the birth of the son of Zeus, Jesus, a single male figure in a tripartite god of father, son, and holy ghost. (Rhea had been a tripartite female god.)

burned off, and out of the mountain mists the valley suddenly materialized, an immense, ravishing patchwork of green and gold—of barley and oat fields, apple and pear orchards, almond and olive trees. More astonishing was the sight of a thousand windmills with white sails turning in the breeze. The entire valley floor was dotted with windmills—thousands of slender, graceful metal towers with white canvas sails. It was one of the most dazzling landscapes I had ever seen. The valley seemed out of time. I had the sense of moving very slowly, as if I were underwater. As the bus chugged across the valley floor, I glimpsed women in black separating wheat from chaff by tossing it in the air with long wooden pitchforks, just as I had seen on the bus crossing the Anatolian plain of Turkey.

The bus ride, however, was unexpectedly short; its destination was Heraklion, in the opposite direction from Agios Nicholaos. The soldier and I got out and began hitchhiking again on an empty mountain road, with few vehicles of any kind passing by. Luck was with us. Soon a lone Englishman driving a snappy Rover picked us up. And what a talker he was! Any subject we brought up, he knew something—a lot—about it. Down we went through the rugged mountains, taking hairpin turns, descending from the clouds.

"How did you happen to come to Crete?" the soldier asked.

"I was here in the fifties in the service," said our driver. The two men talked about battles that had taken place in Crete during World War II and why the guides at Zeus's cave spoke only Italian or German. "Terrible fighting in Crete," said the Englishman. "The Germans occupied one half of the island while the Italians occupied the other, until 1943, when the Italians deposed Mussolini. That's why the only foreign languages the guides speak are German or Italian. Germans killed thirty civilians every time the Greek resistance shot one German soldier.

Sixty thousand British troops had to be evacuated from the south side of the island. Have you been to the south side? Mountains go right down to the sea. Not easy to evacuate from that coast. Right now there's a group of American hippies living in the caves. Every time the police try to get rid of them they climb up higher. The Romans used those caves as burial tombs."

I inquired why he had come up into the mountains.

"Olive oil. See that jug of olive oil I've got in the back. It's the best I've found anywhere. Olives, dates, citrus fruits, wheat, barley—they can grow anything up here." And so he talked the entire way down the mountain, telling us how the Minoans had farmed and irrigated this same valley four thousand years ago and how they used wind power as an energy source. I was sitting in the front seat and closed my eyes as he zipped around the curves, with his hand on the horn, but without applying his foot to the brakes. The road next to my side dropped off into a steep gorge. Suppose there was a car coming in the opposite direction? I bit my lip and concentrated on the conversation.

The soldier asked about the resistance movement in Crete. I asked about Knossos.

In no time, we had reached the outskirts of Agios Nikolaos, and, instead of dropping us off, the Englishman asked if we'd like to come to his house for a glass of wine and a spot of lunch, even though it was late afternoon. He said he was enjoying the opportunity to speak English.

"I haven't had anyone except my poor wife to speak to in months."

We, of course, said yes. His blond wife and two blond children, who were about six and four, seemed a bit surprised to have him show up with two scruffy hitchhikers. But she made sandwiches and then said she had to take the children, who were tanned and shirtless, off to do an errand. He opened a bottle of wine that we finished off pretty quickly. Then another.

The house reminded me of Nigel's house on Hydra, but it was better furnished and less temporary. In one corner of the living/dining room I noticed in front of the window a typewriter surrounded by piles of paper and books. "What do you write?" I asked, gazing at the typewriter, which shimmered in the rays of setting sun that came through the window.

"Oh, nothing much," he said offhandedly. "I just finished something up." This, I noted, was the only subject he was not willing to pursue. Instead, he returned to his conversation with the soldier about 1946 and the Greek civil war and the founding of the American CIA.

"It's really good to speak English," he repeated. As we finished off the second bottle of wine, his wife and children returned from their errand and the children began agitating to go somewhere. As we were leaving, I admired a thick walking stick propped up against the doorway. It was twisted and gnarled but with a smooth surface. It looked very old. "Where did you get it?" I asked.

"Up in the Valley of the Windmills," he answered. "Not far from where I picked you up. Please take it," he said, handing it to me.

"Oh, I wouldn't think of it." I was taken aback.

"Please," he insisted. I refused again. But he insisted again. "I can get another one," he said emphatically. Then I had the feeling that the gracious thing might be to take it. So the walking stick came with me to Rhodes, and to other islands whose names I can no longer remember, and finally back to Piraeus, where I absentmindedly left it on a luggage cart.

I did not tell all this to Dr. Sandoz. Instead, I told him the plot of a book I had just finished by John Le Carré. "What surprised me is that the preface is signed in Crete. Agios Nicolaos, August 1964. That's exactly when I was in Crete. In that town even. It was very warm that summer." I was actually struggling with the idea that it might have been John Le Carré's walking stick I had left on the Pireaus luggage cart.

"What's the title?"

"*A Small Town in Germany,* and it takes place in an East German town in the middle of winter. Freezing, actually. It's about a spy. Betrayal. His books are always about betrayal."

I was trying to absorb the epiphany I'd just had: if I was seeing a CIA therapist under the guise of a marriage counselor, I was in the middle of a John Le Carré plot myself. That was my last appointment with Dr. Sandoz. I told Mac that I felt I needed to find my own therapist, and I did.

In January 1974 Mac moved out into a new apartment by himself. His mother came to Washington and made him curtains. He was soon involved with a woman from his office who had two children. It was also the middle of the Arab oil embargo, and he began flying back and forth to Saudi Arabia. One time, after he had refused to return any of my phone calls, I surprised him at the diplomatic gate of the airport and heard the guard ask him if he was carrying a gun. Do economists carry guns? I wondered.

Like Mrs. Post, who had found that Joe Davies was not the man she thought—"He should have been an actor; his whole life was an act"—I had married someone whose real life I knew nothing about. Some wives might not have needed to know. Some might have taken the prescription for Valium that Dr. Sandoz offered me. Some might have been satisfied with the financial rewards, interesting vacations, comfortable status.

I was not one of them.

I concentrated on finishing my book.

One flawless spring morning in April, while walking around Tregaron with my daughter, who was now two and a half, I encountered Senator Joe Tydings, Joe Davies's grandson. Joe Tydings was one of the heirs of Tregaron. (Joe Davies's daughter, Eleanor, had married Senator Millard Tydings of Maryland.) We chatted for a few moments, then Senator Tydings startled me with his next remark.

"I hear you're going to be moving."

I was stunned. Moving? Senator Tydings delivered his message of displacement as a statement, not a question, just in case I was missing the larger lesson that the ground beneath my feet was not firm.

"Oh," I answered breathlessly, trying to get my voice back. "I didn't know." I wanted to ask him where I was going. But Senator Tydings looked at me knowingly, nodded his head from a great height, and walked on, the padrone on his plantation.

It turned out that Mac had canceled the lease with the bank without informing me. Soon I received a notice from the bank telling me that the carriage house was going to be used for other purposes and I would have to move.

Mac was moving on and up in the Treasury Department. More trips to Saudi Arabia. More oil. More status. He was, after all, a man who "negotiated treaties, controlled finance, ruled India. . . ."

I, on the other hand, had a toddler, no money to pay for child care, and soon no home. How could I qualify for an apartment? Mac was not generous. He took everything of value that we owned and denied that he could pay anything but the minimum for child support. I didn't believe him because the woman who did our taxes told me he had inherited a lot of money when his father died. I knew little about the economics of divorce, and the lawyer I consulted, who had excellent feminist credentials, seemed to know even less. The lesson I learned from the divorce negotiations was that whoever has the best lawyer and can afford to negotiate the longest, wins.

My meeting with Joe Tydings made me recall that I had always found it astonishing that, with all her prominence and social position, Mrs. Post had been the one to leave; she had not been able to negotiate a better settlement for herself. What I hadn't understood was how skillfully her eviction had been executed. The story about the estate being a wedding present was a fiction. When it came time to divide property, Davies called in his lawyer, Senator Millard Tydings, his son-in-law and the chairman of the Senate Foreign Relations Committee. No one knows what exactly was said, but when the negotiations were over, Mrs. Post had to pack up and leave. I suspect that Tydings senior negotiated with the same imperial certainties he brought to foreign affairs. Mrs. Post might have gotten her first glimpse of the back room of American politics, where they let her know that she was just a girl from Battle Creek, Michigan, who had inherited a lot of her daddy's money.

Before I left Washington, I held a big yard sale. I was selling off the artifacts of my life. But even in the chaos, Mrs. Post's presence insinuated itself. I became not only retailer and cashier but local historian. "My grandmother worked in Mrs. Post's kitchen," a West Indian woman from Florida Avenue told me, while she pored over the story of my life spread out on card tables in the courtyard. "I've always wanted to own something from Tregaron," another woman announced, enthusiastically holding up a wicker chair. I started to tell her that my odd pieces of furniture, old wedding presents, records, books, and miscellany were hardly "from Tregaron." But then I stopped; after all, they were.

My Mrs. Ramsay theory is that isolation and emotional

disconnection can kill you. I had watched the wives of many of Mac's friends come down with life-threatening illnesses. While the husbands, concerned about the trajectories of their careers, turned themselves into the intellectual clerks organizing the paperwork of the war, they also projected their anxieties, their repressed conscience, and their paralyzed awareness onto their wives and children. Women and children first is still a relevant slogan.

I agreed with Alice Walker when she wrote, "No person is your friend . . . who demands your silence or denies your right to grow and be perceived as fully blossomed as you were intended."

So ten years later, when my daughter asked about that photograph and the disconnect between then and now, I told her that was a girl I had to leave behind.

EPILOGUE: Conversations with History

1977

Lowell, Massachusetts, once the urban industrial nightmare that my grandmother and mother told me about, was America's first planned industrial city. Chosen for its proximity to the Merrimac River, the city was designed around a series of canals that allowed every mill to have access to water. Its spaciousness and utopian design, lauded by Charles Dickens on his trip through the United States in the 1840s, lasted only a short time. By the twentieth century, it was a city that inspired everyone with the slightest bit of ambition and talent—among them Jack Kerouac and Leonard Bernstein—to leave and never return.

So why, in 1977, was I holding my book publication party in a renovated Lowell mill?

One of my first jobs upon returning to Massachusetts (I would have many jobs, not a career) was to work on a federal state commission supervising the restoration of industrial Lowell as a national park, now known as the Lowell National Historic Park.

The canals were restored, the river locks put in working order, some of the mills—like the immense Boott Mill—renovated and fitted out with deafening working looms. The dilapidated boardinghouses and ancillary outbuildings were shored up, painted, and turned into exhibits. Lowell wasn't Williamsburg, but the city revealed working-class history that had never been excavated before. As the first urban national park in the country, Lowell was unique in illustrating the historic choices made in balancing technological creativity and human cost. I arrived on the commission just in time to weigh in on the argument over historical emphasis: the genius of Francis Cabot Lowell or the wages and working conditions for the mostly female labor force.

So in the fall of 1977, when my book on women was published, a friend with whom I had worked on the Lowell Commission arranged for a publication party in one of the restored mills. My daughter, then six years old, danced around one of the looms that my grandmother might have worked on.

On July 4, 1974, I had packed up my child and two suitcases of clothes, put my bicycle on the back of the car, and headed back to the small town in Massachusetts where I came from. I had arrived in Marblehead at the historical moment when the women's movement had reached small-town America, President Richard Nixon was forced to resign, reactionary forces regrouped, and the vitality of the 1960s ended.

In Marblehead, I joined a women's group in which the focus was work—mainly because every woman in the group had to make a living. In presenting my work history (we all had to create a work autobiography), I told the group about the Frenchwoman in Paris who had given me the key to successfully confronting Monsieur Gaya. When I finished, a woman I didn't know spoke up from the back of the room: "Did she have red hair? And did her desk sit in front of a long French window that overlooked a small park?" Against all odds, Ann Monroe of Marblehead had been Madame Gillet's previous American tutor, from five years before me, when Madame was still married to her second husband and had a different name.

At a fund-raiser held in a private home on Marblehead Neck for the Equal Rights Amendment—which at that point was within three states of ratification—I had to walk through a group of demonstrators, more men than women, wearing green hospital scrubs spattered with faux blood and carrying bloodied dolls or fetuses in large jars or signs saying that passage of the ERA meant abortion and murder. Who were these people? No one had ever seen them before. It turned out that some of them were Mormons from out of town; they were part of the religious coalition that had mobilized to defeat the ERA. They also wanted the Supreme Court decision of the previous year that legalized abortion, *Roe v. Wade,* reversed. They were scary. Marblehead Neck is a quiet residential area by the ocean. The swarms of blood-spattered demonstrators were something we hadn't seen before.

The women's movement lost momentum, then slowed, then stopped. The pendulum began its swing in the opposite direction. America is a country of great technological sophistication, but it is also a country of "crude Old Testament literalism, of coarse nationalism, of company towns . . . and the ethics of the frontier." President Jimmy Carter brought religious leaders into the White House for a presidential conference on family and charged them with setting out a "family policy" for America. The spirit of social engagement of the sixties disappeared into the era of the leveraged buyout, the new capitalism, and the entry of fundamentalist religious organizations into electoral politics.

But the institutionalized changes that the women's movement

brought about had fundamentally changed American life. Girls played team sports with coaches and uniforms and away games and athletic scholarships. Women went to law schools and business schools and medical schools and engineering schools. Women became judges and bus drivers and mailpersons. My daughter colored her Easter eggs on the *New York Times* op-ed page that carried my article on the gender gap in voting patterns. These changes did not "just happen." Women actively fought the dynamics of exclusion and in one generation succeeded in enlarging the concept of human rights. The women's movement that came out of the 1960s was the most successful and transformative social movement of the twentieth century.

I wouldn't trade that experience of friends, community, and the exhilaration of seeing a world made fresh for anything. I never looked back. Mac got the career and life he deserved. The laws of history and consequence catch up with everyone. My book didn't go out of print, was expanded in a subsequent edition, and became a staple in American history and women's history classes, from high schools to graduate schools (and is still in print thirty years later).

I left behind big ambitions, and the big raid on success. A happy child, a good book, a creative life—that would do.

Acknowledgments

The seed for this book began with a casual question at the Yaddo dinner table (Has anyone had dinner at Lutèce?) in the fall of 1995. The essay triggered by that question appeared in *American Voice* (a literary journal established by Sally Bingham to encourage women's voices) in the summer of 1996. Over the twelve years it has taken for me to follow the journey of discovery hidden in that essay, many people have helped in many different ways—shared stories of their own experiences in the sixties, sent or loaned me books and articles, given me names of people I should interview, read proposals, critiqued multiple drafts of chapters, analyzed how men's and women's sixties experiences were different, helped me extract my files from the FBI, told me to stop looking for a book that was a model, read the entire manuscript, and confirmed my original idea that the much-misunderstood decade was the source and success of changing women's lives for the better. I, of course, take full responsibility for all judgments, interpretations, and any errors of fact.

Many thanks to: the late Nadya Aisenberg, Kate Auspitz,

Anne Bernays, Elise Boulding, Ben Brooks, Nancy Brooks, Scott Campbell, Kate Canfield, Congressman Michael Capuano, Dick and Dodi Cole, Jill Ker Conway, Charlet and Peter Davenport, Honorable Don Edwards, Dan Ellsberg, Marguerite Feitlowitz, Susie Fisher, Sarah Flynn, Arvonne Fraser, Ann Goodsell, Elizabeth Graver, Mona Harrington, Pat Harrison, Jean Hey, Emily Hiestand, Barbara Hindley, Amy Hoffman, Arlene and Sheldon Holen, Bonnie Howard, Susan Indresano, Susan Jhirad, Miriam Kahn, Justin Kaplan, Jane Katims, Jane Holtz Kay, Susanna Kaysen, Anne Leslie, Linda Malm (and other members of the Tufts class of 1962 who shared their experiences), Cristina McFadden, Jane Midgley, Ellen Miles, Senator Maurine Neuberger, Jack Nies, Laurie Carter Noble, Gina Ogden, Marcus Raskin, Jack Russell, Terry Russell, Charlotte Sheedy, Herman Sinaiko, Patricia and Stuart Snyder, Louise Steinman, Grace Talusan, Maria Van Dusen, Edward Weisband, the late Sarah Wernick, Kate Williams, Rosemary Winfield, Charlene Woodcock.

Special thanks go to Betsy Amster, who patiently shaped the proposal; Jill Ker Conway, who enlarged my mental framework of memoir and history and asked the big questions; Claire Wachtel, who lived up to her reputation as a merciless but brilliant editor. Also many thanks to the HarperCollins team, including Julia Novitch, Katherine Beitner, and Elizabeth Harper.

I am also grateful for institutional support including residency fellowships at Yaddo, MacDowell Artists Colony, and the Rockefeller Foundation's Center in Bellagio, Italy, where I was able to reflect on my Bologna experience of thirty years earlier. The Ludwig Vogelstein Foundation provided a grant for research and interviews in Washington, D.C.

Judith Nies, Cambridge, Massachusetts
January 12, 2008

Notes

Chapter 1 They Want You to Answer Some Questions
   3 **"Who are Southern and Holcomb?":** Letter to Thomas M. Hughes from J. H. McFadden, Jan 31, 1971. 1978 FOIA request.
   4 **"The file was on *you*":** 1976 FOIA request, FBI File; 2000 FOIA request, FBI File.
   9 COINTELPRO and Operation Chaos were two domestic programs aimed at infiltrating dissenting organizations and disrupting activists within the United States. The FBI launched COINTELPRO (Counter Intelligence Program) while the CIA launched Operation Chaos, a domestic espionage program aimed at antiwar resisters and campus radicals. When a special Senate intelligence committee under Frank Church examined the two programs in 1976, they found that the CIA had a computer index of three hundred thousand Americans, the FBI had files on over thirteen thousand, and over one thousand organizations had been infiltrated. See also Frederick Donner, *The Age of Surveillance* (New York: Random House, 1981).

13 **"The Questions":** My husband gave me a list of specific questions to answer. Later, I wrote my answers in a separate letter, but my letter was never submitted. Instead, my husband folded them into his own letter of January 31, 1971. 1978 FOIA request.

Chapter 2 The Most Interesting Job in Washington

15 **considered by many to be a political genius:** Author interview with the Honorable Don Edwards, June 12, 1998, Mayo, Maryland; telephone interview with Arvonne Fraser, February 24, 1999; author interview with Marcus Raskin, March 8, 1999, Washington, D.C. See also, John Jacobs, *A Rage for Justice: The Passion and Politics of Phillip Burton* (Berkeley: University of California Press, 1995).

18 **decided to meet more formally:** author interview with Don Edwards, June 11, 1998.

23 **trade book publisher in New York:** *War Crimes and the American Conscience* (New York: Holt, Rinehart & Winston, 1971). The hearings on which the book was based, the Congressional Conference on War and National Responsibility, took place on February 20–21, 1970, in the Rayburn House Office Building. Reviews in many newspapers and magazines called the subsequent book "the most important book on Vietnam in print."

23 **last-minute addition to the hearing's invitation list:** A photocopy of the letter of invitation to Dan Ellsberg was provided to me by Dan Ellsberg.

25 **potential nominee for the U.S. Supreme Court:** Eckhardt obituary, *New York Times,* November 16, 2001; interview with Marcus Raskin, March 8, 1999. Bob Eckhardt survived for fourteen years in Congress as a liberal Democrat, even though his Houston, Texas, constituency was conservative

and filled with petrochemical plants. Columnist Molly Ivins said, "He believed in representing people, not industry." His reputation as a skillful legislative draftsman is remembered in his authorship of the War Powers Act and in the bill that set up the Superfund to clean up polluted sites.

25 **Cardinal Spellman was homosexual and a cross-dresser:** Mentioned in James Carroll's *An American Requiem* (Boston: Houghton Mifflin, 1996) and in John Cooney's *The American Pope: The Life and Times of Francis Cardinal Spellman* (New York: Times Books, 1984). J. Edgar Hoover, as portrayed in Burton Hersh's *Bobby and J. Edgar* (New York: Carroll & Graf, 2007), was less of a cross-dresser and more of a stable married man whose wife was the ever present Clyde Tolson.

26 **campaign for automobile safety:** Ralph Nader, *Unsafe at Any Speed: The Designed-In Dangers of the American Automobile* (New York: Grossman, 1965). See also the documentary film *An Unreasonable Man* (2007) by Henrietta Mantel and Steve Skrovan.

Chapter 3 The Godfather

32 **I had read Jack Kerouac's *On the Road*:** *On the Road* was published in 1957 by Viking Press and became a phenomenon of the 1950s and early '60s. It quickly sold over a million copies, was read by college students across the country, and *Time* magazine named it one of the most influential one hundred books of the century. (Viking resissued a fiftieth anniversary edition in 2007.) It was a time when the male experience was believed to be the universal experience, so I, of course, had no idea that the adventures of these priapic men had little to do with my life's possibilities.

Their women led lives ranging from difficult to desperate. The word *beat* came from the word "beatific" (meaning "to bless or show exalted joy") and was the catalyst for the 1960s counterculture. Kerouac's novels included characters based on his friendships with Allen Ginsberg, Neal Cassady, and William S. Burroughs.

36 **thesis about the Soviet secret police:** Judith Nies, *Evolution of the Soviet Secret Police, 1917–1938* (thesis, Tufts University, 1962).

42 **articles from the *New York Times* and *Ramparts*:** The J. M. Kaplan Fund was one of the foundations revealed to be funding CIA infiltration of student organizations. Sol Stern, "National Student Association and the CIA," *Ramparts*, March 1967, p. 30.

> *It is widely known that the CIA has a number of foundations which serve as direct fronts or as secret "conduits" that channel money from the CIA to preferred organizations. An intimation of the scope of this financial web was afforded the public on August 31, 1964 when Texas congressman Wright Patman in the course of an investigation into the use of foundations for tax dodges, announced that the J. M. Kaplan fund of New York was serving as a secret conduit for CIA funds. . . . It turned out that during the crucial years 1961–63 a number of other foundations had contributed to the Kaplan fund while the fund was serving the CIA.*

Photo of J. M. Kaplan, *New York Times*, August 11, 1964, p. 6. Caption: "*Under Investigation: J. M. Kaplan, former president of Welch Grape Juice Company. He was accused of using tax-free foundation for business manipulation.*" The body of the article explained how the Kaplan Fund lost its tax exempt status in 1957 and 1958 but regained it in 1959.

"Patman Attacks Secret CIA Link. Says Agency Gave

Money to Private Group Acting as Its Sub Rosa Conduit." *New York Times*, September 1, 1964, p. 1.

The Texas Democrat quoted an unidentified official of the agency as having said that the intelligence agency had had an "arrangement" with the J. M. Kaplan Fund of New York City from 1959 until some time this year.

"Kaplan Fund, Cited as CIA Conduit, Lists Unexplained $395,000 Grant," *New York Times,* September 3, 1964, p. 10.

Michael Wood, Epilogue, *Ramparts*, March 1967, p. 50.

For years the U.S. National Student Association has stood for "a free university in a free society." . . . When I was told of [CIA's] infiltration of NSA, I was also told of numerous other organizations similarly infiltrated. . . .

Robert G. Kaiser, "Work of CIA with Youths at Festivals Is Defended," *Washington Post,* February 18, 1967.

Miss Steinem was co-director of the Independent Research Service with Dennis Shaul, a former president of the National Student Association.

Sol Stern, "A Short Account of International Student Politics and the Cold War with Particular Reference to the NSA, CIA, etc.," *Ramparts*, March 1967, p. 32.

Although the official position of the NSA [National Student Association] was not to participate in the youth festivals, important NSA officers and ex-officers were very active in the Independent

Research Service activities in Vienna and Helsinki. The director of the IRS during the Helsinki Youth Festival was Dennis Shaul, who was elected NSA president shortly thereafter. Shaul has also been the recipient of one of the Independence Foundation's "scholarships" in 1964.

"Talk of the Town," the *New Yorker,* July 22, 1996. p. 24.

Robert Kiley, the president of the New York City Partnership and Chamber of Commerce . . . has the unusual distinction of having served in the CIA from 1963 to 1970. He worked, he says, on the "operations" side, funneling Agency money to "international voluntary" bodies like the National Student Association which he ran after graduating from Notre Dame.

Frederick Donner, *The Age of Surveillance* (New York: Random House, 1981), pp. 268–74. Donner discusses the scale and duration of the CIA's involvement in the National Student Association, the Congress for Cultural Freedom, the AFL-CIO's American Institute for Free Labor, the Center for International Studies at MIT, as well as other labor, business, church, university, cultural, and women's groups.

Marcus Raskin, *Ramparts*, March 1967, "And a Judgment," p. 51.

The best way to understand the CIA's motives is to see it as primarily a commercial institution which deals in buying, renting and selling people.

43 President's Commission on the Status of Women: Executive Order no. 10980, *Establishing the President's*

Commission on the Status of Women. Signed by President John F. Kennedy, December 14, 1961.

45 **Contrary to conventional wisdom:** Formation of the Commission on the Status of Women and the composition of the commission members. Ruth Rosen, *A World Split Open: How the Women's Movement Changed America* (New York: Penguin, 2001), pp. 66–69.

47 **revolution in consciousness about cities, nature, and the home:** Rebecca Solnit, "Three Who Made a Revolution—Rachel Carson, Betty Friedan, Jane Jacobs," *The Nation,* April 3, 2006, pp. 29–32.

48 **the Equal Pay Act:** Telephone interview with Senator Maurine Neuberger, June 5, 1997. Senator Neuberger was elected to the U.S. Senate from Oregon from 1960 to 1966 after the death of her husband. Although she succeeded her deceased husband in the U.S. Senate, she ran her own campaigns for the Oregon legislature and was elected for three consecutive terms. Like Edith Green, she had been a teacher, and said Green's dedication to changing laws for women came from having encountered the unjust conditions for women in teaching positions throughout Oregon's rural school systems.

Chapter 4 *The Honorable Schoolgirl*

51 "**World War III, only this time it will be nuclear**": In Graham Allison's classic study of the Cuban missile crisis, *Essence of Decision: Explaining the Cuban Missile Crisis* (Boston: Addison-Wesley, 1999), he states on page 1:

"The Cuban missile crisis stands as a seminal event. History offers no parallel to those thirteen days of October 1962 when the United States and the Soviet Union paused at the nuclear precipice." Roger Hillsman, in *The Cuban Missile Crisis: The Struggle Over Policy* (Westport, CT: Praeger, 1996), dedicates the book to the Kennedy brothers, "without whose leadership the world might well have suffered nuclear war."

53   Estimates varied widely over fatalities in nuclear war scenarios. Allison speculates, "Had war come, it could have meant the death of 100 million Americans and more than 100 million Russians, and millions of Europeans as well."

53   **"looking uncomfortably to the world we inherit":** Port Huron Statement of 1962. Quoted in Todd Gitlin, *The Sixties: Years of Hope, Days of Rage* (New York: Bantam, 1987), p. 27. The tone of the statement also reflects the authors' awareness of an individual life's limited possibilities in the nuclear age. "Our work is guided by the sense we may be the last generation in the experiment with living."

54   **"the world stands at the brink of a second nuclear age":** January 17, 2007, statement by the board of directors of the *Bulletin of Atomic Scientists,* founded in 1945 by scientists involved in the Manhattan Project. The goal of the *Bulletin* was to provide nontechnical information about global security and dangers posed by nuclear weapons. The current reading of five minutes to midnight on the Doomsday Clock is based on the ongoing existence of twenty-six thousand live nuclear weapons, two thousand of which are ready to launch in minutes. The board of directors and the board of sponsors making the clock determination includes eighteen Nobel laureates in science. www.thebulletin.org/minute-to-midnight/timeline.html (accessed 11/10/2007).

55   **"So gorgeous was the spectacle":** Barbara Tuchman, *The Guns of August* (New York: Macmillan, 1962), p. 1.

56   **"A final Club at Harvard":** Often referred to as the Porc, Porcellian is a male-only final club at Harvard. Its reputation is that it is the club for legacies, rich foreigners, preppies, social climbers. (In 2008, final clubs at Harvard are still all male.)

Porcellian was founded in 1791; its members are chosen on the basis of class, wealth, social position. No women, no racial mix, no public high school grads. Franklin D. Roosevelt was rejected by Porcellian. It has many wealthy alumni who give more money to Porcellian than to Harvard. Evan W. Thomas, "The Clubs: Pale, but Still Breathing," *Harvard Crimson,* September 20, 1971. http://www. thecrimson.com/article.aspx?ref=250877 (accessed 9/25/2007).

58   **connections with organized crime:** Joe Kennedy's connection with crime figures has been a subject of controversy. Arthur Schlesinger, the Kennedy family historian, always dismissed such charges out of hand. But Steven Fox, in *Blood and Power: Organized Crime in Twentieth Century America* (New York: Penguin, 1985), describes Joe Kennedy as an upperworld gangster, and devotes an entire chapter to Joe Kennedy's early and ongoing links with underworld gangsters (pp. 306–46). He quotes Ralph Lowell of the Boston Lowells on the tenth reunion of Joe Kennedy's Harvard College class of 1912: "Joe was our chief bootlegger. He arranged with his agents to have the stuff sent in right on the beach at Plymouth. It came ashore the way the Pilgrims did" (p.14). Recent books such as Burton Hersh's *Bobby and J. Edgar* (New York: Carroll & Graf, 2007) trace Joe Kennedy's mob connections, as well as J. Edgar Hoover's case files on Joe Kennedy.

59   **"The eccentric and colorful Paul Linebarger":** *What is SAIS?* (Washington, D.C.: Johns Hopkins School of Advanced International Studies Publications Office, 1987), p. 12.

62   **strontium 90 . . . caused leukemia and other childhood cancers:** Amy Swerdlow, *Women Strike for Peace: Traditional Motherhood and Radical Politics in the 1960s* (Chicago: University of Chicago Press, 1993), p. 43.

62   **scientists . . . believed there was legitimate cause for alarm:** On the current website maintained by the U.S. government's Centers for Disease Control, the section on

Emergency Preparedness and Response has this to say about potential Strontium 90 effects from nuclear testing, terrorists, or plant accidents: "SR–90 is also *found in the environment from nuclear testing that occurred in the 1950s and 1960s.* . . . SR–90 can be inhaled, but *ingestion through food and water is the greatest health concern* (italics added). Once in the body, SR–90 acts like calcium and is readily incorporated in bones and teeth, where it can *cause cancers of the bone, bone marrow and soft tissues around the bone.* . . . SR–90 can be present in dust from nuclear fission after detonation of nuclear weapons or a nuclear power plant accident." http://www.bt.cdc.gov/radiation/isotopes/strontium.asp (accessed 11/10/2007).

63 Photos of "event Annie" and press reports surrounding nuclear tests at Nevada Testing Grounds. Exhibited at Nevada Museum and Historical Society, Las Vegas, June 2003.

64 **most exciting and pivotal moments in her life:** author interview with Elise Boulding, Wayland, Massachusetts, 1998; "Who Are the Women of Women's Strike for Peace? A Progress Report on a Study of the Women Strike for Peace," Center for Conflict Resolution, University of Michigan, March 5, 1963. See also Swerdlow, *Women Strike for Peace,* p. 70.

66 **"found them sincere":** Swerdlow, p. 85.

66 **"mothers' vote":** Telephone interview with Senator Maurine Neuberger, 1996. The concept had been used by the treaty's opponents to discredit the treaty and its supporters. Senator Neuberger was the only woman on the floor of the Senate in favor of the Test Ban Treaty. (Margaret Chase Smith opposed it.) Neuberger told me the WSP women were "disorganized" but a visible and strong presence in lobbying the senators. Neuberger's speech on the floor of the Senate on September 24, 1963, addressed the issue of the so-called "mothers' vote":

We have been told that Senate ratification of the test ban treaty will be more a tribute to the political potency of the "mothers' vote" than a rational reflection of our national self-interest. There is, indeed, a mothers' vote, but it is not a sentimental vote. It is a vote that flows from the rational concern of any mother for the welfare of her children, and her natural and acute sensitivity to the survival of future generations in recognizable form. It is a vote cast for the genetic future of mankind.

Congressional Record, Maurine Neuberger, September 24, 1963, quoted in newsletter, WSP of New York, New Jersey, Connecticut, October 1963. See also, *Hearings Before the Senate Committee on Foreign Relations on the Treaty Banning Nuclear Weapons Tests in the Atmosphere, in Outer Space, and Underwater,* 88th Cong., 1st sess., August 12–15, 1963, p. 744; also quoted in Swerdlow, *Women Strike for Peace,* p. 94.

67 **America's very first treaties:** Treaty of 1778 with the Delaware Indians. Charles J. Kappler, ed., *Indian Treaties 1778–1883* (New York: Interland Publishing, 1972).

69 **"opportunistic feminist":** Ann Blackman, *Seasons of Her Life: A Biography of Madeleine Korbel Albright* (New York: Simon & Schuster, 1998); Telephone interview with author, March 8, 1999, Washington, D.C.

71 **social capital to become the first woman secretary of state in American history:** A more contempory concept for understanding women's absence from top-level leadership positions is women's "underinvestment in social capital" rather than the "glass ceiling." Psychology professors Alice H. Eagly and Linda L. Carli, in *Through the Labyrinth: The Truth About How Women Become Leaders* (Cambridge: Harvard Business School Press, 2008), see the problem as structural rather than performance-related. "Social capital"

refers to socializing with colleagues, building professional networks, and spending out of work hours in activities which—at upper levels—are composed almost entirely of men. The ongoing gender discrimination lawsuit against Wal-Mart illustrates some of the difficulties for women: one top executive retreat was a quail-hunting expedition at Sam Walton's ranch in Texas; another managers' retreat included visits to strip clubs, a Hooters restaurant, and a football game. A woman executive was told she wouldn't advance because she didn't hunt or fish. The authors analyze how socializing, politicking, and interacting with other leaders is more important to top executive selection than job performance. See also "Leadership" by Alice Eagly and Linda Carli, *Harvard Business Review,* September 2007, pp. 63–71.

71 **"perfect female gentleman":** Lani Guinier, *Radcliffe Quarterly,* Fall 2000.

72 **borrowing a lot of money:** The National Defense Student Loan Program was enacted in 1958 and extended to 1972 to provide low interest, long term federal loans to needy students attending institutions of higher learning.

74 **"on history's clock":** Tuchman, *The Guns of August,* p. 1.

Chapter 5 History's Clock

76 **the first Factory Girls Association:** The first American women workers to participate in a labor action were textile workers in Pawtucket, Rhode Island, in 1824. In 1833, women shoemakers in Lynn, Massachusetts, staged a "walk out" for higher wages. In 1834, the mill girls of Lowell, only twenty-five miles away, walked off the job to protest a cut in wages. The "walk-outs" lasted for a few hours and then the women returned to work. They were not strikes. The loose

collaborations of workers eventually developed into more formal organizations. The Factory Girls Associations in both Lynn and Lowell formed in 1836 around the issues of the ten-hour day, better pay, reduced boardinghouse fees, and improved working conditions.

See also, Thomas Dublin, "The Industrial Revolution in the United States," State University of New York, Binghamton. http://www.uwgb.edu/teachingushistory/images/pdfs/2005_ lectures/dublin-industrialrevolutionlecture.pdf (accessed 6/22/2007).

Also Christine Lunardini, *What Every American Should Know About Women's History: 200 Events that Shaped Our Destiny* (Holbrook, MA: Adams Media Corp., 1997), pp. 41–42, 61–62. http://www.pinn.net/~sunshine/whm2002/bagley. html (accessed 6/22/2007).

77 **"not so wholesome things":** Author copy of personal correspondence between Stratton Brophy and his father, James Brophy, president of Brophy Brothers Shoe Company of Lynn.

78 **"Don't think I am neglecting you":** Ibid.

79 **"in the factory up to 3600 pairs daily":** Letter #24, February 15, 1918, Brophy collection.

83 Alfred Grosser is a French political scientist, sociologist, and historian who was born in Germany in 1925, escaped to France during World War II, and became one of the leading French intellectuals advising on Franco-German policies in the postwar era. A professor at Science Po in Paris (Institut d'etudes politique de Paris) and Johns Hopkins Bologna while writing a weekly column for *Le Monde,* he published over a dozen books on politics and philosophy. His awards include the French Legion of Honor. http://fr.wikipedia.org/wiki/Alfred_Grosser (accessed 6/22/2007).

Chapter 6 The Failure Theory of Success

85 **an artist actually counted and duplicated 768 different hues:** Artist Angela Lorenz installed a work at Mass MOCA (Massachusetts Museum of Contemporary Art, North Adams, MA) entitled *Bologna* in October 2000 as part of a series of artists' books. Her work in "Off the Shelf" was on the theme of travel, "ability of a book to transport the reader through the geography of time," and a metaphorical museum. Viewing the work online, she actually was able to duplicate 768 hues of Bologna's colors. www.massmoca.org/event_details.php?id=64 (accessed 7/9/2007).

92 **Mrs. Baity and her husband came from Chapel Hill:** According to Doug Eyre, in *Chapel Hill News,* January 20, 2007, Elizabeth Chesley Baity (1907–1989) "was an award-winning author of books, a poet and painter. In Geneva she was a newspaper art critic. . . . Her thirst for learning propelled her to University of North Carolina master's degrees in English, Educational Psychology and Anthropology and a doctorate in Anthropology, more UNC degrees than held by any other alumnus. Chesley had a passion for studying the relationship of natural disasters and the collapse of ancient Mediterranean culture centers. That led her to become a pioneer in creating a new study sub-field, archaeo-astronomy." The article described her husband, Herman Glenn Baity, as an international expert in sanitary engineering and head of the environmental health section of the World Health Organization in Geneva, Switzerland. http://www.chapelhillnews.com/features/v<->print/story/4943.html. (accessed 6/19/2007).

92 **Mrs. Baity was fond of the French anthropologists:** Claude Lévi-Strauss, *Tristes Tropiques* (Paris: Plon, 1955, or New York: Criterion, 1961); Claude Lévi-Strauss, *Structural Anthropology* (New York: Basic Books, 1963); and

Paul Mus, *Vietnam, Sociologie d'une guerre* (Paris, Èditions du Seuil, 1952).

102 **I was recalling the scene in *Zorba the Greek:*** Nikos Katzanzakis, *Zorba the Greek* (New York: Simon & Schuster, 1953).

107 **Italians started developing their own theories:** Over the years conspiracy theories became more respectable within the United States. By 2003, the fortieth anniversary of the Kennedy assassination, national polls showed that the majority of the American public no longer believed that Lee Harvey Oswald was a lone assassin. Among the public notables to have said, privately or publicly, that President Kennedy was killed as the result of a conspiracy were Presidents Lyndon Johnson and Richard Nixon; Attorney General Robert Kennedy; William Attwood, special adviser dealing with Cuba at the United Nations; FBI director J. Edgar Hoover; Senator Richard Russell, a member of the Warren Commission; Senators Richard Schweiker and Gary Hart, both of the Senate Intelligence Committee; and the twelve congressmen and women on the House Select Committee on Assassinations. Based in part on the sound of four gunshots recorded over an open police cruiser radio, the committee issued a report in 1979 stating, "The Committee believes, on the basis of evidence available to it, that President John F. Kennedy was probably assassinated as a result of a conspiracy." http://www.archives. gov/research/jfk/select-committee-report (accessed 1/11/2008).

116 **I had discovered the words of theologian:** Howard Thurman, author of *The Creative Encounter: An Interpretation of Religion and the Social Witness* (Richmond, IN: Friends United Press, 1954), quoted by Lani Guinier in "Learning from Losing: The Failure Theory of Success," *O Magazine*, December 2003, p. 217.

Chapter 7 Citizen of the World

123   *The Second Sex* . . . **had a great impact on me:**
Simone de Beauvoir, *The Second Sex*, trans. H. M. Parshley
(New York: Knopf, 1953).

123   **The format for our English lessons:** Harold
Robbins, *The Carpetbaggers* (New York: Simon & Schuster,
1961). Motion picture based on the novel released in 1964 by
Paramount Pictures.

124   *Who's Afraid of Virginia Woolf?* Edward Albee's play
opened on Broadway on October 13, 1962, at the Billy Rose
Theater and won a Tony for 1962 and New York Drama Critics
awards for 1963. (First published edition of the play *Who's Afraid
of Virginia Woolf?* [New York: Atheneum, 1962]). By 1963, a
French version was being staged in Paris.

125   *Dr. Strangelove, or: How I Learned to Stop Worrying
and Love the Bomb,* a film directed by Stanley Kubrick, was
released in 1964 at the height of the cold war. The film satirized
the cold war mentality and the Soviet and American nuclear
policies of mutual assured destruction. The character of
Strangelove was supposedly based on Herman Kahn, whom
Kubrick had met. Kubrick instructed all his writers to read *On
Thermonuclear War* (1960). (Other real-life candidates for
Strangelove were Edwin Teller, Robert McNamara, and Curtis
LeMay.) The Hudson Institute, a think tank cofounded by
Kahn in 1961, constructed nuclear scenarios that projected
nuclear war consequences with hundreds of millions of casualties, contaminated food, and global radiation poisoning. Kahn's
next book, *Thinking the Unthinkable,* came out the same year as
the movie's release. *Dr. Strangelove* is listed in the top
twenty-five of the most important one hundred films of the
twentieth century, and the Library of Congress has preserved it
in its National Film Registry of culturally significant films.

126 **It was a Frenchman:** Roger Trinquier, *Modern Warfare: A French View of Counterinsurgency* (New York: Praeger, 1964).

132 **She asked if I had read:** Jean Lacouture, *Le Vietnam Entre Deux Paix* (Paris, Editions du Seuil, 1965); Jean Lacouture and Philippe de Villiers, *Fin d'une Guerre: Indochine 1954* (1960); Philippe de Villiers, *Histoire du Vietnam de 1940–1952* (Paris: Edition du Seuil, 1952). In a three-hour conversation about the Vietnam War with Doris Kearns Goodwin, which she summarizes in *Lyndon Johnson and the American Dream* (New York: Harper and Row, 1976), p. 329, Lyndon Johnson dismisses the arguments of Lacouture, saying he is a French journalist who makes his money by selling papers and who emphasizes history over security and intelligence reports. "You see, we just read different histories, that's all."

133 **"There are only two colors":** Henry Miller, *The Colossus of Marousi* (San Francisco: Colt Press, 1941), p. 55.

136 **"Listen to this. The Tonkin Gulf Resolution":** Stanley Karnow, *Vietnam: A History* (New York: Viking Press, 1983). His account of events in the Gulf of Tonkin, pp. 366–73; see also, *The Gulf of Tonkin, 1964 Incidents,* Senate Committee on Foreign Relations (Washington, D.C.: U.S. Government Printing Office, 1968). The Gulf of Tonkin incident became the template for a manufactured incident required to extract a war resolution from the U.S. Congress.

Chapter 8 Honest Work Is Hard to Find

142 **one of the first woman graduates of the University of Michigan business school:** Author interview with Bonnie Howard, July 29, 2005.

143 **"What's that book you're reading":** Tom Wolfe,

The Kandy-Colored Tangerine-Flake Streamline Baby (New York: Farrar, Straus and Giroux, 1965).

144 **later to be called the New Journalism:** Joan Didion, *Slouching Toward Bethlehem* (New York: Farrar, Straus and Giroux, 1968); Hunter S. Thomson, *Hell's Angels: A Strange and Terrible Saga* (New York: Random House, 1967).

146 **"We are at a moment":** Martin Luther King quoted in Terry Anderson, *The Movement and the Sixties* (New York: Oxford University Press, 1996), p. 160.

156 **I know the man he sent:** E-mail correspondence with Steve Hirst, February 23, 2007.

158 Mildred Scott Olmstead profile. Catherine Foster, *Women for All Seasons: The Story of the Women's International League for Peace and Freedom* (Athens: University of Georgia Press, 1989), pp.120–29.

162 **"I always made it a point to dress stylishly":** author interviews with Mildred Scott Olmstead, 1966.

Chapter 9 The Good Wife and Other Double Binds

166 **"The SDS . . . was essentially a young boys' network":** Todd Gitlin, *The Sixties: Years of Hope, Days of Rage* (New York: Random House, 1987) quoted in Ruth Rosen, *The World Split Open* (New York: Penguin, 2001), p. 118.

168 **"By the time I started writing for women's magazines":** Betty Friedan, *The Feminine Mystique* (New York: Bantam, 1983), p. 50.

170 **"did more to shape American attitudes":** James Carroll, *House of War: The Pentagon and the Disastrous Rise of American Power* (New York: Houghton Mifflin, 2006), p. 181. Carroll's chapter on Nitze's authorship of the document known as NSC–68 (National Security Council "United States Objectives and Programs for National Security") and its purpose—to influence Truman into increasing the defense

budget—puts a human face on doctrines that are usually treated as the impersonal product of an institutional mind. Carroll writes:

> *Paul Nitze would serve every president, in one capacity or another, from Franklin Roosevelt to Ronald Reagan. It may not be too much to say that he did more to shape American attitudes toward military power, and nuclear weapons in particular, than any other figure. Over four decades, especially with the Committee on the Present Danger, founded in the early fifties and revived in the seventies, he would be unrelenting in raising his anti-Soviet warnings.*

Paul Wolfowitz came to Nitze's attention in 1969 when he went to Washington from the University of Chicago to do research for Nitze's Committee to Maintain a Prudent Defense Policy. The Committee on the Present Danger was revived in 2004 to support the global war on terror. Its members include a number of men that Nitze mentored in the national security bureaucracies. See www.fightingterror.org. NSC-68 is available at www.fas.org/irp/offdocs/nsc-hst/nsc-68-htm.

170   **wealthy wife:** Marriage is a much neglected influence in shaping America's foreign policy class. When Paul Nitze married Phyllis Pratt in 1932, he married into a Rockefeller/Standard Oil fortune. Charles Pratt of Cleveland was an early founder of Standard Oil, with John D. Rockefeller Sr., and was the leader of the conservative group of Standard Oil's directors. According to Rockefeller Senior's biographer, Ron Chernow (*Titan: The Life of John D. Rockefeller Sr.* [New York: Random House, 1998]), Pratt presided over the meetings of Standard Oil's board of directors. Chernow estimates that $1 million of Standard Oil stock in 1888 was worth $990 million by 1930. The Rockefeller Foundation proved to be

helpful in many of Nitze's endeavors, including the founding of SAIS.

172   **One bright young man:** Nitze, Wolfowitz, and the Committee to Maintain a Prudent Defense Policy of 1969; Wolfowitz and Team B in 1976: James Mann, *Rise of Vulcans* (New York: Penguin, 2004), pp. 31–33, 74–75.

175   On dioxin and the effects of Agent Orange used as a defoliant in Vietnam, see Elmo Zumwalt Jr. and Elmo Zumwalt III, with John Pekkanen, *My Father, My Son* (New York: Macmillan, 1986) http://www.wellesley.edu/Polisci/wj/Vietnam/Readings/zumwalt.htm. See also interview with Admiral Zumwalt posted on Center for Defense Information www.cdi.org/ADM/1251/zumwalt.html (accessed 2/20/2004).

178   **Paul Gorman was a seeker:** Paul Gorman and Ram Dass, *How Can I Help? Stories and Reflection on Service* (New York: Knopf, 1985).

178   **Another Mother for Peace** was founded in 1967, became inactive in 1979, sent out its last newsletter in 1985, then revived in 2003 in opposition to the Iraq war. From 1986 to 2003, art director Gerta Katz, who had designed its famous Sunflower logo and tagline "War is not healthy for children and other living things," was trustee of the trademark and copyright. In 2003, spurred by the the U.S. invasion of Iraq, Another Mother for Peace logos became visible again. www.anothermother.org/history.html (accessed 7/4/2007).

183   **For the first time, . . . HUAC members confronted:** For the account of the WSP appearance before the House Un-American Activities Committee, see Amy Swerdlow, *Women Strike for Peace: Traditional Motherhood and Radical Politics in the 1960s* (Chicago: University of Chicago Press, 1993), pp. 108–20.

183   **"Which is it that is un-American, peace or**

women?": Herb Block cartoon, *Washington Post,* December 13, 1962, cited in Swerdlow, *Women Strike for Peace,* first section of illustrations.

185 **"What is your budget"**: Donna Allen obituary, *Washington Post,* July 20, 1999. In 1972, Donna Allen led an innovative campaign to create a more democratic press for women and founded Women's Institute for Freedom of the Press. For the next thirteen years, she put out *Media Report to Women* (www.wifp.org).

187 **Riesman had predicted, "If anything remains unchanged"**: *Time* magazine, July 21, 1967.

Chapter 10 The Rise of the Bra Burners

189 **"Picket Lines; Guerrilla Theater"**: Terry H. Anderson, *The Movement and the Sixties: Protest in America from Greensboro to Wounded Knee* (New York: Oxford University Press, 1995), p. 228.

190 **"Peggy Dobbins from New Orleans"**: Carol Giardina, "Women's Studies or Women's Liberation Studies," speech given at the University of Florida, Gainesville, March 1, 1991; also Giardina, *The Making of the Women's Liberation Movement, 1953–70,* PhD dissertation, CUNY Graduate Center, 2004.

192 **"In a breast-obsessed society"**: Ruth Rosen, *The World Split Open: How the Women's Movement Changed America* (New York: Penguin, 2001), pp. 160–61.

195 **"for a strong black male"**: Anderson, *The Movement and the Sixties,* p. 341.

195 **"met far more discrimination as a woman than as a black"**: Shirley Chisholm, *Unbought and Unbossed: An Autobiography* (New York: Houghton Mifflin, 1970); and *Shirley Chisholm '72,* a documentary film by Shola Lynch, winner of 2006 Peabody Award, chronicling Chisholm's 1972 bid for the Democratic presidential nomination.

199 **"The papers they helped us produce ran rings around":** Nitze quoted at www.en.wikipedia.org/wiki/Paul_Wolfowitz (accessed 7/4/2007).

200 **the job requirements:** The congressional hearing took place on March 28–29, 1969, and was called "A Congressional Conference on the Military Budget and National Priorities." Over a fourth of the hearing was devoted to the antiballistic missile system. The proceedings were published as Erwin Knoll and Judith Nies McFadden, eds., *American Militarism 1970* (New York: Viking Press, 1969).

201 **"We must sustain pessimism of the intellect":** Gramsci quoted in Bill Luders, *An Enemy of the State: The Life of Erwin Knoll* (Monroe, ME: Common Courage Press, 1996), p. 236.

203 **"Feminism is a vision of a different kind of society":** Rosen, *The World Split Open,* p. 69.

207 **"acquired the skills":** Alice Echols, "We Gotta Get Out of This Place: Notes Toward a Remapping of the Sixties" in *Cultural Politics and Social Movements,* eds. Marcy Darnovsky, Barbara Epstein, and Richard Flacks (Philadelphia: Temple University Press, 1995), p. 117. Also see Alice Echols, *Shaky Ground: The Sixties and Its Aftershocks* (New York: Columbia University Press, 2002).

Chapter 11 Extraordinary Times

212 **"There is a point":** Clausewitz quoted in Barbara Tuchman, *The March of Folly: From Troy to Vietnam* (New York: Knopf, 1984), p. 234. In further defining the folly of America's Vietnam policy, she writes,

The folly consisted not in pursuit of a goal in ignorance of the obstacles but in persistence in the pursuit despite accumulating

*evidence that the goal was unattainable . . . this is the classic
symptom of folly: refusal to draw conclusions from the evidence,
addiction to the counter-productive.*

217 **"I was lucky in everything"**: quoted in Cecil B.
Currey, *Edward Lansdale: The Unquiet American* (Boston:
Houghton Mifflin, 1998).

219 Thirty years later Dan Ellsberg was able to provide me
with a copy of his original signed conference invitation dated
December 1969. He said he worked on a special pacification
team in Vietnam that Lansdale headed. He described their
relationship as "very close" and said he considered himself
Lansdale's protégé. Author interview with Daniel Ellsberg,
Gabriel's restaurant, Washington, D.C., March 17, 1999.

220 **"single best book on Vietnam to date"**: "Agony
of Questions on War," Herbert A. Kenny, *Boston Globe,*
January 19, 1971, p. 29.

220 **"The most important book on Vietnam in print
today"**: James Reston Jr., *Saturday Review,* January 9, 1971, pp.
26–27.

220 **"The most valuable and important
single-volume collection of relevant source material
available on this crucial subject . . . should be read
soberly by Americans of every shade of conviction"**:
Publishers Weekly, September 14, 1970, p. 65.

225 **crowd of Capitol Hill women:** Val Fleischauer told
the behind-the-scenes lobbying effort required to release the
Equal Rights Amendment from committee after thirty years.
Judith Nies McFadden, "Women's Lib on Capitol Hill," *The
Progressive,* December 1970, pp. 22–25; Author telephone
interview with Arvonne Fraser, February 24, 1999.

228 **"up until then my religion"**: Judith Nies, *Nine*

Women: Portraits from the American Radical Tradition (New York: Viking Press, 1977; reprint, Berkeley: University of California Press, 2002), p. 193.

228 ***In my letter I mentioned:*** Author interviews with Abigail McCarthy, Jenny Moore, and Dwight Macdonald in 1975.

229 **"like a wind from another land":** Jenny Moore, quoted in Nies, *Nine Women,* p. 199.

230 **"This is not temporary":** author interview with Dorothy Day, 1975.

230 **"If the Chancery":** Nies, *Nine Women,* p. 202.

232 The original Executive Order 10980, "Establishing the President's Commission on the Status of Women," signed by John F. Kennedy on December 14, 1961, stipulated that the commission would submit its final report by October 1, 1963, and go out of existence after twenty months. http://www.lib. umich.edu/govdocs/jfkeo/10980.htm (accessed 12/7/2006).

235 **A thirty-page mimeographed document:** *Notes from the First Year* (New York: New York Radical Women, June 1968).

236 **most radical piece of literature:** *Our Bodies, Ourselves*: The book began as a 30-cent, 138-page booklet called "Women and Their Bodies." Published in 1970 by the New England Free Press, it was written by twelve Boston feminist activists as source material for a women's health course, organized in 1969 by Nancy Miriam Hawley at Boston's Emmanuel College. "We weren't encouraged to ask questions, but to depend on the so-called experts," Hawley told Women's eNews. "Not having a say in our own health care frustrated and angered us. We didn't have the information we needed, so we decided to find it on our own." Wendy Sanford wrote about abortion, Jane Pincus and Ruth Bell about pregnancy, and Paula Doress and Esther Rome about postpartum depression. The booklet sold 250,000 copies in New England without any formal advertising.

As a result of their success, the founders incorporated as the nonprofit Boston Women's Health Book Collective (which now goes by the name Our Bodies Ourselves) and published the first trade version 276-page *Our Bodies, Ourselves* in 1973. Featuring first-person stories from women, it tackled many topics then regarded as taboo. Since then, more than 4 million copies have been sold in English and millions more in translated versions in Spanish, Polish, Korean, Armenian, Bulgarian, Serbian. See Molly M. Ginty, "Our Bodies, Ourselves Turns 35 Today," Women's eNews, May 4, 2004; *Our Bodies, Ourselves: A Book by and for Women* (Boston: New England Free Press, 1970; reprint, New York: Simon & Schuster, 1973, 1976, 1984, 1998, 2005, 2007).

237 **sued Robin Morgan over her anthology:** In a February 2001 interview in *Off Our Backs*, Robin Morgan said Cisler sued her because she hadn't received a grant from a fund Morgan set up. Letters regarding *Sisterhood Is Powerful* and lawsuit brought by Lucinda Cisler, 1974, in the records of Women's Community Health Center, Schlesinger Library, Radcliffe Institute.

239 **the first article I ever published:** Judith Nies McFadden, "Women's Lib on Capitol Hill" *The Progressive*, December 1970, p. 22.

Chapter 12 The Ghost of Marjorie Merriweather Post

245 **"What I have in mind":** Arvonne Fraser, phone interview with author, February 24, 1999; e-mail to author, May 15, 2007. See also Arvonne S. Fraser, "Insiders and Outsiders: Women in the Political Arena," in *Women in Washington,* Irene Tinker, ed. (London: Sage Publications, 1983), pp. 120–39.

250 **My "aha" moment was this:** *Women and Fellowships* (Washington, D.C.: Women's Equity Action League, 1974, 1976, 1981). Although I was always listed as author and chair,

between the first and last edition my name changed from
Judith Nies McFadden to Judith Nies. (The 1981 edition was
underwritten by the Ford Foundation.)

257 **one of seven "named defendants":** Eileen Shanahan obituary, *New York Times,* November 3, 2001.

264 **"extended make-believe":** Justin Kaplan e-mail to
author, May 18, 2007.

Kaplan called *Mission to Moscow* a "silly book," and said
Davies almost ruined the career of the *Herald-Tribune Moscow*
bureau chief, Joe Barnes, by reporting in a footnote that
Barnes was often seen playing tennis with KGB people. The
unpublished Joseph Davies memoir had also been a
long-running problem for a previous editor, Quincy Howe.
See also, Anne Bernays and Justin Kaplan, *Back Then: Two
Literary Lives in 1950s New York* (New York: HarperCollins,
2002), pp. 284–85.

264 **"Joe should have been an actor":** Nancy Rubin,
American Empress: The Life and Times of Marjorie Merriwether Post
(New York: Villard Books, 1995), p. 315.

268 **if an open society wasn't a key element of a
democracy:** Mark Mazzetti and Tim Weiner, "Files on Illegal
Spying Show CIA Skeletons from Cold War," *New York Times,*
June 27, 2007, page 1. Operation Chaos was characterized as "the
CIA doing its Stasi imitation" by Tom Blanton, of the National
Security Archive, the research group that filed a Freedom of
Information request in 1992. As a result, in June 2007, the CIA
released 702 pages of documents cataloguing domestic wiretap-
ping, failed assassination plots, mind-control experiments, domes-
tic spying, and a computer database it compiled on 300,000
Americans from 1967 to 1974. (It compiled extensive files on
7,200 citizens.) The CIA and the FBI began working in
secret with police departments all over the United States.

www.nytimes.com/2007/06/27/washington/27cia.html (accessed 6/28/2007).

268 **I remembered where I had first seen Gloria Steinem's name:** Gloria Steinem's CIA connections were well documented in the 1960s by the *New York Times* and *Washington Post.*

"The Independent Research Service, the other New York based organization that received funds from the CIA-connected Independence Foundation of Boston . . . was founded in 1958 by Paul Sigmund, now a professor at Princeton, and Gloria Steinem, a New York journalist . . ." *New York Times*, February 16, 1967.

"Gloria Steinem, a New York freelance writer, acknowledged in an interview yesterday that she worked closely with the Central Intelligence Agency to organize groups of American young people to attend World Youth Festivals in Vienna and Helsinki. . . . She . . . had great praise for the CIA agents with whom she collaborated. . . . At the Helsinki Festival in 1962, Miss Steinem was co-director with Dennis Shaul, a former president of the National Student Association."

Robert Kaiser, "Work of CIA with Youths at Festivals Is Defended," *Washington Post,* February 18, 1967, p. A4.

Chapter 13 Moral Hazard

272 **"Pentagon Study Traces":** *New York Times*, June 13, 1971, p. 1.

274 **Ellsberg had a Zelig-like presence:** Marty Garbus, the lawyer representing Ellsberg in the threatened suit of the congressional group over Ellsberg's edited remarks, was later quoted as saying, "He [Ellsberg] thought it [the Pentagon Papers] would end the war. . . . I thought his perspective was

naïve and grandiose." Tom Wells, *Wild Man* (New York: Palgrave/St. Martin's, 2001), p. 340.

277 **"You were pregnant"**: author interview with Ellen Miles, March 20, 1999.

281 **"A nice guy, but not exactly a pushover"**: John Brooks, *New Yorker*, August 13, 1973, "The Go-Go Years III," p. 40. Renchard set up an eleven-man force to devise strategy against any takeover attempt and put it under the direction of Chemical's chief loan officer J. A. McFadden. Renchard described him later as "a bright fellow, good at figures, not exactly a tough guy, but no pushover."

282 **"I always knew there was a club . . ."** *New Yorker*, August 13, 1973, p. 53.

286 **"(Mr. Ramsay, stumbling along a passage")**: Virginia Woolf, *To the Lighthouse* (New York: Oxford University Press, 1992).

Chapter 14 Leave the Gun; Take the Cannoli

291 **A short article about Cecil Rhodes:** Judith Nies, "Not for Men Only: Cecil Rhodes," *Ms.*, April 1973, p. 114. (Although this piece ran after the Abzug article, it had been written months earlier.)

292 **I had violated a tribal taboo by writing about Bill Ryan:** Judith Nies, "The Abzug Campaign: A Lesson in Politics," *Ms.*, February 1973, pp. 76–79, 107–12.

300 **"takes place in an East German town"**: John Le Carré, *A Small Town in Germany* (New York: Coward McCann, 1968), p. ii.

Epilogue

308 **my article on the gender gap:** op ed, *New York Times*, July 31, 1980.

Selected Bibliography

I am particularly indebted to Ruth Rosen's indispensable history of the modern women's movement in the United States, *The World Split Open*, published in 2002. A new generation of historians, among them Alice Echols and Terry Anderson, are revaluating the 1960s and the transformation of modern life by women. Many earlier histories of the 1960s, which historians bracket as a long decade from 1960 to 1974, barely mention women. I have cited some of them below because they highlight old historical assumptions—that what happens to women is culture; what happens to men is politics. Of necessity, the twenty-first century and our understanding of women and modernity have changed that assumption permanently.

Books

Anderson, Terry. *The Movement and the Sixties*. New York: Oxford University Press, 1995.

_____ *The Sixties*. New York: Pearson Longman, 2004.

Bauer, Nancy. *Simone de Beauvoir, Philosophy and Feminism*. New York: Columbia University Press, 2001.

Belfrage, Sally. *Freedom Summer.* New York: Viking Press, 1965.

Bernays, Anne and Justin Kaplan. *Back Then: Two Literary Lives in 1950s New York.* New York: HarperCollins, 2002.

Bird, Kai. *The Color of Truth: McGeorge Bundy and William Bundy: Brothers in Arms.* New York: Simon & Schuster, 1998.

Biskind, Peter. *Easy Riders, Raging Bulls: How the Sex-Drugs-and-Rock'n Roll Generation Saved Hollywood.* New York: Simon & Schuster, 1998.

Blackman, Ann. *Seasons of Her Life: A Biography of Madeleine Korbel Albright.* New York: Scribners, 1998.

Blewett, Mary H. *Men, Women and Work: Class, Gender, and Protest in the New England Shoe Industry, 1780–1910.* Chicago: University of Illinois Press, 1988.

Blumenthal, Karen. *Let Me Play: The Story of Title IX, the Law That Changed the Future of Girls in America.* New York: Atheneum, 2005.

Branch, Taylor. *Parting the Waters: America in the King Years.* New York: Touchstone, 1989.

Burner, David. *Making Peace with the 60s.* (Princeton, NJ: Princeton University Press, 1996.

Burton, Phillip. *Memorial Services Held in the House of Representatives: Eulogy for Phillip Burton, late a Representative of California, 98th Congress.* Washington, D.C. Government Printing Office, 1983.

Callahan, David. *Dangerous Capabilities: Paul Nitze and the Cold War.* New York: HarperCollins, 1990.

Carroll, James. *House of War: The Pentagon and the* Diastrous Rise of American Power. Boston: Houghton Mifflin, 2006.

Cassell, Justine and Henry Jenkins. *From Barbie to Mortal Kombat: Gender and Computer Games.* Cambridge: MIT Press, 1998.

Conway, Jill Ker. *The Road from Coorain*. New York: Random House, 1990.

_____. *When Memory Speaks: Reflections on Autobiography*. New York: Alfred A. Knopf, 1998.

Davidson, Sara. *Loose Change: Three Women of the Sixties*. New York: Doubleday, 1977.

DeBeauvoir, Simone. *The Second Sex*. New York: Penguin, 1972.

Didion, Joan. *Slouching Toward Bethlehem*. New York: Farrar, Straus and Giroux, 1968.

Domhoff, G. William. *The Higher Circles: The Governing Class in America*. New York: Random House, 1970.

Donner, Frank. *The Age of Surveillance: The Aims and Methods of America's Political Intelligence System*. New York: Random House, 1981.

Echols, Alice. *Daring to Be Bad: Radical Feminism in America, 1967–1975*. (Foreword by Ellen Willis.) Minneapolis: University of Minnesota Press, 1989.

_____ *Shaky Ground: The Sixties and Its Aftershocks*. New York: Columbia University Press, 2002.

Ellsberg, Daniel. *Papers on the War*. New York: Simon & Schuster, 1972.

Enloe, Cynthia. *Bananas, Beaches and Bases: Making Feminist Sense of International Politics*. Berkeley: University of California Press, 1990.

Faler, Paul G. *Mechanics and Manufacturers in the Early Industrial Revolution: Lynn, Massachusetts, 1780–1860*. Albany, NY: State University of New York Press, 1981.

Fitzgerald, Frances. *Fire in the Lake: The Vietnamese and the Americans in Vietnam*. Boston: Little, Brown/Atlantic Monthly Press, 1972.

Fox, Stephen. *Blood and Power: Organized Crime in Twentieth-Century America*. New York: Penguin, 1989.

Fussell, Paul. *Class: A Guide Through the American Status System*. New York: Summit Books, 1983.

Gitlin, Todd. *The Sixties: Years of Hope, Days of Rage*. New York: Bantam, 1987.

_____. *The Twilight of Common Dreams. Why America Is Wracked by Culture Wars*. New York: Henry Holt & Co., 1995.

Gosse, Van and Richard Moser, eds. *The World the 60s Made*. Philadelphia: Temple University Press, 2003.

Hampl, Patricia. *A Romantic Education*. Boston: Houghton Mifflin, 1981.

Herr, Michael. *Dispatches*. New York: Avon, 1978.

Hinckle, Warren. *If You Have A Lemon, Make Lemonade*. New York: G.P. Putnam's Sons, 1973. (The story of the founding of *Ramparts* magazine by its first editor.)

Jacobs, John. *A Rage for Justice: The Passion and Politics of Phillip Burton*. Berkeley: University of California Press, 1995.

Karnow, Stanley. *Vietnam: A History*. New York: Viking Press, 1983.

Kastenmeier, Robert. *Vietnam Hearings: Voices from the Grassroots*. New York: Doubleday, 1966. (This documents one of the first town meetings or teach-ins on the conduct of the Vietnam War held in 1965 at the First Methodist Church in Madison, Wisconsin by Congressmen Bob Kastenmeier and Ben Rosenthal. The *New York Times* called it "A new political phenomenon.")

Klein, Naomi. *The Shock Doctrine: The Rise of Disaster Capitalism*. New York: Henry Holt, 2007.

Knoll, Erwin. *No Comment*. New York: Vintage Books, 1984.

Knoll, Erwin and Judith Nies McFadden, eds. *War Crimes and the American Conscience*. New York: Holt, Rinehart and Winston, 1970.

_____. *American Militarism, 1970.* New York: Viking Press, 1969.

Kunin, Madeleine. *Living A Political Life.* New York: Knopf, 1994.

Kurlansky, Mark. *1968: The Year That Rocked the World.* New York: Random House, 2004.

Marwick, Arthur. *The Sixties: Cultural Revolution in Britain, France, Italy, and the United States, c.1958–1974.* New York: Oxford University Press, 1998.

McAdam, Doug. *Freedom Summer.* New York and London: Oxford University Press, 1988.

McCoy, Alfred W. *The Politics of Heroin: CIA Complicity in the Global Drug Trade.* New York: Lawrence Hill Books, 1991. (Published in 1972 as *The Politics of Heroin in Southeast Asia.*)

Mikva, Abner J. and Patti B. Saris. *The American Congress: The First Branch.* New York: Franklin Watts, 1983.

Moynihan, Daniel Patrick. *Secrecy: The American Experience.* New Haven: Yale University Press, 1998.

Nies, Judith. *Nine Women: Portraits from the American Radical Tradition.* Berkeley: University of California Press, 2002. Viking edition, 1977.

Nitze, Paul H. *From Hiroshima to Glasnost: A Memoir of Five Perilous Decades.* New York: Grove Weidenfeld, 1989.

O'Brien, Tim. *The Things They Carried.* New York: Penguin, 1991.

O'Reilly, Jane. *The Girl I Left Behind: The Housewife's Moment of Truth and Other Feminist Ravings.* New York: Macmillan, 1980.

Peter, Grace Dunlop. *Cleveland Park, An Early Residential Neighborhood of the Nation's Capital.* Washington, D.C.: Cleveland Park Community Library Committee, 1958.

Redstockings, *Feminist Revolution*. New York: Redstockings, Inc., 1975. (Random House reprint, 1978, does not include "Agents, Opportunists, and Fools" with articles about Gloria Steinem and the CIA).

Robinson, Judith. *You're In Your Mother's Arms: The Life and Legacy of Phillip Burton*. San Francisco: J. Robinson, 1995.

Rosen, Ruth. *The World Split Open: How the Modern Women's Movement Changed America*. New York: Penguin, 2001.

Rosenthal, Benjamin S. *Turbulent Era: The Year of Europe in Retrospect, Florence 1974*. Report of the 5th Meeting of Members of Congress and of the European Parliament, March 17–24, 1974. U.S. Government Printing Office.

Rubin, Nancy. *American Empress: The Life and Times of Marjorie Merriweather Post*. New York: Villard Books, 1995.

Swerdlow, Amy. *Women Strike for Peace: Traditional Motherhood and Radical Politics in the 1960s*. Chicago: University of Chicago Press, 1993.

Talbot, Strobe. *The Master of the Game: Paul Nitze and the Nuclear Peace*. New York: Alfred A. Knopf, 1988.

Thomas, Evan. *The Very Best Men: Early Years of the CIA*. New York: Simon & Schuster, 1995.

Tickner, J. Ann. *Gender in International Relations: Feminist Perspectives on Achieving Global Security*. New York: Columbia University Press, 1992.

Tinker, Irene, ed. *Women in Washington, Advocates for Public Policy*. "Insiders/Outsiders" by Arvonne Fraser, pp. 120–139. London: Sage Publications, 1983.

Trillin, Calvin. *Remembering Denny*. New York: Farrar, Straus, and giroux, 1993.

Wolfe, Tom. *The Kandy-Kolored, Tangerine-Flake, Streamline Baby*. New York: Farrar, Straus and Giroux, 1965.

Index

About the author

About the book

Read on

Insights,
Interviews
& More...

Meet Judith Nies

© Kim Indresano

JUDITH NIES has worked as a speechwriter, journalist, teacher, historian, secretary, market researcher, and communications consultant. Her third book, *The Girl I Left Behind: A Personal History of the 1960s,* draws on her experience as one of the few women working as a congressional speechwriter in the late 1960s and '70s. Her first book was *Nine Women: Portraits from the American Radical Tradition,* originally published in 1977 as *Seven Women* and continuously in print for more than thirty years. Her articles and reviews have dealt with the relationship between culture and politics and have appeared in the *New York Times,* the *Boston Globe,*

the *Christian Science Monitor, Ms.,
Harvard Review, Women's Review of
Books,* and other publications. Her
widely known essay "The Black Mesa
Syndrome" was a finalist for the John
B. Oakes Award for Distinguished
Environmental Journalism and was
selected by editor Barry Lopez for
inclusion in the 2007 anthology *The
Future of Nature* (Milkweed). Nies's
second book, *Native American History:
A Chronology,* winner of the Phi Alpha
Theta Award in history, is a parallel
timeline of Native American and world
history. Other awards include a Bunting
Fellowship at the Radcliffe Institute for
Advanced Study, a Ludwig Vogelstein
Foundation grant, and residency
fellowships at the MacDowell and
Yaddo artists' colonies and the
Rockefeller Foundation Bellagio
Center.

Nies received her bachelor's degree
in history from Tufts University and
a graduate degree in international
studies from Johns Hopkins School
of Advanced International Studies.
She teaches writing at Massachusetts
College of Art and Design and is
a member of PEN America. A
Massachusetts native, she grew up
in Swampscott, has traveled widely
outside the United States, and lives
in Cambridge. She has one daughter,
an opera singer. ❧

A Conversation with Judith Nies

Adapted from an interview conducted by novelist Jonatha Ceely for the Women's National Book Association's official publication The Bookwoman, *Winter 2009.*

Jonatha Ceely: *I enjoyed* The Girl I Left Behind *last June when it first came out and recently read it again with my book group. It gave rise to a lively exchange of ideas and of our own memories of growing up in the sixties and seventies. Where and how did the impetus to write it begin?*

Judith Nies: The seed for the book was planted at the dinner table in Yaddo, in 1995, when an editor asked if anyone had ever had dinner at the famous New York restaurant Lutèce. I had, but couldn't remember a single detail. As a kind of warm-up writing exercise in the morning, I began drafting an essay called "The Girl I Left Behind," which was later published in the journal *American Voice.* In the process of writing, I discovered that my memory block occurred about the same time I learned from my husband that I was the subject of a rather large FBI file.

> " My memory block occurred about the same time I learned from my husband that I was the subject of a rather large FBI file. "

JC: *How did the file influence the writing?*

JN: That essay launched a twelve-year journey of exploration and several unsuccessful efforts to get my FBI file. But the book took shape only after I was able to read my full FBI file in 2000. Previously, I had received copies of redacted pages—almost all blacked out. With the help of Congressman Mike Capuano, who put in a Congressional request, I finally saw the full text. The file had wonderful notes that reminded me of people I knew and work I had done and places I had lived. I felt the need to reexamine some important concepts about democracy and protection of dissent. I guess I should have thanked J. Edgar Hoover for his help with material and for keeping such good notes for me.

JC: *The book is such an interesting and unusual combination of memoir and history.*

JN: The poet Czeslaw Milosz was critical of the fact that so much American memoir focused on mother-father-siblings under a bell jar and generally had so little sense of history. His memorable observation about memoir was, "It made no difference to the people on the trains to Auschwitz if father was cold or mother drank." ▶

A Conversation with Judith Nies *(continued)*

So I took a cue from European memoir in which the narrator is expected to understand the historical era she or he is traveling through. That focus allowed me to frame my personal experience in larger historical terms.

JC: *Was it difficult to find a publisher?*

JN: The big obstacle was the mixed genre of memoir and history. Several editors were interested but didn't know if the book would find its audience or would get reviewed. Originally, I wrote a lot about growing up in Swampscott, Massachusetts, but most of that got cut. It was more important to keep the narrative moving and to see the larger picture for women than to unpack family history or sacrifice my daughter's privacy. When editors liked the writing style but were reluctant to buy the work because there was no book like it, Jill Conway offered to write a letter saying the book was important precisely *because* no one else had done it. That made a huge difference. She really mentored the book. She's also a historian and a scholar of memoir (as well as the first female president of Smith College), and she gave me some great advice.

JC: *Like what?*

66 The big obstacle was the mixed genre of memoir and history. Several editors were interested but didn't know if the book would find its audience or would get reviewed. 99

6

JN: Like don't expect to get it right the first time around. And imagine you are writing for your perfect reader.

JC: *How have readers responded to the book? And who has surprised you?*

JN: I have met such a variety of people through readings and book clubs and my e-mail address. Women have sent me their wonderful stories through e-mail and my Web site. I received an e-mail from someone I knew forty years ago. ("Greetings from page 39," she said.) Women of a certain age have said it has made them rethink their lives during that period. Younger women have said it helped them understand their parents' generation, especially why their parents divorced. The biggest surprise, however, has come from men, fathers who said they needed to know about the women's movement in order to better guide their daughters. And from their point of view, they felt I wasn't tough enough on how inequitable society was toward women and how men maintained their privileges. After the book talk I gave at Porter Square Books was broadcast on C-Span's *Book TV,* I heard from a woman in Missouri who wrote to say that she saw my work on a par with *The Feminine* ▶

Mystique because I told the story of an entire generation.

JC: *And it is! What else do you think women are responding to?*

JN: Women tend not to think of themselves as vehicles for history or their lives as having been shaped by forces outside their control. A work like *The Greatest Generation*: that's about men, and men take that historical framework for granted. How often have you heard a woman say, "She's the best of her generation." Women are not taught to think historically; we tend to have amnesia about our own time. Friends who have read the book say, "I hardly knew you at all," because we have never talked about the 1960s and '70s except in terms of individual choices. A recent reader said, "You really captured what women were up against." So it's both memories and the context of the times—the history—that give women a fresh way of looking at their own lives.

JC: *Did you see yourself as a feminist in the sixties and seventies?*

JN: The word *feminist* didn't mean much until the late sixties. There were many strands to women's lives. For

66 Women tend not to think of themselves as vehicles for history or their lives as having been shaped by forces outside their control. 99

most women at that time, the model was marriage, motherhood, and home. We were supposed to be like Betty Draper in the television series *Mad Men* (a television drama about Madison Avenue in the 1960s). For a while during my time in Washington, I was one of only four professional women working in Congress. But I'm not sure *feminist* is a word that conveys a lot. For younger women now, feminism is like the word *suffragist* for my generation. I think we need new language.

JC: *Do you think the issues are different now for young women?*

JN: Women have far more career choices but they struggle with all of the same complexities of work and family and missing support systems. They are told they can do it all, until they can't. The issues are the same but more nuanced. Younger women now seem to be concerned but not politicized. Change doesn't come from benevolent people up above. In the late '60s and early '70s, women got together and analyzed systems and found leverage points to force institutional change. That history has been silenced. And without history, it's hard to shape a future. Now there is ▶

> " Now there is awareness of issues. But awareness is not politics. "

awareness of issues. But awareness is
not politics.

JC: *Speaking of politics and history
too, we are talking during an election
year. Do you think the candidacies of
Hillary Clinton and Sarah Palin have
enhanced the status of women in
politics?*

JN: One of the wonderful images
from the 2008 campaign was a
touched-up 1917 photo of women
demonstrating in front of the White
House with the caption, "Mr. McCain,
America's women have not waited 232
years for Sarah Palin." Sarah Palin raises
questions about the educational system
in Alaska, John McCain's judgment,
and Alaska voters. How can any
responsible pubic figure say that
dinosaurs walked the earth four
thousand years ago? I haven't even
mentioned her opposition to sex
education, birth control, or abortion
rights. Hillary Clinton's candidacy
was of a different order and shows
real change in people's attitudes. Even
though there were big problems in her
campaign, and many people objected
to the racial issues she and her husband
raised at the end, she was a truly viable
candidate. America still has a long
way to go. In 2007 women made up
16 percent of the U.S. Congress, but

we still rank fortieth in the world among parliamentary democracies. I don't think we'll have a woman president until the percentage of women in politics is closer to 30 percent.

JC: *Where can readers who want more information or who have other questions find you online?*

JN: On my website at www.judithnies .com. My e-mail address is there too, and I am in the process of making the blog interactive so readers can have a larger conversation. ∽

Author's Picks:
Women in the Sixties

THE HISTORY OF THE 1960S has been written mostly by men. I discovered this when I was updating my first book, *Nine Women*, to include portraits of civil rights leader Fannie Lou Hamer, feminist Bella Abzug, and women leaders of the environmental movement. Most of the 1960s histories I read either omitted the activism of American women or attributed the women's movement successes to impersonal economic trends.

It was that historical silence that motivated me to expand a personal essay about my life in 1960s Washington, D.C., (published in *American Voice* in 1996) into a book that combined memoir and history.

While much of the material was drawn from the personal details of my own life, I read many memoirs that dealt with larger themes of the 1960s such as class in America, the so-called sexual revolution, race and sex in the South, and how a climate of war affects women. Readers might find that some of these books stimulate their own memories, too.

At a Nieman journalism panel on memoir, Richard Rodriquez (*Hunger of Memory: The Education of Richard Rodriguez*, 1982) and Adam Hochschild

(*Half the Way Home*, 1986) pointed out that class attitudes in America are hidden, powerful, and either not written about or confused with money. (Or as the Mafia saying goes, "There's a million dollars worth of groceries or a million dollars worth of influence.") This concept led me to authors who grew up in poverty or in anti-intellectual, blue-collar environments but who later became middle-class journalists, professors, writers, and intellectuals: Mary Karr (*The Liars' Club: A Memoir*, 1995), bell hooks (*Bone Black: Memories of Girlhood*, 1996), and Roxanne Dunbar-Ortiz (*Red Dirt: Growing Up Oki*, 1997). Anne Moody (*Coming of Age in Mississippi*, 1968) tells the story of a poor, black Mississippi girl growing up in the middle of the civil rights revolution in the South. Tim O'Brien's award-winning work *The Things They Carried* (1990) deals with the moral confusion of the Vietnam foot soldier and memories that never go away.

I owe my discovery of the distinction between American and European memoir to Patricia Hampl (*I Could Tell You Stories: Sojourns in the Land of Memory*, 1999), who introduced poet Czeslaw Milosz's dictum that "memory lives to serve history." She characterized American memoir as largely ahistorical, written by authors who often confuse memory with nostalgia. (This was long before the ▶

flurry of forged memoirs that talk-show television has recently produced.) The author who illustrated how to be a citizen historian was Howard Zinn (*You Can't Be Neutral on a Moving Train: A Personal History of Our Times*, 1994).

The silences growing out of the two World Wars cast such a long shadow in my own family that I was curious to learn how the experience of war lived on in other families, particularly how it affected daughters. Louise Steinman (*The Souvenir: A Daughter Discovers Her Father's War*, 2001) recounts the story of discovering a Japanese soldier's flag in her father's belongings after he died and her ten-year effort to return it to the soldier's village in Japan. Danielle Trussoni (*Falling Through the Earth*, 2006) weaves her family story with a long trip to Vietnam to unravel how post-Vietnam trauma changed her father and the course of their family life. Alexandra Fuller (*Don't Let's Go to the Dogs Tonight*, 2003) grew up in a white British tenant-farmer family with many upper-class attitudes while living in the war zones of African countries throwing off white colonial rule. These women's stories influenced how I thought about the context of what the political world does—or does not—make possible for women's lives.

Jill Ker Conway's *The Road from*

Coorain, True North, and *A Woman's Education* are excellent examples of memoirs written from a feminist perspective that skillfully integrate the personal with the public life. As a scholar of memoir as a genre (*When Memory Speaks: Reflections on Autobiography,* 1998), Conway is also a shrewd critic of how women often shape their personal stories to fit "master narratives" acceptable to social convention.

For a historical perspective on the 1960s, there is a wealth of material, but surprisingly little that deals with the changes in the lives of 50 percent of the population. Ruth Rosen's *The World Split Open: How the Modern Women's Movement Changed America* (2001) corrects that omission and is the indispensable history of the rise of the women's movement in the 1960s and '70s. Other favorites include the provocative essay " 'We Gotta Get Out of This Place': Notes Toward a Remapping of the Sixties" by Alice Echols, who later published *Shaky Ground: The Sixties and Its Aftershocks* (Columbia University Press, 2002). I also recommend Terry Anderson's *The Sixties* (Pearson Longman, 2004) as a comprehensive overview of the 1960s that incorporates the women's movement "as the most successful ▶

Author's Picks: Women in the Sixties
(continued)

social change movement of the twentieth century." And just so we don't place the United States at the center of the world, Mark Kurlansky (*1968: The Year That Rocked the World*, 2004) reminds us that the 1960s involved social and political upheavals in many countries throughout the industrialized world. ⁓

Don't miss the next book by your favorite author. Sign up now for AuthorTracker by visiting www.AuthorTracker.com.